AF552612

VEDIC LITERATURE

Encyclopaedic History of India Series

VEDIC LITERATURE

Dr. Mahesh Vikram Singh
Professor, Deptt. of History
Mahatma Gandhi Kashi Vidyapeeth
Varanasi (UP)

Dr. Brij Bhushan Shrivastava
Head of Deptt., Ancient History, Archeology & Culture
SMMTPG College, Ballia (UP)

CENTRUM PRESS
NEW DELHI-110002 (INDIA)

CENTRUM PRESS
H.O.: 4360/4, Ansari Road, Daryaganj,
New Delhi-110002 (India)
Tel: 23278000, 23261597, 23255577, 23286875
B.O.: No. 1015, Ist Main Road, BSK IIIrd Stage,
IIIrd Phase, IIIrd Block, Bangalore-560085 (INDIA)
Tel: 080-41723429
Email: centrumpress@gmail.com
Visit us at: www.centrumpress.com

Vedic Literature

First Edition, 2011

ISBN 978-93-80836-56-0

PRINTED IN INDIA

Printed at Mehra Offset Press, Delhi

प्रो. विपिन चंद्रा
अध्यक्ष
Prof. Bipan Chandra
Chairman

नेशनल बुक ट्रस्ट, इंडिया
नेहरू भवन
5 इंस्टीट्यूशनल एरिया, फेज़-II, वसंत कुंज, नई दिल्ली-110 070
फोन/ Phone: 011-26121880 फैक्स/ Fax: 011-26121883
NATIONAL BOOK TRUST, INDIA
Nehru Bhawan
5 Institutional Area, Phase II, Vasant Kunj, New Delhi-110 070
ई-मेल / E-mail: chairman@nbtindia.org.in
वेबसाइट / Website: www.nbtindia.org.in

FOREWORD

The term 'history' is derived from the Greek word 'historia' that means knowledge acquired through investigation. Obviously, this knowledge can be correct if the method of investigation is objective and not vitiated by any kind of bias. In other words, if the study of human past is comprehensive and obtained through scientific inquiry, it can provide perspective on the present day problems and help one plan for the future.

A true historian has to identify the sources that can be most useful in a given context. Documents, coins, archaeology, anthropology, geography, travel accounts, oral traditions, mythology and so on can be useful but they can be used only after their veracity is tested and they are critically examined. They should be checked and counter-checked.

Over the centuries, one finds the study and writing of history vitiated by biases. There are numerous instances in which historical data have been distorted to support or oppose certain preconceived ideas and purposes. Strictly speaking such history is just like fiction to accord with preconceived notions and serve some ulterior purposes.

The study of the past has never been static. Conclusions go on changing because of the discovery of new materials and tools of investigation. To give a concrete example, the carbon 14 or radiocarbon dating test has revolutionized the study of civilizations and settlements, especially of prehistoric times, for which written documents, coins, etc. are seldom available. This method has enabled historians to determine more accurately than before the time period of a particular civilization or settlement. This method was discovered only 70 years ago by American scientists.

In our country, excavations brought to light the Indus Valley Civilization and its various features, hitherto unknown. Similarly, no complete text of Kautilya's Arthashastra was available before it was discovered by Shamasastry, the chief of the Mysore Government Oriental Library in the first decade of the last century. Likewise, people's knowledge of the history of the Buddhist period got extended after excavations at Sarnath and the ruins of the Asokan period at Patna. In the future, if the Harappan inscriptions are deciphered, our knowledge of the Indus Valley Civilization will increase enormously. All these instances underline the fact that our knowledge of history is never static and its frontiers go on extending.

In the light of what has been said above the encyclopedic history is going to be of great help to students interested in Indian history. It is comprehensive and as far as possible free from biases. It includes the latest materials, and objective conclusions.

Prof . Bipan Chandra

Professor Emeritus, JNU

Chairman, National Book Trust, India

Contents

Preface

The people of India have had a continuous civilization since 2500 B.C., when the inhabitants of the Indus River valley developed an urban culture based on commerce and sustained by agricultural trade. This civilization declined around 1500 B.C., probably due to ecological changes. During the second millennium B.C., pastoral, Aryan-speaking tribes migrated from the northwest into the subcontinent. As they settled in the middle Ganges River valley, they adapted to antecedent cultures.

The political map of ancient and medieval India was made up of myriad kingdoms with fluctuating boundaries. In the 4th and 5th centuries A.D., northern India was unified under the Gupta Dynasty. During this period, known as India's Golden Age, Hindu culture and political administration reached new heights. Islam spread across the Indian subcontinent over a period of 500 years. In the 10th and 11th centuries, Turks and Afghans invaded India and established sultanates in Delhi. In the early 16th century, descendants of Genghis Khan swept across the Khyber Pass and established the Mughal (Mogul) Dynasty, which lasted for 200 years. From the 11th to the 15th centuries, southern India was dominated by Hindu Chola and Vijayanagar Dynasties. During this time, the two systems—the prevailing Hindu and Muslim—mingled, leaving lasting cultural influences on each other.

The first British outpost in South Asia was established in 1619 at Surat on the northwestern coast. Later in the century, the East India Company opened permanent trading stations at Madras, Bombay, and Calcutta, each under the protection of native rulers. The British expanded their influence from these footholds until, by the 1850s, they controlled most of present-day India, Pakistan, and Bangladesh. In 1857, a rebellion in north India led by mutinous Indian soldiers caused the British Parliament to transfer all political power from the East India Company to the Crown. Great Britain began administering most of India directly while controlling the rest through treaties with local rulers.

In the late 1800s, the first steps were taken toward self-government in British India with the appointment of Indian councillors to advise the British viceroy and the establishment of provincial councils with Indian members; the British subsequently widened participation in legislative councils. Beginning in 1920, Indian leader Mohandas K. Gandhi transformed the Indian National Congress political party into a mass movement to campaign against British colonial rule.

—Authors

1

Introduction

The *Vedas* are the main scriptural texts of Hinduism, also known as the Sanatana Dharma, and are a large corpus of texts originating in Ancient India. The Vedas, regarded as *Aaruti* ("that which is heard"), form part of an oral tradition in the form of an ancient teacher-disciple tradition. As per Hindu tradition the Vedas were 'revealed' to the Rishis referred to in the texts, not composed or written by them. Even though many historians have tried to affix dates to the Vedas there is as yet no common consensus as there is for the scriptures of other religions.

The Vedas are arguably the oldest surviving scriptures in the world. The Vedanta and Mimamsa schools of Hindu philosophy assert that the Vedas are apaurusheya ("unauthored"), that is, they have neither human nor divine origin, and are eternal in nature. As per Hindu tradition, the sage Vedavyasa divided the Vedas into Rigveda, Yajurveda, Samaveda and Atharvaveda at the beginning of the Kali Yuga.

Overview: The sacred books of ancient India. The Sanskrit word "Veda" means "knowledge", more particularly "sacred book". In its widest sense the term designates not only the sacred texts, but also the voluminous theological and philosophical literature attached thereto, the Brahmanas, Aranyakas, Upanishads, and Sutras. But usually the term veda applies only to the four collections (Samhitas) of hymns and prayers composed for different ritualistic purposes: the Rigveda, Samaveda, Yajurveda, and Atharvaveda. Of these only the first three were—originally regarded as canonical; the fourth attained to this position after a long struggle. Though differences exist in the language of the four

Vedas, still there is such agreement on cardinal points as against later Sanskrit that the term Vedic, which is in common use for the oldest form of the language of India, is amply justified.

The Rigveda: The Rigveda ("Veda of verses"; from *ric,* or before sonants *rig,* "laudatory stanza") is the oldest and most important of these collections. In its present form it contains 1028 hymns (including eleven supplementary ones in the eighth book), arranged in ten mandalas (cycles), or books, which vary in extent, only the first and tenth being approximately equal. The poems themselves are of different authorship and date from widely different periods.

The actual date of these ancient scriptures is a nebulous topic. Yet, the description of an extremely cold climate leads some to believe that the Vedas are close to 20,000 years old, but there are some modern scholars who think that the number is exaggerated and should be about 5000. No matter what the age, it is the belief by many these texts were and are the oldest in the world. They express philosophies, realities and truths about life. The texts themselves show that the collection is the result of the work of generations of poets, extending over many centuries. Books II to VII inclusive are each the work of a single poet, or Rishi (seer), and his descendants; hence they are aptly called "family books". Book III is attributed to the family of Vishvamitra, IV to that of Vamadeva, V to that of Vasishtha. The hymns in books I and X are all composed by different families. The ninth consists exclusively of hymns addressed to Soma, the deified plant, the juice of which was used for the Soma sacrifice. Books II to VII are the oldest, and Book X the most recent, in point of origin.

Hymns to the same deity are usually grouped together. Thus, approximately 500 hymns are addressed to two gods alone: Indra, the god of lightning and storms, and Agni, the god of fire. The term god is actually false, the "gods" (devas) being only highly, elevated prophets, angels, or phenomenons. The Vedas clearly state that there is only one God, the same as Jews, Muslims, Christians belief alike. One Vedic missionary is the Arya Samaj, its churches are located all over the world, especially in India, the USA, and can teach those who search the Vedas.

The element of nature-worship is a marked feature in most of the hymns, which are invocations of different deities. The value of the great collection as presenting the earliest record of the mythology of an Indo-European people is apparent. Several of the gods go back to the time of Indo-Iranian unity, *e.g.* Yama (the Avestan Yima), Soma (haoma), Mitra (the later Persian Mithra). Some of the divinities, especially the higher ones, still exhibit the attributes which enable us to trace their origin to the personification of natural phenomena.

Thus, Indra personified thunder, Agni-fire, Varuna-the sea, Surya-the sun, Usha-the dawn, the Maruts the storm, and others were of a somewhat similar character. Indra was the favourite god of the Vedic Aryans; almost one fourth of all the hymns in the Rigveda are addressed to him and they are among the best in the collection. Next to Indra stands Agni. Many hymns are in honour of Soma. Other gods invoked are the two Ashins, somewhat resembling the Diocsuri of ancient Greece, the terrible Rudra, Parjanya the rain-god, Vayu the wind-god, Surya the sun-god, Pushan the protector of roads and stray kine. Prayers are also addressed to groups of divinities like the Adityas and the Vishve Devas (all the gods). Only a few hymns sing the praise of Vishnu and of Shiva in his earlier form as Rudra, though these two deities became later the chief gods of the Hindu pantheon. Goddesses play a small part, only Ushas, the goddess of dawn, has some twenty hymns in her honour; these poems are of exceptional literary merit.

The number of secular hymns are small, but many of them are of particular interest. They are of various content. In one (book X, 34) a gambler laments his ill luck at dice and deplores the evil passion that holds him in his grasp. In the same book (X, 18) there occurs a funeral hymn, from which important information may be gained concerning the funeral rites of the Vedic age. Evidently cremation was most in vogue, though burial was also resorted to. There are also some riddles and incantations or prayers exactly like those in the Atharvaveda. Historical references are occasionally found in the so-called danastutis (praises of gifts), which in most cases are not independent poems, but laudatory stanzas appended to some ordinary hymn, and in which the poet gives thanks for generosity shown to him by some prince. Some six or seven hymns deal with cosmogonic speculations.

It is significant that some of the hymns, chiefly in book X, are cast in the form of a dialogue. Here we may possibly discern the beginnings of the Sanskrit drama. The poetry of the Rigveda is neither popular nor primitive, as it has been erroneously considered, but is the production of a refined sacerdotal class and the result of a long period of cultural development. It was intended primarily for use in connection with the Soma sacrifice, and to accompany a ritual, which, though not so complicated as at the time of the Brahmanas, was far from simple. The Rigveda has come down to us in only one recession, that of the Shakala school. Originally there were several schools: The "Mahabhashya" (great commentary), about the second century B.C., knows of twenty-one, while some later writings know of two only. In these schools the transmission of the hymns was most carefully attended to; a most elaborate mnemonic system was devised to guard against any changes in the sacred text, which has thus come down to us practically without variants.

Editions of the Rigveda were published by Max Muller, "Rigveda-Samhita with the Commentary of Sayancharya" (6 vols., London, 1849-74; 2nd ed., 4 vols., 1890-95); "The Hymns of the Rigveda in the Samhita and Pada Texts" (2nd ed., 2 vols., London, 1877); Aufrecht, "Samhita Text", in Roman characters (2nd ed., Bonn, 1877); selections in Lanman's "Sanskrit Reader" (Boston, 1884); Bothlingk, "Sanskrit-Chrestomathie" (3rd ed., Leipzig, 1897); Windisch, "Zwolf Hymnen des Rigveda", with Sayana's commentary (Leipzig, 1883). Translations were made into: English verse by Griffith (2 vols., Benares, 1896-97); selections in prose by Max Muller in "Sacred Books of the East", XXXII (Oxford, 1891); continued by Oldenburg, ibidem, XLVI (1897); German verse by Grassmann (2 vols., Leipzig, 1876-77); German prose by Ludwig (6 vols., Prague, 1876-88). On the Rigveda in general see: Kaegi, "The Rigveda", tr. Arrowsmith (Boston, 1886); Odenberg, "Rigveda", books I-VI in "Gottinger Gesellschaft der Wissenschaften", new series, XI (Berlin, 1909).

Righteousness (Dharma) in the Rig Veda : The Vedic sages created the institution of sacrificial fires (yadnya) as the point of union of God and man, on the earth. Later that very institution became the central focus of the spread of Vedic culture (sanskruti). A sacrificial fire is the very core of social life and the formation of social organisations. According to the Vedic sages The Supreme God exists in the form of a sacrificial fire. Performing sacrificial fires was Their sole code of Righteousness. Somyag is a sacrifice which is accorded the central focus in the Rigveda. Som represents vision and fire symbolises light. It is because of the sun and the rain that all living beings survive. Food too is generated from them. This being the attitude of Vedic sages towards sacrificial fires They linked every important action of life to them.

The Samaveda: The Samaveda ("Veda of chants") consists of 1549 stanzas, taken entirely (except 75) from the Rigveda, chiefly from books VIII and IX. Its purpose was purely practical, to serve as a textbook for the udgatar or priest who attended the Soma sacrifice. The arrangement of the verses is determined solely by their relation to the rites attending this function. The hymns were to be sung according to certain fixed melodies; hence the name of the collection. Though only two recensions are known, the number of schools for the veda is known to have been very large. The Samaveda was edited: (with German tr.) by Benfey (Leipzig, 1848); by Satyavrata Samashrami in Bibl. Ind. (Calcutta, 1873); Engl. tr. by Griffith (Benares, 1893).

The Yajurveda: The Yajurveda ("Veda of sacrificial prayers") consists also largely of verses borrowed from the Rigveda. Its purpose was also practical, but, unlike the Samaveda, it was compiled to apply to the entire sacrificial rite, not merely the Soma offering. There are two recensions of this Veda known as the "Black" and "White" Yajurveda. The origin and meaning of these designations are not clear. The White (Shukla) Yajurveda contains only the verses and sayings necessary for the sacrifice, while explanations exist in a separate work; the Black incorporates explanations and directions in the work itself, often immediately following the verses. Of the black there are again four recensions, all showing the same arrangement, but differing in many other respects, notably in matters of phonology and accent. By the Hindus the Yajurveda was regarded as the most important of all the Vedas for the practice of the sacrificial rites. The four recensions of the Yajurveda have been separately edited: (1) "Vajasaneyi Samhita" by Weber (London and Berlin, 1852), tr. Griffith (Benares, 1899); (2) "Taittiriya S." by Weber in "Indische Studien", XI, XII (Berlin, 1871-72); (3) "Maitrayani S." by von Schroeder (Leipzig, 1881-86); (4) "Kathaka S." by von Schroeder (Leipzig, 1900-09).

The Atharvana-Veda: The Atharva-Veda ("Veda of the atharvans or fire priests") differs widely from the other Vedas in that it is not essentially religious in character and not connected with the ritual of the Soma sacrifice. It consists chiefly of a variety of spells and incantations, intended to curse as well as to bless. There are charms against enemies, demons, wizards, harmful animals like snakes, against sickness of man or beast, against the oppressors of Brahmans. But there are also charms of a positive character to obtain benefits, to insure love, happy family-life, health and longevity, protection on journeys, even luck in gambling. Superstitions from primitive ages were evidently current among the masses. To some of the spells remarkably close parallels can be adduced from Germanic and Slavic antiquity.

The Atharvana-Veda is preserved in two recensions, which, though differing in content and arrangement, are of equal extent, comprising 730 hymns and about 6000 stanzas, distributed in twenty books. Many of the verses are taken from the Rigveda without change; a considerable part of the sayings is in prose. The books are of different age; the first thirteen are the oldest, the last two are late additions. Book XX, consisting entirely of hymns in praise of Indra, all taken from the Rigveda, was undoubtedly added to give the Atharvana's connection with the sacrificial ceremonial and thus to insure its recognition as a canonical book. But this recognition was attained only after a considerable lapse of time, and after the period of the Rigveda.

In the "Mahabharata" the canonical character of the Atharvana is distinctly recognized, references to the four Vedas being frequent. Though as a whole this collection must have come into existence later than the Rigveda, much of its material is fully as old and perhaps older. For the history of religion and civilization it is a document of priceless value. The Atharvana-Veda has been edited by Roth and Whitney (berlin, 1856); Engl. tr. in verse by Griffith (2 vols., Benares, 1897); prose by Bloomfield in "Sacred Books of the East", XLII; by Whitney, revised by Lanman (2 vols., Cambridge, Mass, 1905). Consult Bloomfield, "The Atharaveda" in "Grundriss der Indoarischen Philologie", II (Strasburg, 1899).

Organization: The Mantras are collected into anthologies called Samhitas. There are four Samhitas: the *Rk* (poetry), *Saman* (song), *Yajus* (prayer), and *Atharvan* (a kind of priest). They are commonly referred to as the Rigveda, Samaveda, Yajurveda, and Atharvaveda respectively. Each Samhita is preserved in a number of versions or recensions (*shakhas*), the differences among them being minor, except in the case of the Yajurveda, where two "White" (*shukla*) recensions contain the Mantras only, while four "Black" (*krishna*) recensions interspersed the Brahmana parts among the Mantras.

The Rigveda contains the oldest part of the corpus, and consists of 1028 hymns. The Samaveda is mostly a rearrangement of the Rigveda for musical rendering. The Yajurveda gives sacrificial prayers and the Atharvaveda gives charms, incantations and magical formulae. In addition to these there are some stray secular material, such as legends. The next category of texts are the Brahmanas. These are ritual texts that describe in detail the sacrifices in which the Mantras were to be used, as well as comment on the meaning of the sacrificial ritual. Each of the Brahmanas is associated with one of the Samhitas. The Brahmanas may either form separate texts, or in the case of the Black Yajurveda, can be partly integrated into the text of the Samhita. The most important of the Brahmanas is the Shatapatha Brahmana of the White Yajurveda.

The Aranyakas and Upanishads are theological and philosophical works. They are mystic or spiritual interpretations of the Vedas, and are considered their putative end and essence, and thus known as Vedanta ("the end of the Vedas"). They often form part of the Brahmanas (*e.g.* the Brhadaranyaka Upanishad). They are the basis of the Vedanta school of Darshana.

Position and Compilation: Hindu tradition regards the Vedas as shruti: uncreated, eternal and being revealed to sages (rishis). The rishi Krishna Dwaipayana, better known as Veda Vyasa – "Vyasa" meaning "editor" or "compiler" – reputedly distributed this mass of hymns into the four books of the Vedas, each book being supervised by one of his disciples. Paila arranged the hymns of the Rigveda. Those that were chanted during religious and social ceremonies were compiled by Vaishampayana under the title *Yajus mantra Samhita* (see Yajurveda). Jaimini is said to have collected hymns that were set to music and melody — "Saman" (see *Samaveda*). The fourth collection of hymns and chants known as the *Atharva Samhita* was collated by Sumanta.

Philosophies and sects that developed in the Indian subcontinent have taken differing positions on the Vedas. In Buddhism and Jainism, the authority of the Veda is repudiated, and both evolved into separate religions. The sects which did not explicitly reject the Vedas remained followers of the Sanatana Dharma, which is known in modern times as Hinduism.

'Vedic Shakhas and their Geographical Distribution'

Shakha	*Samhita*	*Brahmana*	*Aranyaka*	*Upanishad*
Shakala RV	Oral and Printed	Printed (=Aitareya Brahmana) and Oral	Printed (Aitareya Aranyaka) and Oral	Printed (Aitareya Upanishad) and Oral
Bashkala RV	Manuscript exists with accents and Padapatha.	-	-	-
Shankhayana RV	Manuscript exists with accents and Padapatha.	Printed (=Shankhayana Brahmana)	Printed (=Shankhyana Aranyaka)	Printed as a part of the Aranyaka
Kaushitaki RV	X	Printed (=Kaushitaki Brahmana) and Oral	Manuscript exists	Printed (=Kaushitaki Upanishad)
Ashvalayana RV	Manuscript exists, with accents and Padapatha.	Same as Shakala	Same as Shakala shakha	Same as Shakala shakha
Paingi RV	X	Manuscript might exist	'Rahashya Brahmana' lost.	X
Madhyandina YV	Oral and Printed	Oral and Printed (Madhyandina Shata-patha) with accents.	Oral and Printed (=Shatapatha XIV.1-8) with accents,	Oral and Printed (=Brihadaranyaka Upanishad= Shatapatha XIV. 3-8) with accents.

Contd...

Kanva YV	Oral and Printed	Oral and Printed partially (=Kanva Shatapatha Brahmana) with accents.	Oral and Printed (Book XVII of Kanva Shatapatha) with accents.	Oral and Printed (with numerous commentaries, as 'Brihadaranyaka Upanishad') with accents.
Katyayana YV	Manuscript (?)	Manuscript (only first 6 books, rest lost)	X	X
Taittiriya YV	Oral and Printed	Oral and Printed: =Taittiriya Br. and Vadhula Br. (part of Vadhula Srautrasutra)	Oral and Printed (=Taittiriya. Aranyaka) with accents	Oral and Printed (=Taittiriya Upanishad, Mahanarayana Upanishad) with accents.
Maitrayani YV	Oral (partial?) and Printed	Lost	Oral and Printed (=Maitrayani Aranyaka/ Upanishad) with accents.	Oral and Printed (virtually same as Aranyaka)

Contd...

Kathaka YV	Printed. Accents survive only on 1/3 on the text.	Fragments printed and in manuscript)	Printed as 'Katha Aranyaka' (almost the entire text from a solitary manuscript)	Printed as Kathaka Upanishad with numerous commentaries. Katha Shiksha Upanishad also published.
Kapishthala YV	Printed (from a fragmentary manuscript. Accents left out)	Small fragment extant in manuscript	X	X
Charaka	Manuscript exists (?)	Lost	In Manuscript	X
Kauthuma SV	Samhita and Samans printed/ recorded	Printed (8 Brahmanas in all). Accents lost long back.	None. The Samhita itself has the 'Aranyaka'.	The famous Chhandogya Upanishad with numerous commentaries
Ranayaniya SV	Manuscripts of Samhita exist. Samans recorded but not printed	Same as Kauthuma with minor differences.	None. The Samhita itself has the 'Aranyaka'.	Same as Kauthuma.

Contd...

Jaiminiya/ Talavakara SV	Samhita published. Two distinct styles of Saman recitation, partially recorded and published.	Brahmana published (without accents) – Jaiminiya Brahmana, Arsheya Brahmana	Tamil Nadu version of Talavakara Aranyaka (=Jaiminiya Up. Brahmana) published.	Famous Kena Upanishad
Shatyayana SV	X (traditions might be similar to Jaminiya SV)	Manuscript	X	X
Paippalada AV	Two versions: Kashmirian (published) and Orissan (partly published, in manuscript, unaccented)	Lost	X	Famous Prashna Upanishad, Sharabha Upanishad etc. – all published.
Shaunaka AV	Printed and Oral traditions alive	Fragmentary Gopatha Brahmana (extant and published). No accents.	X	Mundaka Upanishad published.

Study: Elaborate methods for preserving the text (memorizing by heart instead of writing), subsidiary disciplines (Vedanga), exegetical literature, etc., were developed in the Vedic schools. Sayana, from the 14th century, is known for his elaborate commentaries on the Vedic texts.

While much evidence suggests that everyone was equally allowed to study the Vedas and many Vedic "authors" were women, the later dharmashastras, from the Sutra age, dictate that women and Shudras were neither required nor allowed to study the Veda.

These dharmashastras regard the study of the Vedas a religious duty of the three upper varnas (Brahmins, Kshatriyas and Vaishyas). In modern times, Vedic studies are crucial in the understanding of Indo-European linguistics, as well as ancient Indian history.

Many forms of Hinduism encourage the Vedic mantras to be interpreted as liberally and as philosophically as possible, unlike the texts of the three Abrahamic religions. In fact, over-literal interpretation of the mantras is actually discouraged, and even the three layers of commentaries (Brahmanas, Aranyakas, and Upanishads), which form an integral part of the Aaruti literature, interpret the seemingly polytheistic, ritualistic, and highly complex Samhitas in a philosophical and metaphorical way to explain the "hidden" concepts of God (Ishwara), the Supreme Being (Brahman) and the soul or the self (Atman).

Many Hindus believe that the very sound of the Vedic mantras is purifying for the environment and the human mind. Each may contain a thousand layers of meaning.

Cosmogony: The Vedic view of the world and cosmogony sees one true divine principle self-projecting as the divine word, *Vaak*, 'birthing' the cosmos that we know from 'Hiranyagarbha' or Golden Womb, a primordial sun figure that is equivalent to Surya.

The varied gods like Vayu, Indra, Rudra (the Destroyer), Agni (Fire, the sacrifical medium) and the goddess Saraswati (the Divine Word, or Vaak) are just some examples of the myriad aspects of the one underlying nature of the universe.

The word Veda is often derived from 5 roots these days:

- *Vid Jnaane:* To know

- *Vid Sattaayaam*: To be, to endure
- *Vid Labhe*: To obtain
- *Vid Vichaarane*: To consider
- *Vid Chetanaakhyaananiveseshu*: To feel, to tell, to dwell.

To these roots is added the suffix 'ghaw' according to Ashtadhyayi 3.3.19, the celebrated text of Sanskrit grammar of Panini. Accordingly, the word Veda means 'the means by which, or in which all persons know, acquire mastery in, deliberate over the various lores or live or subsist upon them.'

Traditionally, the Vedic literature as such signifies a vast body of sacred and esoteric knowledge concerning eternal spiritual truths revealed to sages (Rishis) during intense meditation. They have been accorded the position of revealed scriptures and are revered in Hindu religious tradition. Over the millennia the Vedas have been handed over generation to generation by oral tradition and hence the name "shruti" or "that which is heard". According to tradition they are unauthorised (apaurusheya) and eternal.

The Vedic literature is also called by several other names:

- *Nigama*: Traditional wisdom transmitted from generation to generation
- *Amnaaya*: The root texts or primordial texts of (Hindu) tradition
- *Trayi*: The Vedic texts comprising of Versified mantras, prose mantras, and melodies.

Dating: The Hindus fundamental belief is that the Vedas are sanatan-eternal-and apaurusheya-not composed by human entity. At the beginning of every cosmic cycle of Brahma, Paramatma utters the divine words. Later, at various periods great rishis perceive these divine words and imparted this knowledge orally through generations.

It is believed that this Vedic knowledge totally disappeared at the end of Brahmas cosmic cycle and reappeared again in Brahma's next cycle of creation. Later a part of vedic knowledge was written. Maha Rishi Veda Vyas simplified this one Veda by dividing it into four: Rig, Sam, Yajur, Atharva. In Bharatvarsh as true tradition the Vedas are eternal. In the light of these beliefs, the historical dating of these texts is a concept foreign to Hinduism and the province of secular (academic) philology.

Many historians regard the samhitas as one of the oldest oral traditions. The newest parts of the Vedas are estimated to date to around 500 BC, the oldest text (Rugveda) may be assumed to have been completed orally by 1500 BC after being composed over hundreds of years, but most Indologists agree that a long oral tradition possibly existed before it was written down by the second century BC.

Some parts of the Rigveda as well as the other Vedas are written in Sanskrit. Some writers have used astronomical references in the Rigveda to date it to as early as the 4th millennium BC. This astronomical evidence has often been claimed to support the out of India theory in relation to origins of the Indo-European languages.

Etymology: The word "veda" means "knowledge", and is derived from the root "vid", Sanskrit for "know", reconstructed as being derived from the Proto-Indo-European root "weid-", meaning "see" or "know". "Weid" is also the source of the English word "wit", as well as "vision" through Latin. The Czech and Slovak words for "science" are "vìda" resp. "veda", derived from western Slavic "videt" resp. "vedie" for "know".

Upavedas: The Upavedas are derived from the Vedas and are specific applications of the teachings of the Vedas. The main Upavedas are:

1. *Ayurveda:* Indian healing system, it lays more stress on living with nature instead of fighting it, hence preventive instead of corrective medicine.
2. *Dhanur Veda:* Martial arts.

   Ayurveda and Dhanurveda have points in common. They both work with Marma, or natural Pran (Life Energy) that flows in the body. Ayurveda heals the body, while Dhanurveda is used for defending the body. This concept is also known to Chinese as Acupuncture and related Chinese Martial Arts.
3. *Stahapatya Veda:* Architecture, sculpture and geomancy. Used especially for Temple design.

4. *Gandharv-Veda:* Music, poetry and dance.

Some other fields like Jyotish (Indian Astrology), Tantra (based on the Puranas, which are in turn based on Vedas), Shiksha and Vyakara (Grammar and pronunciation) are also based on the Vedas.

The Six Schools of Vedic Philosophy

1. *Nyaya:* The Logical School, founded by Gautama
2. *Vaishesika:* Atomic school, founded by Kannada
3. *Samkhya:* Cosmic Principle School, founded by Kapila
4. *Yoga:* Yoga school (includes Raj, Hatha, Kundalini, and Tantra Yoga), supposedly founded by Hiranyagarbha, although the Bhagavad Gita, Patanjali's Yoga Sutras, and Hatha Yoga Pradipika are the most popular treatises that have survived.
5. *Mimamsa (also Purva Mimamsa):* Ritualistic School, founded by Jamini
6. *Vedant (also Uttara Mimasa):* Theological School, founded by Badarayana.

Vedanta was made popular by Adi Shankara also called Shankaracharya, who founded the Swami Order of Monks, and established 4 schools (or Maths) in 4 parts of India to carry on teachings of the Vedas in the 7th century.

Modern Writers Opinions

Sri Aurobindo

One of the best commentaries to the Vedas in the modern times is written by Sri Aurobindo. Rigveda is considered by many to be a book written by barbaric culture worshipping violent Gods. Sri Aurobindo realised that this was due to the biased view of Westerners who had some preconceived views on Hindu culture.

Taking the cue from Swami Dayananda Saraswati, founder of the Arya Samaj, Sri Aurobindo decided to look for hidden meanings in the Vedas. He looked at the Rigveda as a psychological book, inspiring the people to move towards God, but in a hidden language.

So Indra is the God of Indriya, or the senses (sight, touch, hear, taste, etc.). Vayu means air, but in esoteric terms means Prana, or the Life force. So when the Rigvedas says "Call Indra and Vayu to drink Soma Rasa" they mean use the Mind senses and Prana to receive Divine Bliss (Soma means wine of Gods, but in several texts also means Divine Bliss, as in Right-handed Tantra).

Agni, or God of Fire, is the hidden Divine Spark in us, which we have to fan, so it grows and engulfs our whole body. So the sacrifice of the Vedas actually means sacrificing one's ego to the internal Agni, or Divine spark.

2

The Vedic Literature

Rigveda

The *Rigveda* is a collection of Vedic Sanskrit hymns dedicated to the gods. It is counted as the holiest among the series of four Hindu canonical texts known as the Vedas. Geographical and ethnological passages in the Rigveda provide evidence that the Rigveda was composed between 1700–1100 BCE (the early Vedic period) in the Punjab (Sapta Sindhu) region of the Indian subcontinent. The Rigveda is the oldest of all known religious books, and the oldest book in Vedic Sanskrit or any Indo-European language. The composition of the Rigveda is conventionally dated to before 1500 BC. Some writers have traced astronomical references in the *Rigveda* dating it to as early as 4000 BC, a date well within the late Mehrgarh culture.

Today, this text is revered by Hindus around the world, primarily in India and Nepal. Its verses are recited at prayers, religious functions and other auspicious occasions.

Text: The Rigveda consists of 1,028 hymns (or 1,017 discounting the apocryphal *valakhilya* hymns 8.49–8.59) composed in Vedic Sanskrit, many of which are intended for various sacrifical rituals. This long collection of short hymns is mostly devoted to the praise of the gods. It is organized in 10 books, known as Mandalas. Each Mandala consists of hymns, called *sukta,* which in turn consist individual verses called, plural. The Mandalas are by no means of equal length or age: The "family books", mandalas 2-7, are considered the oldest part of the Rigveda, being the shortest books, arranged by length, accounting for 38% of the text. RV 8 and RV 9, likely comprising hymns of mixed age, account for 15% and 9%, respectively. RV 1 and RV 10, finally, are both the latest and the longest books, accounting for 37% of the text.

Preservation: The *Rigveda* is preserved by two major shakhas ("branches", *i.e.* schools or recensions), *Uakala* and *Backala*. Considering its great age, the text is spectacularly well-preserved and uncorrupted, the two recensions being practically identical, so that scholarly editions can mostly do without a critical apparatus. Associated to *Uakala* is the Aitareya-Brahmana. The *Backala* includes the Khilani and has the Kausitaki-Brahmana associated to it.

This compilation or redaction included the arrangement in books as well as orthoepic changes, such as regularization of sandhi (called by Oldenberg *orthoepische Diaskeunase*). It took place centuries after the composition of the earliest hymns, about coeval to the redaction of the other Vedas.

From the time of its redaction, the text has been handed down in two versions: The *Samhitapatha* has all Sanskrit rules of sandhi applied and is the text used for recitation. The Padapatha has each word isolated in its pausa form and is used for memorization. The Padapatha is, as it were, a commentary to the *Samhitapatha,* but the two seem to be about coeval. The original text as reconstructed on metrical grounds (*viz.* "original" in the sense that it aims to recover the hymns as composed by the Rishis) lies somewhere between the two, but closer to the Samhitapatha.

Organization: The most common numbering scheme is by *book, hymn and verse (and pada* (foot) *a, b, c...,* if required). *e.g.* the first *pada* is

- "Agni I laud, the high priest" and the final *pada* is
- "for your being in good company"

Hermann Grassmann had numbered the hymns 1 through to 1028, putting the *valakhilya* at the end. The entire 1028 hymns of the *Rigveda,* in the 1877 edition of Aufrecht, contain a total of 10,552 verses, or 39,831 padas. The Shatapatha Brahmana gives the number of syllables to be 432,000, while the metrical text of van Nooten and Holland (1994) has a total of 395,563 syllables (or an average of 9.93 syllables per pada); counting the number of syllables is not straightforward because of issues with sandhi. Most verses are jagati (padas of 12 syllables), trishtubh (padas of 11 syllables), viraj (padas of 10 syllables) or gayatri or anushtubh (padas of 8 syllables).

Contents: The chief gods of the *Rigveda* are Agni, the sacrificial fire, Indra, a heroic god who is praised for having slain his enemy Vrtra, and Soma, the sacred potion, or the plant it is made from. Other prominent gods are Mitra-Varuna and Ushas (the dawn). Also invoked are Savitar, Vishnu, Rudra, Pushan, Brihaspati, Brahmanaspati, as well as deified natural phenomena such as Dyaus Pita (the sky), Prithivi (the earth), Surya (the sun), Vayu (the wind), Apas (the waters), Parjanya (the rain), Vac (the word), many rivers (notably the Sapta Sindhu, and the Saraswati River). Groups of deities are the Ashvins, the Maruts, the Adityas, the Rbhus, the Vishvadevas (the all-gods).

It contains various further minor gods, persons, concepts, phenomena and items, and fragmentary references to possible historical events, notably the struggle between the early Vedic people (known as Vedic Aryans, a subgroup of the Indo-Aryans) and their enemies, the Dasa.

Rigveda manuscript in Devanagari, early 19th century:

- Mandala 1 comprises 191 hymns. Hymn 1.1 is addressed to Agni, and his name is the first word of the *Rigveda*. The remaining hymns are mainly addressed to Agni and Indra. Hymns 1.154 to 1.156 are addressed to Vishnu.
- Mandala 2 comprises 43 hymns, mainly to Agni and Indra. It is chiefly attributed to the Rishi *gatsamda aunohotra.*
- Mandala 3 comprises 62 hymns, mainly to Agni and Indra. The verse 3.62.10 has great importance in Hinduism as the Gayatri Mantra. Most hymns in this book are attributed to *viuvamitra gathina.*
- Mandala 4 consists of 58 hymns, mainly to Agni and *Indra. Most hymns in this book are attributed to Vamadeva* Gautama.
- Mandala 5 comprises 87 hymns, mainly to Agni and Indra, the Visvadevas (gods of the world), the Maruts, the twin-deity Mitra-Varuna and the Asvins. Two hymns each are dedicated to Ushas (the dawn) and to Savitar. Most hymns in this book are attributed to the *atri* family.
- Mandala 6 comprises 75 hymns, mainly to Agni and Indra. *Most hymns in this book are attributed to the barhaspatya* family of Angirasas.

- Mandala 7 comprises 104 hymns, to Agni, Indra, the Visvadevas, the Maruts, Mitra-Varuna, the Asvins, Ushas, Indra-Varuna, Varuna, Vayu (the wind), two each to Saraswati (ancient river/goddess of learning) and Vishnu, and to others. Most hymns in this book are attributed to *vasicmha maitravaurgi.*
- Mandala 8 comprises 103 hymns to different gods. Hymns 8.49 to 8.59 are the apocryphal *valakhilya.* Most hymns in this book are attributed to the *kagva* family.
- *Mandala 9 comprises 114 hymns, entirely devoted to Soma* Pavamana, the plant of the sacred potion of the Vedic religion.
- Mandala 10 comprises 191 hymns, to Agni and other gods. It contains the Nadistuti sukta which is in praise of rivers and is important for the reconstruction of the geography of the Vedic civilization and the Purusha sukta which has significance in Hindu tradition. It also contains the Nasadiya sukta (10.129), probably the most celebrated hymns in the west, which deals with creation.

Rishis: Each hymn of the Rigveda is traditionally attributed to a specific rishi, and the "family books" (2-7) are said to have been composed by one family of rishis each. The main families, listed by the number of verses ascribed to them are:

- Angirasas: 3619 (especially Mandala 6)
- Kanvas: 1315 (especially Mandala 8)
- Vasishthas: 1267 (Mandala 7)
- Vaishvamitras: 983 (Mandala 3)
- Atris: 885 (Mandala 5)
- Bhrgus: 473
- Kashyapas: 415 (part of Mandala 9)
- Grtsamadas: 401 (Mandala 2)
- Agastyas: 316
- Bharatas: 170

Translations: The *Rigveda* was translated into English by Ralph T.H. Griffith in 1896. Partial English translations by Maurice Bloomfield and William Dwight Whitney exist. Griffith's translation is good, considering its age, but it is no replacement for Geldner's

1951 translation (in German), the only independent scholarly translation so far. The later translations by Elizarenkova depends heavily on Geldner, but Elizarenkova's translation (in Russian) is valuable in taking into account scholarly literature up to 1990. Partial translations exists in many other languages.

Hindu Tradition: According to Indian tradition, the Rigvedic hymns were collected by Paila under the guidance of Vyasa, who formed the Rigveda Samhita as we know it. According to the Uatapatha Brahmana, the number of syllables in the *Rigveda* is 432,000, equalling the number of muhurtas (1 day = 30 muhurtas) in forty years. This statement stresses the underlying philosophy of the Vedic books that there is a connection (bandhu) between the astronomical, the physiological, and the spiritual.

The authors of the Brahmana literature described and interpreted the Rigvedic ritual. Yaska was an early commentator of the *Rigveda*. In the 14th century, Sayana wrote an exhaustive commentary on it. Other *Bhacyas* (commentaries) that have been preserved up to present times are those by Madhava, Skacdasvamin and Veckatamadhava.

Dating and Historical Reconstruction: Geography of the Rigveda, with river names; the extent of the Swat and Cemetery cultures are also indicated.

The *Rigveda* is far more archaic than any other Indo-Aryan text. For this reason, it was in the centre of attention of western scholarship from the times of Max Muller. The *Rigveda* records an early stage of Vedic religion, still closely tied to the pre-Zoroastrian Persian religion. It is thought that Zoroastrianism and Vedic Hinduism evolved from an earlier common religious—Indo-Iranian—culture.

The Rigveda's core is accepted to date to the late Bronze Age, making it the only example of Bronze Age literature with an unbroken tradition. Its composition is usually dated to roughly between 1700–1100 BC. The text in the following centuries underwent pronunciation revisions and standardization (samhitapatha, padapatha). This redaction would have been completed around the 7th century BC.

Writing appears in India around the 5th century BC in the form of the Brahmi script, but texts of the length of the Rigveda were likely not written down until much later, the oldest surviving manuscript dating to the 11th century. While written manuscripts were used for teaching in medieval times, they were written on bark or palm leaves, which decomposed quicker in the tropical climate, until the advent of the printing press from the 16th century. The hymns were thus preserved by oral tradition for up to a millennium from the time of their composition until the redaction of the Rigveda, and the entire Rigveda was preserved in shakhas *for another 2,500 years from the time of its redaction until the editio* princeps by Muller, a collective feat of preservation unparalleled in any other known society.

Puranic literature names Vidagdha as the author of the Pada-text. Other scholars argue that Sthavira Sak of the Aitareya Aranyaka is the padakara of the RV. After their composition, the texts were preserved and codified by a vast body of Vedic priesthood as the central philosophy of the Iron Age Vedic civilization.

The *Rigveda* describes a mobile, nomadic culture, with horse-drawn chariots and metal (bronze) weapons. According to some scholars the geography described is consistent with that of the Punjab (Gandhara): Rivers flow north to south, the mountains are relatively remote but still reachable (Soma is a plant found in the mountains, and it has to be purchased, imported by merchants). Nevertheless, the hymns were certainly composed over a long period, with the oldest elements possibly reaching back before the split of Proto-Indo-Iranian (around 2000 BC). Thus there is some debate over whether the boasts of the destruction of stone forts by the Vedic Aryans and particularly by Indra refer to cities of the Indus Valley civilization or whether they hark back to clashes between the early Indo-Aryans with the BMAC in what is now northern Afghanistan and southern Turkmenistan (separated from the upper Indus by the Hindu Kush mountain range, and some 400 km distant).

In any case, while it is highly likely that the bulk of the Rigveda was composed in the Punjab, even if based on earlier poetic *traditions, there is no mention of either tigers or rice in the Rigveda* (as opposed to the later Vedas), suggesting that Vedic culture only penetrated into the plains of India after its completion. Similarly, it is assumed that there is no mention of iron although the term ayas (metal) occurs in the Rigveda. The Iron Age in northern India begins in the 12th century BC with the *Black and Red Ware* (BRW) culture. This is a widely-accepted timeframe for the beginning codification of the *Rigveda* (*i.e.* the arrangement of the individual hymns in books, and the fixing of the samhitapatha (by applying Sandhi) and the padapatha (by dissolving Sandhi) out of the earlier metrical text), and the composition of the younger Vedas. This time probably coincides with the early Kuru kingdom, shifting the centre of Vedic culture east from the Punjab into what is now Uttar Pradesh.

Some of the names of gods and goddesses found in the Rigveda are found amongst other belief systems based on Proto-Indo-European religion as well: Dyaus-Pita is cognate with Greek Zeus, Latin Jupiter (from deus-pater), and Germanic Tyr; while Mitra is cognate with Persian *Mithra*; also, Ushas with Greek Eos and Latin Aurora; and, less certainly, Varuna with Greek Uranos. Finally, Agni is cognate with Latin *ignis* and Russian *ogon*, both meaning "fire".

Some writers have traced astronomical references in the Rigveda dating it to as early as 4000 BC, a date well within the Indian Neolithic. Claims of such evidence remain controversial, but are a key factor in the development of the Proto-Vedic Continuity theory.

N. Kazanas in a polemic against the "Aryan Invasion Theory" suggests a date as early as 3100 BC, based on an identification of the early Rigvedic Saraswati River as the Ghaggar-Hakra and on glottochronological arguments. Being a polemic against mainstream scholarship, this is in diametral opposition to views in mainstream historical linguistics, and supports the controversial Out of India theory, which assumes a date as late as 3000 BC for the age of late Proto-Indo-European itself.

Flora and Fauna in the Rigveda: The horse (Ashva) and cattle play an important role in the Rigveda. There are also references to the elephant (Hastin, Varana), Camel (Ustra, especially in Mandala 8), Buffalo (Mahisa), lion (Simha) and to the Gaur in the Rigveda. The peafowl (Mayura) and the Chakravaka (*Anas casarca*) are birds mentioned in the Rigveda.

Indian Views of Recent Past

The Hindu perception of the *Rigveda* has moved away from the original ritualistic content to a more symbolic or mystical interpretation. For example, instances of animal sacrifice are not seen as literal slaughtering but as transcendental processes. The Rigvedic view is seen to consider the universe to be infinite in size, dividing knowledge into two categories: *lower* (related to objects, beset with paradoxes) and *higher* (related to the perceiving subject, free of paradoxes). Swami Dayananda, who started the Arya Samaj and Sri Aurobindo have emphasized a spiritual (adhyatmic) interpretation of the book.

The Saraswati river, lauded in RV 7.95 as the greatest river flowing from the mountain to the sea is sometimes equated with the Ghaggar-Hakra river, which went dry perhaps before 2600 BC or certainly before 1900 BC. Others argue that the Saraswati was originally the Helmand in Afghanistan. These questions are tied to the debate about the Indo-Aryan migration (termed "Aryan Invasion Theory") vs. the claim that Vedic culture together with Vedic Sanskrit originated in the Indus Valley Civilisation (termed "Out of India theory"), a topic of great significance in Hindu nationalism, addressed for example by Amal Kiran and Shrikant G. Talageri. Subhash Kak has claimed that there is an astronomical code in the organization of the hymns.

Bal Gangadhar Tilak, also based on astronomical alignments in the Rigveda, in his "The Orion" (1893) claimed presence of the Rigvedic culture in India in the 4th millennium BC, and in his "Arctic Home in the Vedas" (1903) even argued that the Aryans originated near the North Pole and came south during the Ice Age

Rigvedic Deities: There are 1028 hymns in the *Rigveda,* most of them dedicated to specific deities.

Indra, the heroic god and slayer of Vrtra and Vala, liberator of the cows and the rivers, *Agni,* the sacrificial fire and messenger of the gods, and *Soma,* the ritual drink dedicated to Indra are the *most prominent deities by far. Invoked in groups are the Vishvedevas* (the "all-gods"), the *Maruts,* violent storm gods in Indra's train and the *Ashvins,* the twin horsemen.

There are two major families of gods, the *Devas* and the *Asuras. Unlike in later Hinduism, the Asuras are not yet demonized, Mitra* and *Varuna* being their most prominent members. Aditi is the mother both of Agni and of the *Adityas,* a group of Asuras, led by Mitra and Varuna, with Aryaman, Bhaga, Daksha, Ansa and Savitar. Surya is the personification of the Sun, but Savitar, the Ashvins and the Rohus, semi-divine craftsmen, also have aspects of solar deities. Other natural phenomena deified include Vayu, (the wind), Dyaus and Prithivi (Heaven and Earth), Dyaus continuing Dyeus, the chief god of the Proto-Indo-European religion, and Ushas (the dawn), the most prominent goddess of the Rigveda, and Apas (the waters).

Rivers play an important role, deified as goddesses, most prominently the Sapta Sindhu and the Saraswati River.

Yama is the mythical first ancestor, also worshipped as a deity, and the god of the underworld and death.

Vishnu and Rudra, the prominent deities of later Hinduism (Rudra being an early form of Shiva) are already present as marginal gods.

The names of Indra, Mitra, Varuna and the Nasatyas are also attested in a Mitanni treaty, suggesting that the religion of the Indo-Aryan Mitanni ruling class was very close to that of the Rigveda.

Deities by Prominence: List of Rigvedic deities by number of dedicated hymns, after Griffith (1888). Some dedications are to twin-deities, such as Indra-Agni, Mitra-Varuna, Soma-Rudra, here counted doubly.

- Indra 289
- Agni 218
- Soma 123 (most of them in the Soma Mandala)
- Vishvadevas 70
- The Asvins 56
- Varuna 46
- the Maruts 38
- Mitra 28
- Ushas 21
- Vayu (Wind) 12
- Savitar 11
- The Rohus 11
- Pushan 10
- The Apris 9
- Brhaspati 8

- Surya (Sun) 8
- Dyaus and Prithivi (Heaven and Earth) 6, plus 5.84 dedicated to Earth alone
- Apas (Waters) 6
- Adityas 6
- Vishnu 6
- Brahmanaspati 6
- Rudra 5
- Dadhikras 4
- The Saraswati River/Saraswati 3
- Yama
- Parjanya (Rain) 3
- Vac (Speech) 2 (mentioned 130 times, deified *e.g.* in 10.125)
- Vastospati 2
- Vishvakarman 2
- Manyu 2
- Kapinjala (the Heathcock, a form of Indra) 2

Minor deities (one single or no dedicated hymn)

- Manas (Thought), prominent concept, deified in 10.58
- Dakshina (Reward), prominent concept, deified in 10.107
- Jnanam (Knowledge), prominent concept, deified in 10.71
- Purusha ("Cosmic Man" of the Purusha sukta 10.90)
- Aditi
- Bhaga
- Vasukra
- Atri
- Apam Napat
- Ksetrapati
- Ghrta
- Nirrti
- Asamati
- Urvasi
- Pururavas

- Vena
- Aranyani
- Mayabheda
- Tarksya
- Tvastar
- Saranyu

Anukramani

An ***Anukramani*** is an index of Vedic hymns, recording poetic meter, content, and traditions of authorship.

The most important Anukramani is Katyayana's Sarvanukramani of the Rigveda (ca. 2nd century BC), recording the first word, the number of verses, name and family of poets (Rishis), names of deities and metres for each of the 1,028 hymns of the Rigveda.

Mayrhofer (2003) discusses the personal names contained in the Rigveda Anukramani, counting 543 items. Academic opinion regarding the age and authenticity of the tradition of these names is not unanimous. Mayrhofer suggests that Hermann Oldenberg (1888) was essentially correct in assuming that "the editors of the lists of authors [...] [possessed] a correct notion of the families associated with these Mandalas [the Rigvedic "family books" 2–7], *possibly* rooted in tradition. Beyond this, they do not betray as much as the slightest sign of any genuine tradition on the hymn authors" (p. 229).

Yajurveda

The ***Yajurveda*** is one of the four Hindu Vedas. It contains religious texts focusing on liturgy, rituals and sacrifices, and how to perform the same.

Collections: There are two primary collections or *samhitas* of the Yajurveda: Shukla (white) and Krishna (black). Both contain the verses necessary for rituals, but the Krishna Yajurveda has additional prose commentary and detailed instructions within the work itself.

Shukla Yajurveda: There are two (nearly identical) *shakhas* or recensions of the Shukla (White) Yajurveda, both known as Vajasaneyi-Samhita (VS):

- *Vajasaneyi Madhyandiniya* (VSM)
- *Vajasaneyi Kanva* of Kosala (VSK)

The former is popular in North India, Gujarat, parts of Maharashtra (north of Nasik) and northern parts of Orissa, and thus commands a numerous following. The Kanva Shakha is popular in Maharashtra (south of Nasik), most of Orissa, Karnataka, Andhra Pradesh and Tamil Nadu. Sureshvaracharya, one of the four main disciples of Jagadguru Adi Shankara, is said to have followed the Kanva *shakha*. The Guru himself followed the Taittiriya Shakha with the Apastamba Kalpasutra. The Vedic rituals of the Ranganathaswamy Temple at Srirangam, the second biggest temple in India, are performed according to the Kanva *shakha*. The White Yajurveda has two Upanishads associated with it: the Isa Vasya and the Brihadaranyaka upanishads. The Brihadaranyaka Upanishad is the most voluminous of all Upanishads.

The VS has forty chapters or *adhyayas*, containing the formulas used with the following rituals:

1-2: New and Full Moon sacrifices
3: Agnihotra
4-8: Somayajna
9-10: Vajapeya and Rajasuya, two modifications of the Soma sacrifice
11-18: Construction of altars and hearths, especially the Agnicayana
19-21: Sautramani, a ritual originally counteracting the effects of excessive Soma-drinking
22-25: Ashvamedha
26-29: Supplementary formulas for various rituals
30-31: Purushamedha
32-34: Sarvamedha
35: Pitriyajna
36-39: Pravargya
40: The final adhyaya is the famous Isha Upanishad

Krishna Yajurveda

There are four recensions of the Krishna ("black" or "dark") Yajurveda:

- *taittiriya sachita* (TS) of Panchala
- *maitrayani sachita* (MS)
- *caraka-katha sachita* (KS) of Madra
- *kapicmhala-katha sachita* (KapS) of Bahika

Each of the recensions has a *Brahmana* associated with it, and some of them also have associated Shrautasutras, Grhyasutras, Aranyakas, Upanishads and Pratishakhyas.

The Taittiriya Shakha: The best known of these recensions is the TS, named after Tittiri, a pupil of Yaska. It consists of 8 books or *kandas*, subdivided in chapters or *prapathakas*, further subdivided into individual hymns. Some individual hymns in this Samhita have gained particular importance in Hinduism; *e.g.* TS 4.5 and TS 4.7 constitute the Shri Rudram Chamakam, while 1.8.6.i is the *Shaivaite Tryambakam mantra. The formula bhur bhuva, suva,* prefixed to the (rigvedic) Gayatri mantra is also from the Yajurveda, appearing four times. The Taittiriya recession of the Black Yajurveda *shakha* most prevalent in southern India. Among the followers of this Shakha, the Apastamba Sutras is the common Shrautasutra associated with the Shakha.

The Taittiriya Shakha consists of Taittiriya Samhita (having seven kaandas), Taittiriya Braahmana (having three kaandas), Taittiriya Aaranyaka (having seven prashnas), Taittiriya Upanishad (having three *prashnas* or *vallis*-Sheeksha valli, Ananda valli and Bhrigu valli) and the Mahanarayana Upanishad. The Taittiriya Upanishad and Mahaanaarayana Upanishad are considered to be the seventh, eighth, ninth and tenth prashnas of the Aaranyaka. The words *prapaathaka* and *kaanda* (meaning sections) are interchangeably used in the Vedic literature. *Prashna* and *valli* refer to sections of the Aaranyaka.

Legend: Legend has it that the vedic seer Yajnavalkya studied the Yajurveda collection under the tutelage of sage Vaishampayana maternal uncle of Yajnavalkya. Yajnavalkya's birth was with a purpose as purported by Gods. He was an 'Ekasandhigraahi', meaning he learnt anything with just once teaching. The two came to have serious differences in interpretation. On one occasion, Vaishampayana was so enraged that he demanded the return of all the knowledge he has imparted to Yajnavalkya. Yagnavalkya regurgitated all the knowledge he had learnt in the form of flesh.

The other disciples of Vaishampayana, eager to receive this knowledge, assumed the form of *tittiriya* birds and ate that flesh. Thus, that knowledge came to be called the Taittiriya Samhita (from the word *tittiriya*). There is a secret meaning in this. As we know, it is impossible to regurgiate knowledge or learning, but the words are used in 'srimad bhaagavata'.

It is also of interest to know why the Guru himself did not take the vedaas he taught Yajnyavalkya, but instead asked his deciples to eat the flesh. Any way, after having regurgitated out the knowledge acquired from his teacher, Yajnavalkya worshipped Surya (the Sun God) and acquired new knowledge directly from God Narayana (suryantargata narayana) who preached Shukla yajurveda by taking vaaji rupa, (god with horse face) which was compiled to become the *Shukla Yajurveda.* This is recorded in srimad bhaagavata.

Large Numbers: The Yajurveda documents the earliest known use of numbers up to a trillion (*parardha*). It even discusses the concept of numeric infinity (*purna* "fullness"), stating that if you subtract *purna* from *purna,* you are still left with *purna.*

Samaveda

The *Samaveda* is third in the usual order of enumeration of the four Vedas, the ancient core Hindu scriptures.

The Samaveda ranks next in sanctity and liturgical importance to the Rigveda or Veda of Recited praise. Its Sanhita, or metrical portion, consists chiefly of hymns to be chanted by the Udgatar priests at the performance of those important sacrifices in which the juice of the Soma plant, clarified and mixed with milk and other ingredients, was offered in libation to various deities. The Collection is made up of hymns, portions of hymns, and detached verses, taken mainly from the Rigveda, transposed and rearranged, without reference to their original order, to suit the religious ceremonies in which they were to be employed.

The verses are not intended to be chanted, but to be sung in specifically indicated melodies using the seven *svaras* or notes. Such songs are called *Samagana* and in this sense the Samaveda is really a book of hymns.

In these compiled hymns there are frequent variations, of more or less importance, from the text of the Rigveda as we now possess it which variations, although in some cases they are apparently explanatory, seem in others to be older and more original than the readings of the Rigveda. In singing, the verses are still further altered by prolongation, repetition and insertion of syllables, and various modulations, rests, and other modifications prescribed, for the guidance of the officiating priests, in the Ganas or Song-books.

Two of these manuals, the Gramageyagana, or Congregational, and the Aranyagana or Forest Song-Book, follow the order of the verses of part I, of the Sanhita, and two others, the Uhagana, the Uhyagana, of Part II. This part is less disjointed than part I, and is generally arranged in triplets whose first verse is often the repetition of a verse that has occurred in part I.

The Samaveda survives in a single shakha or recession, the Kauthuma shakha, with a second shakha, Jaiminiya (or Talavakara), surviving fragmentarily, the Jaiminiya Samhita. From the Jaiminiya shakha, we also have the Jaiminiya Brahmana, the Jaiminiya Upanishad Brahmana and the Kena Upanishad.

Since the Samaveda is written in verse it can be sung. This decade has seen a poetic translation of Samveda in Hindi. This translation was done by Dr. Mridul Kirti and is called "Samveda Ka Hindi Padyanuvad"

Samaveda had originally 1000 shakhas. Here are the names of some of them:

- Ranayana
- Shatyamukhya
- Vyasa
- Bhaguri
- Oulundi
- Goulgulvi
- Bhanuman-oupamayava
- Karati
- Mashaka Gargya
- Varsgagavya
- Kuthuma
- Sgakugitra

- Jaimini

One of the leading exponents of Samaveda was Pandit Rewashankar Shastri of Padadhari, Gujarat India. He was awarded with the title of 'Samaveda Martanda' by His Holiness Paramacharya Sankaracharya of Kanchi Kamakoti Peetam. This honour was conferred on Pt. Rewashankar Shastri in Madras, India in late 1960s.

Atharvaveda

The *Atharvaveda* (Sanskrit, *Atharvaveda*, a tatpurusha compound of *atharvan*, a type of priest, and *veda* meaning "knowledge") is a sacred text of Hinduism, and one of the four Vedas, often called the "fourth Veda". According to tradition, the Atharvaveda was mainly composed by two groups of rishis known as the Bhrigus and the Angirasas. Additionally, tradition ascribes parts to other rishis, such as Kauuika, Vauicmha and Kashyapa. There are two surviving recensions (uakhas), known as *aunakiya* (*AVS*) and *Paippalada* (*AVP*).

Status: The Atharvaveda, while undoubtedly belonging to the core Vedic corpus, in some ways represents an independent parallel tradition to that of the Rigveda and Yajurveda.

The Jaina and Buddha texts are considerably more hostile to the AV (they call it Aggvana or Ahavana Veda) than they are to the other Hindu texts. The Atharva Veda is less predominant than other Vedas, also the Gayatri mantra used in Atharva Veda is different from other 3 Vedas a special initiation of Gayatri is required to learn the Atharva Veda. The Hindus believe the mantras are highly powerful, the Atharvan Pariihthas (appendices) themselves state that specific priests of the Mauda and Jalada schools should be avoided or strict discipline should be followed as per the rules and regulations laid by the Atharva Veda. It is even stated that women associated with Atharvan may suffer from abortions if pregnant women remain while the chants for warfare are pronounced.

Recensions: The *Caraavyuha* (attributed to Shaunaka) lists nine shakhas or Schools of the Atharvaveda:

1. Paippalada
2. stauda

3. mauda
4. aunakiya
5. jajala
6. jalada
7. brahmavada
8. devadarea
9. charaavidya

Of these, only the Ceaunakiya (AVS) and the Paippalada (AVP) recensions have survived. The core Paippalada text is considered earlier than the Ceaunakiya, but both also contain later additions and corruptions. In places where the Ceaunakiya and the Paippàlada agree, it is likely the original version. Often, the two recensions in corresponding hymns have a different verse order, or either has additional verses missing from the other.

Additionally, from the Vicgu and Vayu Puranas (older Hindu texts on the gods, goddesses and their histories) it may be possible to glean a few more ancient schools that were not listed in the *Caragavyuha*.

These are:

- sumantu
- kabandha
- kumuda
- uaulkayana
- babhravya
- munjakeœa
- saindhavayana
- nakœatrakalpa
- uantikalpa
- sahitavidhi

At least some of these may have evolved into the other schools mentioned in the Caraavyuha list. Sahitavidhi, Uantikalpa and Nakoeatrakalpa are the five *kalpa* texts adduced to the Ceaunakiya tradition and not separate schools of their own.

There are two main circum-vedic texts associated with the AV, the vaitana sutra and the Kauuika sutra. These serve the same purpose as the vidhana of the Rigveda and are of greater value in studying the Puranic-Vedic link than the AV text itself. There are several Upanishads that are associated with the AV, but appear to be relatively late additions to the tradition. The most important amongst these are the munaka and the pracna Upanishads.

Issues of Note

- The AV is the first Indic text dealing with medicine. It identifies the causes of disease as living causative agents such as the yatudhanya, the kimidi, the krimi and the durgama. The atharvans seek to kill them with a variety of drugs in order to counter the disease (see XIX.34.9). This approach to disease is surprisingly advanced compared to the trihumoral theory developed in the puragic era. Remnants of the original atharvanic thought did persist in the puragic era as can be seen in suruta's medical. Here following the atharvan theory the puragic text suggests germs as a cause for leprosy. In the same chapter sucruta also expands on the role of helminths in disease. These two can be directly traced back to the AV sachita. The hymn AV I.23-24 describes the disease leprosy and recommends the rajani aucadhi for its treatment. From the description of the aucadhi as black branching entity with dusky patches, it is very likely that is a lichen with antibiotic properties. Thus the AV can stake a claim to being one of the earliest texts to record uses of the antibiotic agents.
- The AV also informs us about warfare. A variety of devices such as an arrow with a duct for poison (apaskambha) and castor bean poison, poisoned net and hook traps, use of disease spreading bugs and smoke screens find a place in the AV sachita (eg. hymns IX.9, IX.10, the trioeacdi and nyarbudi hymns). These references to military practices and associated koeátriya rites were what gave the AV its formidable reputation. In the Mahabharata era that shortly followed after the end of the atharvan period there is a frequent comparison between weapons and the mantras of the heroes. Probably, this comparison was initially supposed to mean the application of deadly weapons as mentioned in the atharvan tradition.

- Several regular and special rituals of the Aryans are a major concern of the AV, just as in the three other vedas. The major rituals covered by the AV are marriage in kaC a-XIV and the funeral in kaC a-XVIII. There are also hymns that are specific to rituals of the bhigu-agnirasas, vatyas and khatriyas. One of the most important of these rites is the Viuhasahi Vrata, performed to invoke the icdra and Vicgu with the mantras of the XVIIth kaC a. The Vatya rituals were performed by individuals who took on a nomadic ascetic way of living and were generally sent into neighbouring states by the ruler of a particular state. They appear to have served a role in reconnaissance and negotiations with neighbouring states (compare with Arjuna's Vatya-like journey into the Yadu principality to woo Subhadra). Finally, there are some rituals aimed at the destruction of the enemies (Abhicharika hymns and rites) particularly using the closing mantras of the XVIth kaC a. While these support traditional negative views on the AV, in content they are mirrored by several other hymns from the Rig as well as the Yajuces. Moreover, Abhicharika rites were an integral part of the vedic as amply attested in the brahmaga literature (see the tale of Yavakrd a in the Jaiminiya brahmaga). Thus the AV as such began fully within the classic Vedic fold, though it was more specific to certain clans of fire priests. The development of the Abhicharika rites to their more 'modern' form was seen only in the vidhana literature and in fact began within the Rigvedic tradition in the form of the Vigvidhana. The author of the (igvidhana provides passing reference to the development of similar rites in the AV tradition (the references to the Agnirasa Krityas). These rites reached their culmination in the Kauhika and Vaitana Sutra and in some of the Pariihthas (appendices) of the atharvan literature. However, these are far removed from the actual hymns themselves suggesting that they represent an encrustation on the atharvanic practice rather than its original form. While in its most extreme form Atharvanic Abhicharika faded away, it did seed the mainstream Hindu culture resulting in the origin of the Puranic form of the fire ritual (yaga-s). It also provided the launching pad for the worship of late evolving popular deities like Kumara and Ganapati to capture the mainstream Hindu ritual.

Philosophical Excursions: The AV made the most important contributions to Aryan philosophical thought of all the Sachitas. One of the most spectacular expressions of this is seen in the hymn XII.I, the Hymn to goddess Earth or the Prithvi Suktam used in the Aghrayana rite. The foundations of Vaiceuika, the highest of the Hindu Darœanas is expressed in the mantra XII.1.26 in which the atoms (Pamsu) are described forming the stone, the stones agglutinating to form the rocks and the rocks held together to form the Earth. An early pantheistic thought (somewhat convergent to the latter day Vicihthadvaitins) is seen in the hymn X.7 that describes the common thread running through all manifest and un-manifest existence as the skaCbha. This skaCbha is described as what poured out of the Hiranya Garbha, that was the precursor of the *complex world in a very simple form (X.7.28). (Hiranya* Garba = " The radiant or golden egg or womb. Esoterically the luminious 'fire mist' or ethereal stuff from which the Universe was formed.")

This Skambha is Indra and Indra is the Skambha which describes all existence. The hymn also describes a pantheistic nature of the Vedic gods (X.7.38): skaCbha is the heat (tapa) that spreads through the universe (Bhuvana) as waves of water; the units of this spreading entity are the gods even as branches of one tree. This one theme that repeatedly presents itself in various interpretations that abounded in later Hindu philosophies and can be considered one of the most fundamental expression of Vedic thought.

Dating: From alleged internal astronomical references (AVS XI.7), it has been surmised that the Atharvanic period included the time when the Pleiades occupied the spring equinox (roughly 2200 BC). Further, tradition suggests that paippalada, one of the early collators, and Vaidharbhi, one of the late contributors associated with the Atharvanic text, lived during the reign of prince Hiranyanabha of the Ikshvaku dynasty, interpreted to mean that the core AV composition was at least complete by 1500 BC.

While these approaches are not widely accepted as valid, it is clear that the core text of the AV is not particularly recent in *the Vedic Sachita tradition, and falls within the classical Mantra* period of Vedic Sanskrit in the late 2nd millennium BC—roughly contemporary with the Yajurveda mantras, the Rigvedic Khilani, and the redaction of the Samaveda.

The Atharvaveda is also the first Indic text to mention Iron (as uyama ayas, literally "black metal"), so that scholarly consensus dates the bulk of the Atharvaveda hymns to the early Indian Iron Age, corresponding to the 12th to 10th centuries BC or the early Kuru kingdom. During its oral tradition, however, the text has been corrupted by later additions considerably more than the other Vedas, and it is only from comparative philology of the two surviving recensions that we may hope to arrive at an approximation of the original reading.

Editions: The Shaunakiya text was edited 1960–62 by Vishva Bandhu, Hoshiarpur.

The bulk of the paippalada text was edited by Leray Carr Barret from 1905 to 1940 (book 6 by Edgerton, 1915) from a single Kashmirian uarada manuscript (now in Tübingen). This edition is outdated, since various other manuscripts were discovered in Bihar, Bengal and Orissa since. Some manuscripts are in the Orissa State Museum, but many manuscripts are in private possession, and are kept hidden by their owners. Many manuscripts were collected by Prof. Durgamohan Bhattacharya of Bengal by deceiving their owners, as told by his son Dipak Bhattacharya in 1968 (below), who describes the theft as valiant daredevilry:

"The knowledge of the villagers, in whose possession many important manuscripts remain, about their possession is often very hazy [...] Prof. Bhattacharya secured a manuscript from an illiterate Brahmin on promise of return..." (see: Zehnder (1999), p.19)

Books 1–15 were edited by Durgamohan Bhattacharya (1997). There is a provisional edition of book 20 by Dipak Bhattacharya. Book 2 and 5 were edited and translated by Thomas Zehnder (1999) and Alexander Lubotsky (2002), respectively.

Samhita

The *Samhita* (Sanskrit: "joined" or "collected") is the basic text of each of the *Vedas*, comprising collections of hymns and ritual texts. This term was originally used in reference to the style of recitation used during hymns and chants. In the Vedas the Samhitas are supplemented by later explanatory commentaries, notably the Brahmanas and Upanishads. The term is also sometimes spelled 'Sanhita'.

Other Samhitas: In later times, the term Samhita also came to be applied to the names of texts belonging to various fields of *knowledge, not directly connected to the Vedas. e.g.*

- Gherand Samhita
- Charak Samhita
- Ashtavakra Samhita
- Yogayajnavalkya samhita
- Brahma Samhita

Gherand Samhita

Gheranda Samhita is one of the three classic texts of Hatha Yoga (the other two being the Hatha Yoga Pradapika and the Shiva Samhita). It is a late 17th Century text and is considered to be the most encyclopedic of the three classic texts on Hatha Yoga. Gheranda Samhita is a manual of Yoga taught by Gheranda to Chanda. Unlike other Hatha Yoga texts, the Gheranda Samhita focuses upon the *Shat Kriyas* or internal body cleansing, *i.e., Ghatastha Yoga*. The closing stanzas of the Gheranda Samhita deal with Samadhi, but the methods taught are different from Patanjali's methods.

Charaka

Charaka, sometimes spelled *Caraka,* (300 BC) is one of the founders of Ayurveda. According to Charaka, health and disease are not predetermined and life may be prolonged by human effort.

Contributions: According to the Charaka tradition, there existed six schools of medicine, founded by the disciples of the sage Punarvasu Atreya. Each of his disciples, *Agnivesha, Bhela, Jatukarna, Parashara, Harita,* and *Ksharapani,* composed a Samhita. Of these, the one composed by Agnivesha was considered the best. The Agnivesha Samhita was later revised by Charaka and it came to be known as Charaka Samhita. The Charaka Samhita was revised by Dridhbala. Charaka was from India. Ayurveda is traditionally divided into eight branches which, in Charaka's scheme, are:

1. Sutra-Sthana, general principles
2. Nidana-Sthana, pathology
3. Vimana-Sthana, diagnostics
4. Sharira-Sthana, physiology and anatomy
5. Indriya-Sthana, prognosis
6. Chikitsa-Sthana, therapeutics
7. Kalpa-Sthana, pharmacy
8. Siddhi-Sthana, successful treatment

Charak Samhita: The Charak Samhita contains 120 adhyayas (chapters), divided into 8 parts.

1. Sutra Sthana (30 chapters)
2. Nidan Sthana (8 chapters)
3. Viman Sthana (8 chapters)
4. Sharir Sthana (8 chapters)
5. Indriya Sthana (12 chapters)
6. Chikitsa Sthana (30 chapters)
7. Kalpa Sthana (12 chapters)
8. Siddhi Sthana (12 chapters)

Ashtavakra Gita

The *Ashtavakra Gita* (Song of Ashtavakra), also known by the name *Ashtavakra Samhita* is an influential non-dualist Vedic scripture traditionally said to have been spoken by the Sage Ashtavakra, though its authorship is not known with certainty.

There is little doubt though that it is very old, probably dating back to the days of the classic Vedanta period. The Sanskrit style and the doctrine expressed would seem to warrant this assessment. The work was known, appreciated and quoted by Ramakrishna and his disciple Vivekananda, as well as by Ramana Maharishi. Radhakrishnan refers to it with great respect, while even Sri Ravi Shankar has given a commentary on the scripture. Apart from that, the work speaks for itself. It presents the traditional teachings of Advaita Vedanta with a clarity and power very rarely matched.

The *Ashtavakra Gita* does not date itself or brand itself to any region, culture, or peoples, although it does contain Hindu-specific references, especially in the final chapter entitled 'I am Shiva' where it is proclaimed in the final verse that the author is in truth one with God. The essence of the *Ashtavakra Gita* is that there is no such thing as existence or non existence, right or wrong, or moral or immoral. In the eyes of the sage Ashtavakra who is the ostensible author of this text, one's true identity can be found by simply recognizing oneself as Pure Existence and that as individuals we are the awareness of all things.

The *Ashtavakra Gita* teaches that one is already free once one realises they are free. It advocates non-action (similar to the Daoist concept of Wu Wei), the loss of desire and severing of worldly attachments. To free oneself from the cycle of life and death, one should withdraw from all Earthly desires, worries and cares. To continue induldging in Earthly things even after one has realised their true nature is said to be foolish and time wasting. Instead it paints a picture of The Master as someone who continues to keep up their responsibilities in the world, not because they believe they have to or due to any worldy attachments, but simply that it is in their nature to do so. It is important to avoid misinterpretation in this regard, and to that end teachers traditionally recommend that *Ashtavakra Gita* be pursued by only those who have already advanced on the spiritual path. Ashtavakra teaches that emotion, thought and even meditation can lead to further bondage and that religious practice itself is of no meaning to the enlightened.

Brahmana

The *Brahmaas* are part of the Hindu *Shruti;* They are composed in Vedic Sanskrit, and the period of their composition is sometimes referred to as the *Brahmanic period* or *age* (approximately between 900 BC and 500 BC). They are essentially commentaries of the Vedas, explaining Vedic ritual. The earliest Brahmanas may have been written several centuries earlier, contemporary to the Black Yajurveda commentary prose, but they have only survived in fragments.

Each Brahmana is associated with one of the four Vedas, and within the tradition of that Veda with a particular shakha or school:

- Rigveda
  - o Shakala shakha: Aitareya Brahmana (AB)
  - o Bashkala shakha: Kaushitaki Brahmana (KS)

- Samaveda
  - o Kauthuma: PB, SadvB
  - o Jayminiya: Jayminiya Brahmana (JB)
- Yajurveda
  - o Krishna: the Brahmanas are integrated into the samhitas:
    - * Maitrayani (MS)
    - * Carakakatha (CS)
    - * Kapisthalakatha (KS)
    - * Taittiriya (TS). The Taittiriya school has an additional Taittiriya Brahmana (TB)
  - o Shukla
    - * Vajasaneyi Madhyandina: Shatapatha Brahmana, Madhyadina recession (ShB)
    - * Kanva: Shatapatha Brahmana, Kanva recession (ShBK)
- Atharvaveda
  - o Paippalada: Gopatha Brahmana

Aitareya Brahamana

Aitareya Brahmana, also known as the *Ashvalayana Brahmana* is associated to Rigveda, first among the four Vedas. It is believed to have been composed around 600 BC and is perhaps the oldest Brahmana. It deals principally with Soma sacrifices.

Jaiminiya Upanishad Brahmana

The *Jaiminiya Upanishad Brahmana* (JUB) is a Vedic text associated with the Jaiminiya shakha of the Samaveda. It may be considered a very early Upanishad, together with the Brhadaragyaka and Chandogya Upanishads dating to the Brahmana period of Vedic Sanskrit, likely predating the 6th century BC.

It is not to be confused with the Jaiminiya Brahmana (JB), the actual Brahmana commentary of the Jaiminiya school.

Kaushitaki Brahmana

The *Kaushitaki Brahmana* is the Brahmana associated with the Rigveda in the Bashkala shakha.

Panchavimsha Brahmana

The *Tandhya-maha-*(or *Praudha-*) *brahmana,* or "great" Brahmana— usually called *Panchavimsha-brahmana* from its consisting of twenty-five *adhyayas* is a Brahmana of the Samaveda, treating of the duties of the udgatars generally, and especially of the various kinds of chants.

Shatapatha Brahmana

Shatapatha Brahmana is one of the prose texts describing the Vedic ritual, associated with the White Yajurveda. It survives in *two recensions, Madhyandina* (*CEBM,* of the *vajasaneyi madhyandina* shakha) and *Kanva* (*CEBK,* of the *kagva* shakha), with the former having the eponymous 100 brahmanas in 14 books, and the latter 104 brahmanas in 17 books.

The CEB is notable as one of the oldest prose (non-metrical) Sanskrit texts altogether. Linguistically, it belongs to the Brahmana period of Vedic Sanskrit, dated to the first half of the 1st millennium BC (roughly 800 BC).

Among the points of interest are the mythological sections embedded in it, including myths of creation and the Deluge of Manu.

The text describes in great detail the preparation of altars, ceremonial objects, ritual recitations, and the Soma libation, along with the symbolic attributes of every aspect of the rituals.

Some Hindu scholars have dated it to around 1800 BC, based on the reference in it of migration from the Saraswati river area to east India, because the river is said to have dried up around 1900 BC. Archaeoastronomers have dated it to around 2000 BC based on a reference to the Pleiades (Krttikas) "rising in the east" at autumnal equinox (CEBM 2.1.2.1). Such dating interpretations are controversial. (see Hindu astronomy)

The 14 books of the Madhyandina recession can be divided into two major parts. The first 9 books have close textual commentaries, often line by line, of the first 18 books of the corresponding samhita of the Yajurveda. The following 5 books cover supplementary and ritualistically newer material, besides including the celebrated Brhadaranyaka Upanishad as most of the 14th and last book.

Taittiriya Brahmana

The *Taittiriya Brahmana* (TB) is the Brahmana associated with the Taittiriya shakha of the Black Yajurveda. The Taittiriya school is the only school of the Black Yajurveda to have a Brahmana additional to the commentary already interspersed in the Samhita.

Aranyaka

The *Aranyakas* are part of the Hindu Kruti; these religious scriptures are sometimes argued to be part of either the Brahmanas or Upanishads. The name translates to "the forest books", meaning, treatises for hermits or sadhus living in the wilderness. This contrasts with the grhyasutras, treatises intended for domestic life. Their language is early Classical Sanskrit, and together with the bulk of the Upanishads, the Aranyakas form the basis of Vedanta, roughly dating to a few centuries before the Common Era.

Books: The Aranyakas discuss philosophy and sacrifice. They are believed to have originated with the various mystical ascetic groups that developed in post-Vedic India. The Aranyakas constitute a more philosophical and mystical interpretation of the themes presented in the Vedas, as opposed to the Brahmanas, which were primarily concerned with the proper performance of ritual. Like the Upanishads, the Aranyakas may have initially constituted a secret or hidden teaching, not in the sense of being forbidden or restricted, but rather being both a non-obvious expansion on the themes of the Vedas and a teaching that was primarily conveyed individually from teacher to student.

The Aranyakas are associated with and named after individual Vedic shakhas.

- Aitareya Aranyaka belongs to the Shakala Shakha of Rigveda
- Taittiriya Aranyaka belongs to the Taittiriya Shakha of Krishna-Yajurveda
- Katha Aranyaka belongs to the Katha-Charaka Shakha of the Krishna-Yajurveda
- Kaushitaki Aranyaka belongs to the Kaushitaki and Shankhayana Shakhas of Rigveda
- Maitrayaniya Aranyaka belongs to the Maitrayaniya Shakha of Krishna-Yajurveda

- Talavakara Aranyaka belongs to the Talavakara or Jaiminiya Shakha of Samaveda

The Atharvaveda has no surviving Aranyaka, although indications are that there did exist Araynaka works attached to this Veda in the past.

The Secret of the Brahmanas: There is also a certain continuity of the Aranyakas from the Brahmanas in the sense that the Aranyakas go into the subtle esoteric meanings of the ritualistic tilt that the rites detailed in the Brahmanas give to the mantras of the Vedas. It is this leap into subtlety that provides the reason for Durgacharya in his commentary on the Niruktas to say that the Aranyakas are 'Rahasya Brahmana', that is, the Secret of the Brahmanas. In short, the undercurrent of emphasis of the Aranyakas is to point out that through all the different multiplicities that one has to contend with, there is a single thread of continuity, namely, the One Absolute Reality. The language of the Aranyakas is, unlike Vedic Sanskrit, nearer to the ordinary Sanskrit of the layman.

A glimpse into the contents of some of the Aranyakas

Aitareya Aranyaka: There are five chapters each of which is even considered as a full Aranyaka. The first one deals with the regimen known as 'Mahaa-vrata'. The explanations are both ritualistic as well as absolutistic. The second one has six chapters of which the first three are about 'Praana-vidyaa' – meaning, Prana, the Vital Air that constitutes the life-breath of a living body is also the life-breath of all mantras, all vedas and all vedic declarations (cf. 2.2.2 of aitareya Aranyaka). It is in this portion of the Aranyaka that one finds specific statements about how one who follows the vedic injunctions and performs the sacrifices goes to become the God of Fire, or the Sun or Air and how one who transgresses the vedic prescriptions is born into lower levels of being, namely, as birds and reptiles.

It is in Aitareya Aranyaka Praana is recommended to be worshipped in the form of Rishis. Praana is Vishvamitra, because all the universe ('vishwa') is the object of experience of this praana deity. Praana is Vamadeva, because the word "Vaama" indicates respectability and deservingness to be worshipped and served. It is also Atri Maharishi because, the word 'traayate' in Atri indicates the Praana that protects from sins. The Praana enters this body and supports it, therefore it is Bharadvaja – where the 'bhara' word denotes supporting and the 'Vaaja' indicates the mortal body that is made mobile by the residence of praaana. Vashishhta is also Praana because the word 'vas' indicates the dwelling in this body of the senses made possible by praana.

The 4th, 5th and 6th chapters of this second Aranyaka constitute what is known as Aitareya Upanishad.

The third Aranyaka in this chain of Aranyakas is also known as 'Samhitopanishad'. This elaborates on the various ways – like pada-paatha, krama-paatha, etc.—of reciting the Vedas and the nuances of the 'svaras'.

The fourth and the fifth Aranyakas are technical and dwell respectively on the mantras known as 'Mahaanaamnl' and the yajna known as 'Madhyandina'.

Shankhayana Aranyaka: There are fifteen chapters here. From the third to the sixth it constitutes the Kaushitaki Upanishad. The seventh and eighth are known as a Samhitopanishad.

The first two chapters deal with the Mahavrata. The ninth talks about the greatness of Prana. The tenth chapter deals with the esoteric implications of the agnihotra ritual. All divine personalities are inherent in the Purusha, just as Agni in speech, Vayu in Prana, the Sun in the eyes, the Moon in the mind, the directions in the ears and water in the potency.

The one who knows this, says the Aranyaka, and in the strength of that conviction goes about eating, walking, taking and giving, satisfies all the gods and what he offers in the fire reaches those gods in heaven. (cf.10-1).

The eleventh chapter prescribes several antidotes in the form of rituals for warding off death and sickness. It also details the effects of dreams. The 12th chapter elaborates the fruits of prayer. The 13th gets into more philosophical matters and says one must first attitudinally discard one's bodily attachment and then carry on the 'shravana', manana and nidhidhyasana and practise all the disciplines of penance, faith, self-control, etc.

The 14th gives just two mantras. One extols the "I am Brahman" mantra and says it is the apex of all Vedic mantras. The second mantra declares that one who does not get the meaning of mantras but only recites vedic chants is like an animal which does not know the value of the weight it carries. The final chapter gives a long list of genealogy of spiritual teachers from Brahma downwards upto Guna-Sankhayana.

Brihad–Aranyaka: This is the famous Upanishad of that name. The Self is the subject of discussion here from all aspects. For a complete discussion see Brihad-Aranyaka Upanishad.

Taittiriya-Aranyaka: There are ten chapters here. The 7th, 8th and 9th constitute the well-known Taittiriya Upanishad. The tenth is a long Upanishad known as Maha-Narayana-Upanishad; it contains several important mantras culled from the three vedas. Chapters one to six form the Aranyaka proper.

The first one is the famous Surya namaskara chapter. The second one is a description of the five maha-yajnas that every Brahmin has to do daily. Naturally the sacred thread, the yajnopavita, of the Brahmin is extolled and elaborated here. The sandhya worship, the worship of the manes, worship of the brahman through the brahma-yajna, the cleansing homa-sacrifice called the kushmanda-homa are all dealt with in detail. In this chapter the word 'shramana' is used (2-7-1) in the meaning of a doer of penance (tapasvii); this word came to mean in later times, a recluse of the Buddhist and Jain religions.

The third and fourth chapters go into further technicalities of several other homas and yajnas. The fourth chapter has also sections on mantras that may be used for averting (or causing !) havoc. The fifth is an academic treatise on yajnas. The sixth one is a collection of 'pitr-medha' mantras, that is, the mantras recited on the occasion of, and used for, the rituals for the disposal of the dead body.

Upanishad

The *Upanishads* are part of the Vedas and form the Hindu scriptures which primarily discuss philosophy, meditation and nature of God; they form the core spiritual thought of Vedantic Hinduism. The Upanishads are mystic or spiritual contemplations of the Vedas, their putative end and essence, and thus known as *Vedanta* ("the end/culmination of the Vedas").

The Upanishads were composed over several centuries. The oldest, such as the Brhadaranyaka and Chandogya Upanishads, have been dated to around the eighth century BCE. The roots of many Indian religions are built upon the foundation of the Upanishads.

Etymology: The Sanskrit term *upanicad* derives from *upa*-(near), *ni*-(down) and *sad* (to sit), *i.e.* referring to the "sitting down near" a spiritual teacher (guru) in order to receive instruction in the Guru-shishya tradition or parampara. The teachers and students appear in a variety of settings (husband answering questions about immortality, a teenage boy being taught by Yama, etc.).

Traditional Etymology

Upa + ni + cad (sad)

Upa = an *upasarga* (prefix) meaning *Samipyam*-Nearest, *i.e.* Atma (Oneself);

ni = an *upasarga* (prefix) meaning *Niœcaya*-definitely ascertained knowledge;

cad = a *dhatu* (verbal root) which was originally *sad*. It becomes *cad* due to the affix *kvip*, which forms a noun in the sense of the verbal action. *Sad* has three meanings: (1) *Viharagam*-dissolves, disintegrates, destroys, (2) *Gati* or *Prapti*-go, lead, attain, know, (3) *Avasadana*—puts an end to.

Thus, *Upanicad* means:

- Definitely ascertained knowledge of *Atma* (Oneself) which dissolves, disintegrates, destroys ignorance.
- Definitely ascertained knowledge of *Atma* (Oneself) which leads one to *Brahman*; makes one gain, know *Brahman*.
- Definitely ascertained knowledge of *Atma* (Oneself) which puts an end to *sacsara* (a life of becoming, characterized by birth, death, suffering, etc.)

Definition of *Upanicad* based on the Introductory *Uagkarabhacyam* on *Kamha Upanicad* and *Brhadaragyaka Upanicad*. The word *Upanicad* ultimately means Self-knowledge = *Atmavidya*, *Knowledge of Brahman* = *Brahmavidya*. The *Magukya Upanicad* Mahavakya (verse 2) *Ayam Atma Brahma*. "This *Atma* is *Brahman*," confirms the view of the *Upanicad*, that in truth, you (the individual self, free from incidental attributes) are *Brahman* (the infinite and the ultimate basis of all reality).

Major Upanishads: Different Upanishads are affiliated with the four Vedas (Rigveda, Yajurveda, Samaveda and Atharvaveda). The Upanishads were transmitted orally by the Vedic school sakhas. The longest and oldest Upanishad, are the Brhadaragyaka and the

Chandogya respectively. The language of the Upanishads, is Sanskrit, the oldest among them still classifying as late Vedic Sanskrit. The oldest Upanishads, the Brhadaragyaka and the Chandogya are composed in prose. These early texts may date back to the 8th-7th centuries BCE. Later followed a series of Upanishads composed in verse, such as the Ica, Magd.ukya, Katha, and bvetacvatara Upanishads.

According to tradition, there were over two hundred *Upanishads*, but the philosopher and commentator Shankara only composed commentaries to eleven of them. The Upanishads commented on by Shankara are generally regarded as the oldest ones. The Muktika Upanishad lists 108 Upanishads. In 1656, at the order of Dara Shikoh, the Upanishads were translated from Sanskrit into Persian.

These philosophical and meditative tracts form the backbone of Hindu thought. Of the early Upanishads, the Aitareya and Kauoitaki belong to the Rigveda, Kena and Chandogya to the Samaveda, Ioa and Taittiriya and Bhadara yaka to the Yajurveda, and Pracna and Mudaka to the Atharvaveda. In addition, the Madukya, Katho,-'veta'vatara are very important. Others also include Mahanarayaa and Maitreyi Upanishads as key.

Place in the Hindu Canon: Scholars of the Vedic books consider the four Vedas as poetic liturgy, collectively called *mantra* or *samhita*—adoration and supplication to the deities of Vedic religion, in parts already melded with monist and henotheist notions, and an overarching order (Rta) that transcended even the Gods.

The *Brahmana* were a collection of ritual instructions, books detailing the priestly functions (which first were available to all men, and so concretized into strictly Brahmin privilege). These came after the Mantra.

Vedanta, is chiefly composed of *Aranyakas* and Upanishads. The Aranyakas ("of the forest") detail meditative yogic practices, contemplations of the mystic one and the manifold manifested principles. The Upanishad basically realized all the monist and universal mystical ideas that started in earlier Vedic hymns, and have exerted an influence unprecedented on the rest of Hindu and Indian philosophy. However, by adherents they are not considered philosophy alone, and form meditations and practical teachings for those advanced enough to benefit from their wisdom.

Contents: The *Taittiriya Upanishad* says this in the Ninth Chapter:

> *He who knows the Bliss of Brahman, whence words together with the mind turn away, unable to reach It? He is not afraid of anything whatsoever. He does not distress himself with the thought: "Why did I not do what is good? Why did I do what is evil?". Whosoever knows this regards both these as Atman; indeed he cherishes both these as Atman. Such, indeed, is the Upanishad, the secret knowledge of Brahman.*

Taittiriya Upanishad Capt. 9 (II-9-1): The Upanishads hold information on basic Hindu beliefs, including belief in a world soul, a universal spirit, Brahman, and an individual soul, Atman (Smith 10). A variety of lesser gods are seen as aspects of this one divine ground, Brahman (different from Brahma). Brahman is the ultimate, both transcendent and immanent, the absolute infinite existence, the sum total of all that ever is, was, or ever shall be. For Advaita (non-dual) philosophers Brahman is not a God in the monotheistic sense, as they do not ascribe to it any limiting characteristics, not even those of being and non-being, and this is reflected in the fact that in Sanskrit, the word Brahman has no gender (masculine or feminine or neuter). Dvaita philosophy holds that Brahman is ultimately a personal God, Vishnu, or Krishna (*brahmano hi pratisthaham*, Bhagavad Gita 14.27).

"Who is the Knower?" "What makes my mind think?" "Does life have a purpose, or is it governed by chance?" "What is the cause of the Cosmos?"

The sages of the Upanishad try to solve these mysteries and seek knowledge of a Reality beyond ordinary knowing. They also show a preoccupation with states of consciousness, and observed and analysed dreams as well as dreamless sleep.

Philosophy: Due to their mystical nature and intense philosophical bent that does away with all ritual and completely embraces principals of One Brahman and the inner Atman (Self), the Upanishads have a universal feel that has led to their explication in numerous manners, giving birth to the three schools of Vedanta.

The Vedantin philosopher Adi Shankara summed up all the Upanishad in one phrase and said that in the end, the ultimate, formless, inconceivable Brahman is the same as our soul, Atman.

We only have to realize it through discrimination and piercing through Maya.

A distinctive quotation that is indicative of the call to self-realization, one that inspired Somerset Maugham in titling a book he wrote on Christopher Isherwood, is as follows:

Get up! Wake up! Seek the guidance of an Illumined teacher and realize the Self. Sharp like a razor's edge is the path, The sages say, difficult to traverse.

Death Instructing Nachiketa in the Katho (Word) Upanishad: The Upanishads also contain the first and most definitive explications of 'aum' as the divine word, the cosmic vibration that underlies all existence and contains multiple trinities of being and principles subsumed into its One Self. The *Isha* says of the Self (Verses 6, 7 & 8 of Isha Upanishad):

> *Whoever sees all beings in the soul and the soul in all beings does not shrink away from this. In whom all beings have become one with the knowing soul what delusion or sorrow is there for the one who sees unity? It has filled all. It is radiant, incorporeal, invulnerable, without tendons, pure, untouched by evil. Wise, intelligent, encompassing, self-existent, it organizes objects throughout eternity.*

Isha Upanishad Verses 6, 7, & 8: "*Aum Shanti Shanti Shanti*" This, too, is found first in the Upanishads, the call for tranquillity, for divine stillness, for Peace everlasting.

Dara Shikoh, the Muslim sufi, and son of Mughal emperor Shah Jahan, translated the Upanishads in Persian in order to find in it elements of monotheism that might pave the way for a common mystical bond between Islam and Hinduism.

List of Upanishads

"Principal" Upanishads: The following is a list of the eleven "principal" (*mukhya*) Upanishads that were commented upon by Shankara, and that are accepted as shruti by all Hindus. They are listed with their associated Veda (Rigveda (ZV), Samaveda (SV), White Yajurveda (YV), Black Yajurveda (KYV), Atharvaveda (AV)).

1. Aitareya (ZV)
2. Brhadaragyaka (YV)

3. Ica (YV)
4. Taittiriya (KYV)
5. Kamha (KYV)
6. Chandogya (SV)
7. Kena (SV)
8. Muaka (AV)
9. Maukya (AV)
10. Pracena (AV)
11. Uvetauvatara

The Kauuitaki and Maitrayagi Upanishads are sometimes added to extend the canon to 13. They are also the oldest Upanishads, likely all of them dating to before the Common Era. From linguistic evidence, the oldest among them are likely the Brhadaragyaka and Chandogya Upanishads, belonging to the late Vedic Sanskrit period; the remaining ones are at the transition from Vedic to Classical Sanskrit.

Canon by Vedic Shakha: The older Upanishads are associated with Vedic Charanas (Shakhas or schools). The Aitareya Upanishad with the Shakala shakha, the Kauuitaki Upanishad with the Bashakala shakha; the Chandogya Upanishad with the Kauthuma shakha, the Kena Upanishad, and the Jaiminiya Upanishad Brahmana, with the Jaiminiya shakha; the Kamha Upanishad with the Caraka-Katha shakha, the Taittiriya and Uvetauvatara with the Taittiriya shakha; the Maitrayagi Upanishad with the Maitrayani shakha; the Brhadaragyaka and Ica Upanishads with the Vajasaneyi Madhyandina shakha, and the Maukya and Muaka Upanishads with the Shaunaka shakha. Additionally, parts of earlier texts, of Brahmanas or passages of the Vedas themselves, are sometimes considered Upanishads.

The Muktika Canon: The following is a list of the 108 canonical Upanishads of the Advaita school, according to the Muktika Upanishad (number 108), 1:30-39 (which does not list the associated Veda). In this canon,

- 10 Upanishads are associated with the Rigveda and have the Shanti beginning *vagme-manasi.*
- 16 Upanishads are associated with the Samaveda and have the Shanti beginning *apyayantu.*

- 19 Upanishads are associated with the White Yajurveda and have the Shanti beginning *purgamada.*
- 32 Upanishads are associated with the Black Yajurveda and have the Shanti beginning *sahanavavatu.*
- 31 Upanishads are associated with the Atharvaveda and have the Shanti beginning *bhadram-kargebhi.*

The first 10 are grouped as *mukhya* "principal", and are identical to those listed above. 21 are grouped as Samanya Vedanta "common Vedanta", 23 as Sannyasa, 9 as Shakta, 13 as Vaishnava, 14 as Shaiva and 17 as Yoga Upanishads.

1. Ica, (YV, Mukhya) "The Inner Ruler"
2. Kena (SV, Mukhya) "Who moves the world?"
3. Kamha (KYV, Mukhya) "Death as Teacher"
4. Prakna, (AV, Mukhya) "The Breath of Life"
5. Muaka (AV, Mukhya) "Two modes of Knowing"
6. Maukya (AV, Mukhya) "Consciousness and its phases"
7. Taittiriya (KYV, Mukhya) "From Food to Joy"
8. Aitareya, (ZV Mukhya) "The Microcosm of Man"
9. Chandogya (SV, Mukhya) "Song and Sacrifice"
10. Brhadaragyaka (YV, Mukhya)
11. Brahma (KYV, Sannyasa)
12. Kaivalya (KYV, Shaiva)
13. Jabala (YV, Sannyasa)
14. Uvetauvatara (KYV, Sannyasa) "The Faces of God"
15. HaCsa (YV, Yoga)
16. AruGeya (SV, Sannyasa)
17. Garbha (KYV, Sannyasa)
18. NarayaGa (KYV, Vaishnava)
19. Paramahacsa (KYV, Sannyasa)
20. Am[tabindu (KYV, Yoga)
21. Amrtanada (KYV, Yoga)
22. Kira (AV, Shaiva)
23. Atharvakikha (AV, Shaiva)
24. Maitrayagi (SV, Sannyasa)
25. Kauuitaki (ZV, Samanya)
26. Brhajjabala (AV, Shaiva)

27. Nsichatapani (AV, Vaishnava)
28. Kalagnirudra (KYV, Shaiva)
29. Maitreyi (SV, Sannyasa)
30. Subala (KYV, Samanya)
31. Kcurika (KYV, Yoga)
32. Mantrika (KYV, Samanya)
33. Sarvasara (KYV, Samanya)
34. Niralamba (KYV, Samanya)
35. Kukarahasya (KYV, Samanya)
36. Vajrasuchi (SV, Samanya)
37. Tejobindu (KYV, Sannyasa)
38. Nadabindu (ZV, Yoga) [3]
39. Dhyanabindu (KYV, Yoga)
40. Brahmavidya (KYV, Yoga)
41. Yogatattva (KYV, Yoga)
42. Atmabodha (ZV, Samanya)
43. Parivrat (Naradaparivrajaka) (AV, Sannyasa)
44. Trikikhi (KYV, Yoga)
45. Sita (AV, Shakta)
46. Yogachuamagi (SV, Yoga)
47. Nirvaga (ZV, Sannyasa)
48. Maalabrahmaga (KYV, Yoga)
49. Dakcigamurti (KYV, Shaiva)
50. Karabha (AV, Shaiva)
51. Skanda (Tripavibhumi) (KYV, Samanya)
52. Mahanarayaga (AV, Vaishnava)
53. Advayataraka (KYV, Sannyasa)
54. Ramarahasya (AV, Vaishnava)
55. Ramatapagi (AV, Vaishnava)
56. Vasudeva (SV, Vaishnava)
57. Mudgala (ZV, Samanya)
58. Uailya (AV, Yoga)
59. Paiegala (KYV, Samanya)
60. Bhikcu (KYV, Sannyasa)
61. Mahad (SV, Samanya)
62. Uariraka (KYV, Samanya)

63. Yogauikha (KYV Yoga)
64. Turiyatita (KYV, Sannyasa)
65. Sannyasa (SV, Sannyasa)
66. Paramahacsaparivrajaka (AV, Sannyasa)
67. Akcamalika (Malika) (ZV, Shaiva)
68. Avyakta (SV, Vaishnava)
69. Ekakcara (KYV, Samanya)
70. Annapurga (AV, Shakta)
71. Surya (AV, Samanya)
72. Akci (KYV, Samanya)
73. Adhyatma (KYV, Samanya)
74. Kuika (SV, Sannyasa)
75. Savitri (SV, Samanya)
76. Atma (AV, Samanya)
77. Pauupata (AV, Yoga)
78. Parabrahma (AV, Sannyasa)
79. Avadhuta (KYV, Sannyasa)
80. Devi (AV, Shakta)
81. Tripuratapani (AV, Shakta)
82. Tripura (ZV, Shakta)
83. Kamharudra (KYV, Sannyasa)
84. Bhavana (AV, Shakta)
85. Rudrahrdaya (KYV, Shaiva)
86. Yogakualini (KYV, Yoga)
87. Bhasma (AV, Shaiva)
88. Rudrakca (SV, Shaiva)
89. Gagapati (AV, Shaiva)
90. Darkana (SV, Yoga)
91. Tarasara (KYV, Vaishnava)
92. Mahavakya (AV, Yoga)
93. Pancabrahma (KYV, Shaiva)
94. Pragagnihotra (KYV, Samanya)
95. Gopalatapani (AV, Vaishnava)
96. Krcga (AV, Vaishnava)
97. Yajnavalkya (KYV, Sannyasa)
98. Varaha (KYV, Sannyasa)

99. Uamyayani (KYV, Sannyasa)
100. Hayagriva (AV, Vaishnava)
101. Dattatreya (AV, Vaishnava)
102. Gara (AV, Vaishnava)
103. Kali-Sagmaraga (Kali) (KYV, Vaishnava)
104. Jabala (SV, Shaiva)
105. Saubhagya (ZV, Shakta)
106. Sarasvatirahasya (KYV, Shakta)
107. Bahvrca (ZV, Shakta)
108. Muktika (KYV, Samanya)

Aitareya Upanishad

The *Aitareya* Upanishad is one of the older, "primary" Upanishads commented upon by Shankara. It is a Mukhya Upanishad, associated with the Rigveda. It figures as number 8 in the Muktika canon of 108 Upanishads. The Aitareya Upanishad is a short prose text in three chapters and contains 33 verses in total. It comprises 4-6 chapters of the second book of the older vedic text, Aitareya Aranyaka. In the first chapter of the text, atman, the inner self, is portrayed as a divine creator. In the second chapter, the three births of the atman are described. The third chapter deals with the qualities of the Self or Brahman. It contains one of the most famous expressions of the Vedanta, "pragnanam Brahma," which is one of the Mahavakyas.

Brihadaranyaka Upanishad

The *Brihadaranyaka* Upanishad is one of the older, "primary" (*mukhya*) Upanishads commented upon by Adi Shankara. It is contained within the Shatapatha Brahmana, and its status as an independent Upanishad may be considered a secondary extraction of a portion of the Brahmana text.

This makes it one of the oldest (if not the oldest) texts of the Upanishad corpus, possibly dating to as early as the 9th century BCE. It is associated with the White Yajurveda. It figures as number 10 in the Muktika canon of 108 Upanishads.

Isha Upanishad

The *Isha Upanishad* (*iua upanicad*) or *Ishopanishad* (*iuopanicad*), also known as the *Ishavasya Upanishad* (*iuavasya upanicad*), is a

Sanskrit poem (or sequence of mantras) from the Upanishads and is considered shruti by followers of a number of diverse traditions within Hinduism. It is one of the smaller texts of the Upanishads (18 verses in total) but also one of the most often quoted.

Background and Content: The Isha Upanishad is contained in the final *adhyaya* (chapter) of the White Yajurveda (VS). It consists of either 17 or 18 two-line verses covering a wide spectrum of philosophy, religion, ritualism and metaphysics in a concise manner. *The name of the Upanishad derives from its incipit, Iuavasyam* idam sarvam, "This universe is enveloped by the Lord".

According to one Western scholar, it belongs to an advanced stage of monist speculation, assuming a Lord (*ish*) of the universe (Weber 1878:103). One view has it that this is one of the later mukhya Upanishads, dating approximately to Mauryan times. According to Mahidhara's commentary, it is a polemic against the Bauddhas (the predecessors of the later Samkhya doctrines).

Mahatma Gandhi used to say, even if every other scripture of Hinduism vanished and this alone survived, Hinduism will survive.

Text: In the two shakhas of the White Yajurveda, VSM and VSK, the order of verses 1-8 is the same. VSK verses 9–14 correspond to VSM verses 12, 13, 14, 9, 10, 11. VSM 17 is a variation of VSK 15, VSK 16 is lacking in VSM, and VSK 17–18 correspond to VSM 15–16. Verse numbers in this article refer to VSK:

VSK	1	2	3	4	5	6	7	8	9	10	11	12	13	14	15	16	17	18
VSM	1	2	3	4	5	6	7	8	12	13	14	9	10	11	(17)	-	15	16

Verse 1

iuavasyam idam sarva? yat kinca jagatya? jagat
tena tyaktena bhunjitha ma grdha kasya svid dhanam

Transliteration: idam sarvam = all this (this entire universe); Isavasyam = Isasya avasyam = Isasya avasayogyam = pervaded by Isa, the Lord Hari; yat kincha = also whatsoever, and whatever there may be; jagatyam = prakrtyam = in the primordial nature; jagat = the world; tena = by Him (the Lord Hari); tyaktena = dattena vittena = wealth granted, allotted, given; bhunjitha = bhogam kuryah = do experience, enjoy; ma grdhah = ma kanksethah= do not crave for, do not seek; kasyasvid = any one else's; dhanam = wealth.

> *"Everything animate or inanimate that is within the universe is controlled and owned by the Lord. One should therefore accept only those things necessary for himself, which are set aside as his quota, and one should not accept other things, knowing well to whom they belong." (trans. Prabhupada)*
>
> *"The world is swaddled in the glory of the Lord.*
>
> *Renounce it and enjoy it. Do not covet anyone's wealth." (trans. P. Lal)*

Verse 7

> *"One who always sees all living entities as spiritual sparks, in quality one with the Lord, becomes a true knower of things. What, then, can be illusion or anxiety for him?" (trans. Prabhupada)*

Verse 8

> *Sa paryagac chukram akayam avragam asnaviram uuddham apapa-viddham*
>
> *Kavir manici paribhu svayambhur yathatathyato 'rthan vyadadhac chauvatibhya samabhya*

"He hath attained [*paryagat*] unto the Bright [*shukram*], Bodiless, Woundless, Sinewless, the Pure which evil hath not pierced."

"Far-sighted, wise, encompassing, he self-existent hath prescribed aims, as propriety demands, unto the everlasting Years" (trans. Griffith).

"Such a person must factually know [*paryagat*] the greatest of all, the Personality of Godhead [*shukram*], who is unembodied, omniscient, beyond reproach, without veins, pure and uncontaminated, the self-sufficient philosopher who has been fulfilling everyone's desire since time immemorial." (trans. Prabhupada). According to Shankara and Mahidhara, the neuter adjectives *shukram*, etc. relate to Atman (*sas* "He") rather than to Brahma or Highest Essence. Depending on the interpretation of the first line, "Far-sighted", etc. refers either to the man who knows, or to Atman itself.

Verse 18

"O my Lord, as powerful as fire, O omnipotent one, now I offer You all obeisances, falling on the ground at Your feet. O my Lord, please lead me on the right path to reach You, and since You know all that I have done in the past, please free me from the reactions to my past sins so that there will be no hindrance to my progress." trans. Prabhupada.

The Supreme: The *Isha Upanishad* is significant amongst the Upanishads for its description of the nature of the Supreme Person as the controller (Ish) behind our universe. 'He who is unembodied, omniscient, beyond reproach, without veins, pure and uncontaminated' (verse 8). (As stated above, commentators differ as to whether the referrent here is Ish, Atman, or he who has recognized Atman.) He who 'walks and does not walk', who is 'far away, but very near as well', who 'although fixed in His abode is swifter than the mind' (from verses 4 & 5). In this way the Upanishad gives a number of seemingly paradoxical descriptions of the Supreme.

The later verses take the form of a series of prayers requesting that the speaker be able to see past the supreme light or effulgence in order to understand the true nature of the Supreme Lord Himself and be freed of the sins of past misdeeds

Morality: The text also discusses the nature of karma for the living entities, and it promotes a way of life of simple living, 'accepting only those things set aside for oneself' (text 1) and a culture of knowledge over ignorance (text 10). The text also mentions negative reactions for one who kills another living being, and it advises seeing all living entities in connection with the Supreme Person and thus being equipoised towards them (verses 6 & 7).

Worship of devas (demigods) is condemned in favour of worship of the Supreme God only, for worship of anything other than the Supreme brings about different results. The reward for correct worship is given as a future life of eternity, bliss and knowledge.

Taittiriya Upanishad

The *Taittiriya* Upanishad is one of the older, "primary" Upanishads commented upon by Shankara. It is associated with the *Taittiriya* school of the Black Yajurveda. It figures as number 7 in the Muktika canon of 108 Upanishads. Black Yajurveda is also called Taittiriya Samhita. Like all vedas Black Yajurveda consists of Samhita, Brahmana and Aranyaka parts. The eighth and ninth chapters of Taittiriya Aranyaka form the Taittiriya Upanishad. The tenth chapter is famous as Mahanarayana Upanishad or Yajnikee.

It is divided into three sections called Vallis. The *Siksha Valli,* the *Brahmananda Valli* and the *Bhrigu Valli*. For the convenience of study, each Valli is subdivided into smaller verses called Anuvak.

Shiksha Valli: The Siksha Valli deals with the discipline of Shiksha (which is the first of the six Vedangas or "limbs" or auxiliaries of the Vedas). It is concerned with phonetics and pronunciation. Main intention of starting Upanishad with Shiksha seems to be that, though meaning of vedic Mantras is important, one should not give any less importance to the right pronouciation and phonetics of mantras. If Mantras are pronounced correctly then meaning becomes clear to recitor. Also there is a belief that Mantras uttered with incorrect pronouciation loose their power.

First Anuvak of this Valli starts with Shanti Mantra (Peace Prayer) "OM Sham no Mitra..". Purpose of having Shanti mantra in the beginning is to please the gods and remove any obstacles during the study of Upanishads.

Second Anuvak defines the contents of Shiksha discipline.

Third Anuvak tells about the intimate connection between the syllables of vedic verses or mantras using five examples and implicitly tells that one should meditate on those examples to realise connections told in them. Also declares that one who realised those connections will get good fruits including heaven.

Fourth Anuvak consists of Mantras and Homas to be done by those who aspire for devine knowledge (Medha kama) and wealth (Shree kama). In this anuvak teacher prays that " As water flows from high land to low land, as months join to become year, let good desciples come to me from everywhere"

Fifth and Sixth Anuvaks try to describe Brahman in the form of "Vyahruti"s. The words "Bhooh", "Bhuvah", "Suvah", "Mahah", "Janah", "Tapah" and "Satyam" are called seven Vyahruti's or Sapta Vyahrutis. These denote different worlds in Puranas. The term "Vyahruti" means pronounciation, since these above mentioned words are pronounced in Vedic rituals like Agnihotra, these are called Vyahruti's.

Fifth Anuvak states that the fourth Vyahruti "Mahah" was discovered by a Rishi called "Mahachamasya" and "Mahah" is Brahman all other Vyahrutis are its organs. This Anuvak says that "Bhooh" denotes earth, fire, Richa's and Prana. "Bhuvah" denotes space, air, Sama's and Apana. "Suvah" denotes heaven, sun, Yajus and Vyana. "Mahah" denotes sun, moon, Holy Syllable OM and food. This way, each of first four Vyahrutis become four each and in total they are 16. So all these four Vyahrutis should be meditated as all of their sixteen manifestations, this is known as famous vedic term Shodasha Kala Purusha in vedic literature. Finally this anuvak says that one who knows all sixteen manifestations of Vyahrutis knows Brahman and all gods bring gifts to him.

Sixth Anuvak tells that in the space inside the heart there exists an immortal golden being (Hiranmaya Purusha) and states that there is a subtly route through the middle of the head through which a self realized Yogi travels when he/she leaves the body and joins the all-pervading Brahman.

The Seventh Anuvak, is bit difficult to understand, It describes a meditation called "Paanktha Upasana", where Brahman is meditated upon as a set of "five" called "Paanktha". There is also a vedic meter of five lines called Paanktha. Outer world seen is classified into 3 set of five things called "Adi Bootha" and also inner body world into 3 sets of five things called "Adhyaathma". This inner-outer grouping is then meditated upon and meditator realizes both inner and outer paankta are one and the same Brahman and every thing is Paanktha. This Anuvak states that Earth (Prithvi), Space (Antariksha), Heaven (Dyuloka), Directions (North, South, etc.), Subdirections (South-East, North-West, etc..) (Worldly set of Five or Loka-Paankta) and

Fire (Agni), Air (Vayu), Sun (Aditya), Moon (Chandra), Stars (Nakshatra) (Divine-Five or Deva-Paanktha) and

Water, Herbs (Oshadhi), Trees, Sky (Akasha), Self (Atma) (Elemental Five or Dhaatu Paanktha) are called Adibhuta or Outer Elements.

Further it states that:

Prana, Vyana, Apana, Udana, Samana (all these are Five inner Vital currents of the body) and

Eye, Ear, Mind, Speech (Vaak), Outer-Skin (Tvak) (Sensory-Five or Indriya-Paanktha) and

Inner-Skin (Charma), Flesh, tendon-Ligaments, bones, Fat or Bone-Marrow (Elemental Five or Dhaatu Paanktha) are called Adhyaatma or Inner Elements.

The Rishi who realized this says, thus everything is Paankta. It further says that one who realized everything as Paanktha, completes Paanktha with Paanthks itself.

Eighth Anuvak states the greatness of Holy Syllable OM. It says that OM is Brahman and everything.

Ninth Anuvak explains the duties to be performed by persons aspiring realization of Brahman.

Tenth Anuvak is a Mantra for self-practice (Swadhyaya) or meditation. It is stated by a Rishi called Trishanku as an exclamation of awe after he realized that he is one with Brahman. It is also called "Mantramnaya" of Trishanku.

Eleventh Anuvak is a set of instructions that teacher (Acharya) gives to his desciple after completion of vedic education.

Twelveth Anuvak concludes the Shikshavalli with Santi Mantra "OM Sham no mitra.." expressing gratitude toward gods who removed obstacles for study of Upanishad as prayed for in first anuvak of this Valli.

Brahmananda Valli: The statement *"Brahmavida Apnoti Param"* which means "The one who knows Brahman becomes one with Brahman" is the formula (Sutra-Vaakya) to get the high level gist of this Valli. First Anuvak starts with Shanti Mantra "OM sham no mitra" and "Shahana vavatu" pleasing gods and removing obstacles for study of Upanishad being the objective of these Mantras.

Second Anuvak starts with formula sentence "Brahmavida Apnoti Param" as stated above and also tries to define brahman *succintly as "Truth, Devine Knowledge and Infinite " (Satya Jnyanam* Anantam Brahma).

Anuvaks Second to Fifth describe that Five sheaths subtle bodies or (Five Atmans) reside in one another in human body. Starting with grosser, tangible human body called "Annamaya" or "Formed out of Food" to "Pranamaya" or "formed out of Vital life force" to "Manomaya" or "Formed out of Mind" to "Vijnyanamaya" or "One who is of Knowledge" to Final and subtle most being "Anandamaya" or one who is full of *Joy*. In Sixth and Seventh Anuvaks, some of the questions asked by a desciple are answered, such as

"Brahman being equal to both knower and ignorant, who gets the Brahman after death, knower or ignorant and why? "

Eighth Anuvak, compares happiness of various evolved beings starting from Man to that of next higher level till Happiness of Brahman itself.

Ninth Anuvak describes that knower of Brahman doesn't repent for not having done any good because for him/her, the terms good and bad loose their meaning and he/she has equalled them with Brahman since it is the only one which is really existing.

With this completes the "Brahmanada Valli".

Brighu Valli: This Valli describes how son of Varuna (The Water God) the [[*Brighu*]] obtained realization of Brahman through repeated Tapas and his father's guidance.

Rest of the part of Valli describes greatness of donating food, that is feeding the hungry. It also emphasises on greatness of Food. It says that since food is support of all life, food should not be insulted, food should not be declined.

Chandogya Upanishad

The *Chandogya* Upanishad is one of the oldest (perhaps "the oldest"), "primary" Upanishads commented upon by Adi Shankara. It is a Mukhya Upanishad, associated with the Samaveda. It figures as number 9 in the Muktika canon of 108 Upanishads. It is part of the *Chandogya Brahmana* which has ten chapters. The first two chapters of the Brahmana deal with sacrifices and other forms of worships. The other eight constitute the Chandogya Upanishad.

Though there are more than one hundred Upanishads, ten are principal. These are known as Dashopanishads and known for their philosophical depth and because Adi Shankara wrote commentaries on them.

Along with Brhadaranyaka Upanishad the Chandogyopanishad is an ancient source of principal fundamentals for Vedanta philosophy. Number of references made to this Upanishad in Brahma sutras indicates special importance of this Upanishad in Vedantic philosophy. Important spiritual practices like Dahara vidya, Shandilya vidya, etc. are its speciality.

Commentary: Of the available commentaries the oldest is the one written by Adi Shankara. Adi shankara has indicated that his commentary work is a brief book for those who want to know summary of this Upanishad. Commentator Ananda Giri has mentioned in his commentary that one Dramidacharya has written an elaborate and detailed commentary well before Adi Shakara. Very little is known about this Dramidacharya and his work is now lost.

Brahmanandi Tankacharya has written a brief explanation for this upanishad and Dramidacharya wrote an elaborate and detailed commentary on the work of Brahmanandi Tankacharya. Shri Ramanuja makes many references to these two scholars in his *Vedanta Sangraha* and *Shree Bhashya* both of which are commentary works.

The first and the second chapters of this Upanishad discuss the problems of liturgy and doctrine such as the genesis and significance of Aum and the meaning and names of Saman.

First chapter consists of eighteen subchapters in which the following are described:

1. Importance and greatness of universal holy syllable OM
2. Importance and greatness of Vital Life Force or Prana, and a story to explain the holiness of Prana describing how it remained untouched by evil while all other five senses got tainted by evil.
3. Fruits of meditating on holy syllable OM

Kena Upanishad

The *Kena* Upanishad (kenopanicad), is one of the older, "primary" Upanishads commented upon by Shankara. It is associated with the Samaveda. It figures as number 2 in the Muktika canon of 108 Upanishads.

About the Upanishad: Kenopanishad derives its name from the first word *Kena,* meaning 'by whom'. It belongs to the Talavakara Brahmana of Samaveda and is therefore also referred to as

Talavakara Upanishad. It has four sections, the first two in verse and the other two in prose. Adi Shankara who has written commentaries on 12 Upanishads, chose to write two commentaries on Kenopanishad. One is called Kenopanishad Pada Bhashya and the other is Kenopanishad Vakya Bhashya.

Brief Content: The One Power that illumines everything and every one is indivisible. It is the Ear behind the ears, Mind behind the mind, Speech behind speech, Vital Life behind life. The ears cannot hear it; it is what makes the ears hear. The eyes cannot see it; it is what makes the eyes see. You cannot speak about it; it is what makes you speak. The mind cannot imagine it; it is what makes the mind think. It is different from what all we know; yet it is not known either. Those who feel they know Him know Him not. Those who know that anything amenable to the senses is not Brahman, they know it best. When it is known as the innermost witness of all cognitions, whether sensation, perception or thought, then it is known. One who knows thus reaches immortality.

Story Part: Once the divines won a victory over the evil forces. The victory must have been credited to the power of the Absolute Brahman. Instead the divines thought it was theirs. Brahman appeared before them in a visible form of a spirit (*yaksha*) but they did not recognize the Absolute. One by one, Agni the God of fire and Vayu the God of air, came to challenge this new appearance in and tried to show off their powers. The God of Fire could not burn even the straw placed before him. The God of air could not blow even the straw placed before him. Finally Indra the God of all the divines came nearest to that spirit to find out who it is that is presenting these challenges to the divines. And before him stood Mother Goddess Herself in the name and form of Uma.

Final Lesson: This is the truth of Brahman in relation to nature and Man. Whether it is the flash of lightning, or the wink of the eyes or the thinking of the mind, the power that is shown is the power of Brahman. For this reason should a man meditate upon Brahman all the time. The sudden Reality that strikes Man as the power behind everything, must be transformed into a permanent Realization.

Mundaka Upanishad

The *Muaka* Upanishad is one of the older, "primary" (*mukhya*) Upanishads commented upon by Shankara. It is associated with the Atharvaveda. It figures as number 5 in the Muktika canon of 108 Upanishads.

It is a Mantra-upanishad, *i.e.* it has the form of a Mantra. But, as the commentators observe, though it is written in verse, it is not, like other Mantras, to be used for sacrificial purposes. Its only object is to teach the highest knowledge, the knowledge of Brahman, which cannot be obtained either by sacrifices or by worship (Upasana), but by such teaching only as is imparted in the Upanishad. With its beautiful style, lucid metres, serious wording, and lofty feelings each mantra of this Upanishad gives joyous reading. It might have derived its name from the word "Munda" meaning "Shaven Head". The assumption is that if the principle thought of this Upanishad is understood, the illusions of material world will be cut like hairs in the process of shaving or because mostly monks are audience for its teachings, and since usually Hindu monks will have a shaven head, this name might have something to do with that background.

It has three chapters and each chapter is divided into sub-chapters which are called "Khanda". In total this Upanishad has 64 Mantras.

As described in the beginning of this upanishad, it is said to be first told by Brahma to his son Atharva and Atharva taught it to Satyavaha and Satyavaha passed it to Angiras who in turn passes the knowledge to Shaunaka, dialogue between two forms content of this Upanishad.

This Upanishad divides all knowledge into two categories. The knowledge that leads to Self Realization is called Para Vidya or Divine Knowledge and everything else is called Apara Vidya or Knowledge of Material world. It is the first text to mention the six disciplines of Vedanga.

This Upanishad expounds the greatness of Para Vidya.

The Mundaka Upanishad is notable as the source of the phrase *Satyameva jayate,* the national motto of India, appearing in the Nation Emblem of four lions.

Mandukya Upanishad

Mandukya Upanishad is one of the shortest Upanishads, that form the speculative metaphysical parts of the Hindu texts, the

Vedas. It belongs to the Atharva Veda. It devotes itself entirely to the explanation of the mystic syllable Aum. It is in prose.

About the Upanishad: For the very reason that it explains the esoteric meaning of the fundamental syllable *Aum* of Hindu spiritual tradition, the Upanishad has been extolled greatly. The Muktikopanishad, which talks about all other Upanishads, says that if a person cannot afford to study all the hundred and more Upanishads, it will be enough to read just the Mandukya Upanishad. According to Dr.S. Radhakrishnan, in this Upanishad we find the fundamental approach to the attainement of reality by the road of introversion and ascent from the sensible and changing, through the mind which dreams, through the soul which thinks, to the divine within but above the soul.

Commentary by Gaudapada: The first extant commentary on this Upanishad was written by Gaudapada, before the time of Adi Shankara. This commentary, called the Mandukya-karika, is the earliest systematic exposition of the advaita point of view of Vedanta. Its importance can be gauged from the fact that when Shankara wrote his commentary on Mandukya Upanishad, as he did for ten other Upanishads, he merged the Karika of Gaudapada with the Upanishad and wrote a commentary on the Karika also.

Detailing Aum as in Mandukya Upanishad

Three matras: There are three matras in the word *aum* : 'a' as the 'u' in 'but'; 'u' as the 'u' in 'put'; and the 'm'. The term matra is used for the upper limb of Nagari characters and a syllabic instant in prosody.

Esoterically, the 'a' stands for the first stage of wakefulness, where we experience in our gross body the totality of external experiences through our mind and sense organs. The 'u' stands for the dream state of sleep in which mental experiences are available, though erratically, by the mind which is the only thing which is then awake, without the help of the external sense organs or the presence of the rationalising intellect.

Waking State and Dream State: The two kinds of experience, namely those of the waking state and those of the dream state, contradict each other, in the sense that a man may experience hunger in a dream though he has eaten in the waking state a few minutes earlier.

Deep Sleep State: In the state of deep sleep, represented by the sound 'm', there is no consciousness of any experience; even the mind has gone to sleep. But still there is an awareness after the deep sleep is over that one has been sleeping. Mandukya Upanishad says that in the state of deep sleep, the Atman which is always present, has been the witness to the sleep of the body and it is this source from which issues the memory of sleep.

Beyond the Three States: It is the Atman which is also present *beyond the three states of experience. The fourth state (turiya* avastha) (see turiya) corresponds to the silence that ensues after one has steadily pronounced aum. It is the state of no matra (amatra). In that silence Consciousness alone is present; there is nothing else. Therefore there is nothing to be cognized or be conscious of. This is the substratum of even the other three states of experience.

During the silence that follows the recitation of *aum*, one is advised to merge in that Consciousness, in fact, be that Consciousness. That Consciousness is the Atman. That is Brahman. To underscore the point that the 'fourth state' is not another 'state' of consciousness, but consciousness itself, *turiya avastha* is simply called *turiya* (the fourth).

Gaudapada's Thesis: In his karika on the Upanishad, Gaudapada deals with all the outstanding problems of philosophy, such as perception, idealism, causality, truth, and reality. In turiya, he says the mind is not simply withdrawn from the objects but becomes one with Brahman, who is free from fear and who is all-round illumination. In both deep sleep and transcendental consciousness there is no consciousness of objects. But this objective consciousness is present in an unmanifested 'seed' form in deep sleep while it is completely transcended in the *turiya*. Specifically, if one identifies the amatra state of silence with the *turiya* and meditates on it without intermission, one realizes one's self and 'there is no return for him to the sphere of empirical life', says Gaudapada.

Prashna Upanishad

Prashna Upanishad (IAST pracnopanicad) is one of the older, "primary" Upanishads commented upon by Shankara. It is a Mukhya Upanishad, associated with the Atharvaveda. It figures as number 4 in the Muktika canon of 108 Upanishads.

In Sanskrit, "Prashna" means question. This book consists of six questions and their answers, hence the name. It is in the form of question-answers, except first and last questions, all other questions are actually a group of smaller sub-questions. As narrated in the beginning of this Upanishad, Six pupils interested in knowing divinity or Brahman come to sage Pippalada and ask questions of great spiritual importance. Pippalada asks them to take up penance of one year. Upon completion of penance, they again come to sage and ask questions, then the sage answers their questions.

The pupils who ask questions are:

1. The son of Bharadwaja the Sukesha
2. The son of Shibi the Satyakama
3. The descendant of Garga the Sauryayanee
4. The son of Ashwalayana the Kausalya
5. Bhargava of the country of Vidarbha
6. The son of Katya the Kabandhi

Each of them asks one question to Pippalada and answer(s) to it forms a chapter in the Upanishad.

The Questions: The first question is asked by Kabandhi concerned with the root cause of the universe.

The second question asked by Bhargava is concerned with the supremacy of vital Force of Life or Prana over other sense organs of human being.

The third question asked by Kausalya is concerned with the origin and functioning of Vital Force of Life.

The fifth question is concerned with fruits one gets by meditating on holy syllable OM.

The sixth and last question is concerned with the being by whom all this known-unknown universe got created and who has sixteen vital things (kala) or who is called as *Shodasha Kala Purusha*.

The answers to each question are developed by Pippalada, within a perspective of great depth.

The language and concepts of the answers are often abstruse and esoteric, but one may get from them glimpses that are rational and perceptive. Thus, in answering the question on the origin of life, Pippalada starts with the origin of all existence in terms of matter and energy, and develops the answer step by step, till in the last one, he gives as the most direct and immediate origin of life, the sperm of the species. The answer to the last question is, that the ultimate supreme source of all existence is Brahman. This, indeed, is the answer of all the Upanishads.

Shvetashvatara Upanishad

The *Shvetashvatara Upanishad* is one of the older, "primary" Upanishads. It is associated with the Black Yajurveda. It figures as number 14 in the Muktika canon of 108 Upanishads. Adi Shankara has called it the "Mantra Upanishad" of the Vedic Shvetashvatara school in his commentary on Brahma sutras.

This Upanishad contains 113 mantras or verses in six chapters. In the last chapter we find the following verse.

> *" Sage Shvetashvatara got this knowledge of Brahman which is very sacred and revered by many great sages by his penance and god's grace and taught it very well to his disciples"*

By this verse we can make out that this Upanishad was due to a sage called "Shvetashvatara" or his line of ancient spiritual teachers. The name "Shvetashvatara" is not uncommon in vedic literature. It means "White Mule". Mule was a prized animal in ancient vedic India.

The person who owns white horse is called "Shvetashva" and the one who owns white mule can be called "Shvetashvatara". We can notice that Arjuna is called as "Shvetashva" in epic Mahabharata. In Rigveda we find a sage's name as "Shyavashva" meaning "One who owns a black horse". This Upanishad has acquired a high place among the Hindu Kruti.

Commentary Works: There is one commentary available on this upanishad that is said to be written by Adi Shankara. But if we compare it with other commentary works of same author, there is some doubt if it is indeed composed by Adi Shankara. There are other three commentators namely Vijnanatma, Shankarananda and Narayana Thirtha.

Time and Origin: Deciding time of the origin of this Upanishad in not easy because, apart from very ancient content, there are also other verses which look like they were added in at a later point of time.

Many Mantras in this upanishad can also be seen in Rigveda, Black Yajurveda, White Yajurveda. Though it may not be as old as liturgic Upanishads like Chandogya or Brhadaranyaka Upanishad, we can say it belongs to time line of poetic group of Upanishads like Katha Upanishad, Eshavasya or Mandukya Upanishad.

Special Features: This Upanishad is just as much tough to understand as much it is wonderful. It has following specialities which arouse curiosity in the reader of vedic literature.

1. The Supreme God or Brahman is called by various names such as Shiva, Rudra, etc. This feature may give rise to an assumption that it may be a Shaiva Upanishad. But such an assumption is not right because, at the time of this Upanishad, Shaiva Agamas weren't there. Also, at that time the supreme God head or Brahman usedbe called by different names each indicating a particular manifestation of Brahman. Just as names Shiva or Rudra are used to refer Brahman, names such as Vayu, Aditya or Agni are also used for same purpose in this Upanishad. More over, if this Upanishad is indeed a Shaiva Upanishad, other sects of Hinduism such as Vaishnavas wouldn't have quoted its verses/mantras as authority in their respective treatises.
2. Second speciality is concept of *"Devotion"* or Bhakti. In other Upanishads, the concept of devotion (or Bhakti) is indirectly voiced in the form of " *Upasana*". But here, without leaving any room for guesswork, it is explicitly mentioned. The word *"Para Bhakti"* is explicitly used at the end of sixth chapter. There are many words which voice submission to God or Brahman (words such as *"Sharanam"*, *"Prapadye"*). This concept of devotion at later *times found profound and wide meanings in Bhakti Sutras* and other treatises on Bhakti or devotion.
3. Third speciality of this upanishad lies in its giving importance to the *form* fullness (or *Moortitva*) of God or Brahman which is usually described as *formless* in other important upanishads. Since it is difficult to concentrate

mind on and/or show devotion on *formless* Brahman, it is only natural that this book goes ahead and tries to ascribe various *forms* to God. While expounding on devotion, it also ascribes various characteristics or manifestations to God, such as, mentioning that God has knowledge and power. This upanishad also presents that God or Brahman as creator and sustainer of the universe, and while trying to describe various powers of God, to drive home the point, makes use of similes such as God having thousands of heads-to denote endless knowledge of God, thousands of eyes-to denote God as universal witness for everything that is going on in the universe and God having thousands or simply innumerable number of feet—to indicate Gods omnipresence. This Upanishad mentions that, God or " *Parama Purusha*" is shining in his (or "its" since upanishads do not ascibe gender to Brahman) glory beyond the darkness of ignorance or " *Tamas* ". Gods characteristic is " *Maya*" or illusion of the world. But God is not bound by his Maya as humans are, because he has conquered it and became "*Maheshvara*", and he (or it) is capable of giving salvation to human beings.

4. *Fourth speciality is use of words such as "Samkhya",* "Kapila", "*yoga*", "*Prakriti*". Some scholars debate that this indicates assimilation of Saankhya-Yoga-Darshana school of thought into Vedanta happened at some point of time. If this view is right, it means that Vedantic Upanishads were originated later than Saankhya-Yoga-Darshana school of thought. This view is not right because of following reasons.

   (i) Just because certain definitive words are similar, it doesn't imply Upanishads are of later origin than Darshana schools. The definitive words like "*Samkhya, prakriti,* etc. are always used in Vedas earlier than Darshana schools. So, these specific words are taken from Vedanta and later used by proponents of Darshana schools.

   (ii) The proponents of Darshanas like sage kapila describe in their treatises that they are interpreting the Vedanta, so it means Vedantic Upanishads are of earlier origin than these schools of thought.

(iii) In this Upanishad, we don't see any assimilation of principles of those schools but to contrary, the thoughts that are rejected by those schools are expounded and accepted using the same words and definitions of those schools.

The philosophical jargon of Samkhya school of thought originated in vedas well before birth of Saamkhya. The word saamkhya originates from word "samkhya" which means counting or understanding.

There are many verses in this upanishad that have some counting of things in them that is why word "samkhya" got another meaning as knowledge. While Yoga is practical Sammkhya is intellectual. While samkhya is purely dualistic. Upanishads are clearly non-dualistic. In Samkhya the "Purusha" or self is different from "Prakriti" or Nature but in Upanishadic thought, "Prakriti"(Nature) is God derived, or God dependent force, specifically this Upanishad refers to it as "*Devaatma Shakti*", which can be roughly translated as "Gods inner force that manifests itself as nature (*Prakriti*)". One hymn of this Upanishad says,

> *"Sages engaged in deep meditation realized secret 'Atma Shakti' of God."*

It says this *Atma Shakti* of God is hidden secretly in the meditators' own inner nature.

Regarding the usage of the word "Kapila" is concerned, if we see the contexts of hyms that have come before and later of the hymn which uses word kapila, it is clear that it does not denote sage kapila who is proponent of Samkhya. The hymn 5.2 which uses word "kapila" should be seen in the context with other hyms. 4th hymn of 3rd chapter says,

> *"All knower Rudra gave birth to Hiranyagarbha"*

12th hymn of 4th chapter says

> *"Rudra saw the birth of Hiranyagarbha"*

later, 18th hymn of 6th chapter says,

> *"Parameshvara created Brahma"*

Now when seen in context of these hymns, the verse 5.2, which uses the word kapila says,

> *"God saw birth of All-knowing Kapila"*

In Sanskrit, word *kapila* means "golden-coloured". *Hiranya* garbha means "one embodying golden core".

In Upanishads *Hiranya garbha* is also called by other names such as Prajapati, Brahma, etc. based on this context relation, we can conclude this Upanishad when it uses word kapila it means *Hiranya garbha* rather than Samkhya school proponent.

Poetic Style: Normally, Upanishads are sources of serious philosophical thought.

But this Upanishad differs with other Upanishads in being same principles explained in simple, easy-going and poetic way, whereever sage svhetashvatara has his independent hymns, he sees them in a beautiful, heart-catching poetic way, he is not only a seer of Mantras, but also a poet from heart. Here are few examples.

While trying to describe omnipresence of Brahman, Hymn 4.2 says,

> *"You are woman, you are man, you are boy and you are girl, you are the shivering old man helped by stick, you are born in the form of this world"*

Hymn 4.4 says

> *"You are blue-coloured butterfly, green eyed parrot, lightning cloud, you are the seasons, and seas, you are the one without any beginning, you are omnipresent, all the worlds are born out of you"*

The Anukramanis

The Anukramanis or Indices of the Rigveda provide us with the most basic information about each of the 1028 hymns of the Rigveda:

a. The Rishi or composer of each hymn or verse.

b. The Devata or deity of each hymn or verse.

c. The Chhanda or metre of each hymn or verse.

For the purpose of our historical analysis of the Rigveda, we will be concerned only with the index which deals with the most undeniably historical aspect of the Rigveda: the index of Rishis which provides us with details about the living and breathing historical personalities who composed the hymns.

The Rigveda consists of 10 Mandala or Books, which contain 1028 suktas or hymns, consisting of 10552 mantras or verses as follows:

Mandala N	*No. of Hymns*	*No. of verses*
I	191	2006
II	43	429
III	62	617
IV	58	589
V	87	727
VI	75	765
VII	104	841
VIII	103	1716
IX	114	1108
X	119	1754
Total	1028	10552

The Anukramanis give us details, regarding these hymns, which are *so basic and indispensable* that it is *inconceivable* that any serious scholar could consider it possible to analyse the hymns *without* taking the Anukramanis as the very basis for his analysis.

But, ironically, not only are the Anukramanis generally ignored by the scholars, but this ignorance of, and indifference to, the details contained in the Anukramanis is even flaunted by them.

Consider the following statements by eminent scholars who consider themselves qualified to make pronouncements on Rigvedic history:

B.K. Ghosh: "The first Mandala falls naturally into two parts: the first fifty hymns have the Kanvas as authors like the eighth Mandala…".

Actual fact: I.1-11, 24-30 (eighteen hymns) are by Vishvamitra.

I.31-35 (five hymns) are by Angirases

I.12-23, 36-50 (twenty-seven hymns) are by Kanvas

DD Kosambi: "The principal Vedic god is Agni, the god of fire; more hymns are dedicated to him than to any other. Next in importance comes Indra."

Actual fact: The ratio between the number of hymns and verses to the two gods, by any count, is Indra: Agni = 3:2.

The flippant attitude of these scholars towards factual details, when it comes to Rigvedic studies, is underlined by the nature of Kosambi's error: he misinterprets the fact that hymns to Agni are generally *placed before* hymns to Indra, to mean that there are more hymns to Agni than to Indra!

Maurice Bloomfield, in his invaluable work on Rigvedic Repetitions (*i.e.* verses, verse-sections or phrases, which occur more than once in the Rigveda) claims that these repetitions prove the falsity or dubiousness of the information contained in the Anukramanis:

Under the title "Untrustworthiness of Anukramani-statements Shown by the Repetitions", Bloomfield remarks that "the statements of the Sarvanukramani.... betray the dubiousness of their authority in no particular more than in relation to the repetitions.... the Anukramani finds it in its heart to assign, with unruffled insouciance, one and the same verse to two or more authors, or to ascribe it to two or more divinities, according as it occurs in one book or another, in one connexion or another. The AprI stanzas 3.4.8-11 = 7.2.8-11 are ascribed in the third book to Vishvamitra Gathina, in the seventh book to Vasishtha Maitravaruni."

However:

1. The repetitions do *not* disprove the authenticity of the Anukramanis:
    a. The repetitions in the Rigveda are representative of a regular phenomenon in Classical and liturgical literature throughout the world. Consider for example what Gilbert Murray says about similar repetitions in Greek literature: "descriptive phrases...... are caught up ready made from a store of such things: perpetual epithets, front halves of lines, back halves of lines, whole lines, if need be, and long formulae. The stores of the poets were full and brimming. A bard need only put in his hand and choose out a well-sounding phrase. Even the similes are ready-made." Quoting this, B.K. Ghosh notes: "All this may be maintained, *mutatis mutandis*, also of Rigvedic poetry."

In the case of the Rigveda it is significant that *every* single repetition pertains to a literary or liturgical phrase. In fact, the more literary or liturgical the reference, the more the likelihood of repetitions: the longest repetition of three consecutive verses is in the liturgical AprI-suktas of the Vishvamitras and Vasishtha: III.4.8-11 = VII.2.8-11.

Not a single repetition pertains to any historical reference: even when the same historical reference is found in four different verses, the phrasing is different: I.53.10; II.14.7; VI.18.13; VIII. 53.2.

Therefore, regardless of the number of verses or verse-sections common to any two hymns ascribed to two different Rishis, the hymns in question have to be regarded as compositions of the two Rishis to whom they are ascribed: that one Rishi has borrowed from the composition of the other is no criterion in judging the correctness of the Anukramanis.

b. The AprI-suktas of the Vishvamitra and Vasishtha contain the longest repetitions, of three verses, in common: III.4.8-11 = VII. 2.8-11. Bloomfield points to these particular repetitions as evidence in support of his contention that the repetitions disprove the correctness of the Anukramanis. But, ironically, it is these very repetitions which disprove the correctness of his *contention*.

The composers of the Rigveda were members of ten priestly families, and each family had its own AprI-sukta composed by a member of the family. In later times, during the performance of any sacrifice, at the point where an AprI-sukta was to be recited, the conducting Rishi was required to recite the AprI-sukta of his own family.

The AprI-sukta of the Vishvamitra was therefore undoubtedly composed by a Vishvamitra, and that of the Vasishtha by a Vasishtha. If these two hymns contain repetitions in common, it constitutes the ultimate proof that repetitions in common are no evidence of two hymns *not* having been composed by two different Rishis.

2. There is no logical reason to doubt the authenticity of the authorship ascriptions in the Anukramanis, which are corroborated by:
   a. The very existence of the Anukramanis as a part and parcel of the Rigvedic text from the most ancient times.
   b. The very division of the Rigveda into Mandala, many of which are family Mandala.
   c. The uniformity of style in hymns ascribed to single Rishis or families (eg. Parucchepa).
   d. The common refrains occurring in the concluding verses of hymns ascribed to certain Rishis or families (eg. Kutsa).
   e. The common contexts in hymns ascribed to certain Rishis or families (eg. the repeated references to Sudas in hymns by Vasishtha).
   f. Specific statements within the hymns, where the composers refer to themselves by name.
   g. Most important of all, the perfectly logical way in which an analysis of the historical references in the hymns, as we shall demonstrate in this book, produces a pattern of historical correspondences and inter-relationships which fits in perfectly with the ascriptions in the Anukramanis.

With this, we may now turn to the actual details given in the Anukramanis regarding the names of the composers of the different hymns in the Rigveda:

Mandala I (191 hymns)

1-10	Madhucchandas Vishvamitra
11	Jeta Madhucchandas
12-23	Medhatithi Kanva
24-30	Sunahsepa Ajigarti later Devarata Vishvamitra
31-35	Hiranyastupa Angiras
36-43	Kanva Ghaura
44-50	Praskanva Kanva
51-57	Savya Angiras

58-64	Nodhas Gautama
65-73	Parasara Saktya
74-93	Gautama Rahugana
94-98	Kutsa Angiras
99	Kasyapa Marica
100	Rjrasva Varsagira
101-115	Kutsa Angiras
116-126	Kaksivan Dairghatamas
127-139	Parucchepa Daivodasi
140-164	Dirghatamas Aucathya
165-191	Agastya Maitravaruni
	Mandala II (43 hymns)
1-3	Grtsamada Saunahotra, *later* Grtsamada Saunaka
4-7	Somahuti Bhargava
8-26	Grtsamada Saunahotra, *later* Grtsamada Saunaka
27-29	Kurma Gartsamada
30-43	Grtsamada Saunahotra, *later* Gartsamada Saunaka
	Mandala III (62 hymns)
1-12	Vishvamitra Gathina
13-14	Rsabha Vishvamitra
15-16	UtkIla Katya
17-18	Kata Vishvamitra
19-22	Gathin Kausika.
23-35	Vishvamitra Gathina
36	Vishvamitra Gathina, Ghora Angiras
37	Vishvamitra Gathina
38	Vishvamitra Gathina, Prajapati Vishvamitra/Vacya
39-53	Vishvamitra Gathina
54-56	Prajapati Vishvamitra/Vacya
57-61	Vishvamitra Gathina
62	Vishvamitra Gathina, Jamadagni Bhargava

Mandala IV (58 hymns)

1-42	Vamadeva Gautama
43-44	PurumIlha Sauhotra, AjamIlha Sauhotra
45-58	Vamadeva Gautama

Mandala V (87 hymns)

1	Budha/Gavisthira Atreya
2	Kumara/Vrsa Jana Atreya
3-6	Vasusruta Atreya
7-8	Isa Atreya
9-10	Gaya Atreya
11-14	Sutambhara Atreya
15	Dharuna Angiras
16-17	Puru Atreya
18	Dvita Atreya
19	Vavri Atreya
20	Prayasvanta Atreya
21	Sasa Atreya
22	Visvasaman Atreya
23	Dyumna Visvacarsani Atreya
24	Bandhu, Subandhu, Srutabandhu, Viprabandhu (Gaupayanas)
25-26	Vasuyava Atreya
27	Atri Bhauma
28	Visvavara Atreyi
29	GaurivIti Saktya
30	Babhru Atreya
31	Avasyu Atreya
32	Gatu Atreya
33-34	Samvarana Prajapatya
35-36	Prabhuvasu Angiras
37-43	Atri Bhauma

44	Avatsara Kasyapa, various Atreyas
45	Sadaprna Atreya
46	Pratiksatra Atreya
47	Pratiratha Atreya
48	Pratibhanu Atreya
49	Pratiprabha Atreya
50-51	Svasti Atreya
52-61	Syavasva Atreya
62	Srutavida Atreya
63-64	Arcananas Atreya
65-66	Ratahavya Atreya
67-68	Yajata Atreya
69-70	Urucakri Atreya
71-72	Bahuvrkta Atreya
73-74	Paura Atreya
75	Avasyu Atreya
76-77	Atri Bhauma
78	Saptavadhri Atreya
79-80	Satyasravas Atreya
81-82	Syavasva Atreya
83-86	Atri Bhauma
87	Evayamarut Atreya

Mandala VI (75 hymns)

1-30	Bharadvja Barhaspatya
31-32	Suhotra Bharadvaja
33-34	Sunahotra Bharadvaja
35-36	Nara Bharadvaja
37-43	Bharadvaja Barhaspatya
44-46	Samyu Barhaspatya
47	Garga Bharadvaja
48	Samyu Barhaspatya

49-52	Rjisvan Bharadvaja
53-74	Bharadvaja Barhaspatya
75	Payu Bharadvaja
	Mandala VII (104 hymns)
1-31	Vasishtha Maitravaruni
32	Vasishtha Maitravaruni Shakti Vasishtha
33-100	Vasishtha Maitravaruni
101-102	Vasishtha Maitravaruni, Kumara Agneya
103-104	Vasishtha Maitravaruni
	Mandala VIII (103 hymns)
1	Pragatha Kanva, Medhatithi Kanva, Medhyatithi Kanva
2	Medhatithi Kanva, Priyamedha Angiras
3	Medhyatithi Kanva
4	Devatithi Kanva
5	Brahmatithi Kanva
6	Vatsa Kanva
7	Punarvatsa Kanva
8	Sadhvamsa Kanva
9	SaSakarNa Kanva
10	Pragatha Kanva
11	Vatsa Kanva
12	Parvata Kanva
13	Narada Kanva
14-15	Gosuktin Kanva, Asvasuktin Kanva
16-18	Irimbitha Kanva
19-22	Sobhari Kanva
23-25	Visvamanas Vaiyasva
26	Visvamanas Vaiyasva, Vyasva Angiras
27-31	Manu Vaivasvata or Kasyapa MarIca
32	Medhatithi Kanva

33	Medhyatithi Kanva
34	Nipatithi Kanva
35-38	Syavasva Atreya
39-41	Nabhaka Kanva
42	Nabhaka Kanva, Arcananas Atreya
43-44	Virupa Angiras
45	Trisoka Kanva
46	Vasa Asvya
47	Trita Aptya
48	Pragatha Kanva
49	Praskanva Kanva
50	Pustigu Kanva
51	Srustigu Kanva
52	Ayu Kanva
53	Medhya Kanva
54	Matarisvan Kanva
55	Krsa Kanva
56	Prsadhra Kanva
57-58	Medhya Kanva
59	Suparna Kanva
60-61	Bharga Pragatha
62-65	Pragatha Kanva
66	Kali Pragatha
67	Matsya Sammada or Manya Maitravaruni
68-69	Riyamedha Angiras
70	Puruhanman Angiras
71	Suditi PurumIlha
72	Haryata Pragatha
73-74	Gopavana Atreya
75	Virupa Angiras

76-78	Kurusuti Kanva
79	Krtnu Bhargava
80	Ekadyu Naudhasa
81-83	Usidin Kanva
84	Usana Kavya,
85	Krsna Angiras
86	Krsna Angiras, Visvaka Karsni
87	Krsna Angiras, DyumnIka Vasishtha, Priyamedha Angiras
88	Nodhas Gautama
89-90	Nrmedha Angiras, Purumedha Angiras
91	Apala Atreyi
92-93	Sukaksa Angiras
94	Vindu Angiras, Putadaksa Angiras
95-96	Tirasci Angiras
97	Rebha Kasyapa
98-99	Nrmedha Angiras
100	Nema Bhargava
101	Jamadagni Bhargava
102	Prayoga Bhargava, Agni Barhaspatya
103	Sobhari Kanva

Mandala IX (114 hymns)

1	Madhucchandas Vishvamitra
2	Medhatithi Kanva
3	Sunahsepa Ajigarti
4	Hiranyastupa Angiras
5-24	Asita Kasyapa, Devala Kasyapa
25	Drlhacyuta Agastya
26	Idhmavaha Darlhacyuta
27	Nrmedha Angiras
28	Priyamedha Angiras

29	Nrmedha Angiras
30	Bindu Angiras
31	Gotama Rahugana
32	Syavasva Atreya
33-34	Trita Aptya
35-36	Prabhuvasu Angiras
37-38	Rahugana Angiras
39-40	Brhanmati Angiras
41-43	Medhatithi Kaṇva
44-46	Ayasya Angiras
47-49	Kavi Bhargava
50-52	Ucathya Angiras
53-60	Avatsara Kasyapa
61	Amahiyu Angiras
62	Jamadagni Bhargava
63	Nidhruvi Kasyapa
64	Kasyapa Marica
65	Jamadagni Bhargava
66	Sata Vaikhanasa
67	Saptarsis, Pavitra Angiras
68	Vatsapri Bhalandana
69	Hiranyastupa Angiras
70	Renu Vishvamitra
71	Rsabha Vishvamitra
72	Harimanta Angiras
73	Pavitra Angiras
74	Kaksivan Dairghatamas
75-79	Avi Bhargava
80-82	Asu Bharadvaja
83	Pavitra Angiras
84	Prajapati Vacya

85	Vena Bhargava
86	Atri Bhauma, Gartsamada Saunaka, Akrsta Masa, Sikata Nivavari, Prsni Aja
87-89	Usana Kavya
90	Vasishtha Maitravaruni
91-92	Kasyapa Marica
93	Nodhas Gautama
94	Kanva Ghaura
95	Praskanva Kanva
96	Pratardana Daivodasi
97	Vasishtha Maitravaruni, Indrapramati Vasishtha, Vrsagana Vasishtha, Manyu Vasishtha, Upamanyu Vasishtha, Vyaghrapada Vasishtha, Shakti Vasishtha, Karnasrut Vasishtha, Mrlika Vasishtha, Vsukra Vasishtha, Parasara Saktya, Kutsa Angiras. Ambarisa Varsagira, Rjisvan Angiras
98	Rebhasunu Kasyapas
99-100	Andhigu Syavasvi, Yayati Nahusa, Nahusa
101	Manava, Manu Samvarana, Prajapati Vishvamitra. Trita Aptya Dvita Aptya
102	Parvata Kanva, Narada Kanva
103	Agni Caksusa, Caksu Manava, Manu Apsava
104-105	Saptarsis
106	Gauriviti Saktya, Shakti Vasishtha, Uru Angiras,
107	Rjisvan Bharadvaja
108	Agni Dhisnya Aisvaraya Tryaruna Traivrsna, Trasadasyu Paurukutsa
109	Ananata Parucchepi
110	Sisu Angiras
111	Kasyapa Marica
112	
113-114	

Mandala X (191 hymns)

1-7	Trita Aptya
8	Trisiras Tvastra
9	Trisiras Tvastra, Sindhudvipa Ambarisa
10	Yama Vaivasvata, Yami Vaivasvati
11-12	Havirdhana Angi
13	Vivasvan Aditya
14	Yama Vaivasvata
15	Sankha Yamayana
16	Damana Yamayana
17	Devasravas Yamayana
18	Sankusuka Yamayana
19	Matitha Yamayana, or Bhrgu, or Cyavana Bhargava
20-26	Vimada Aindra, Vasukrt Vasukra
27-29	Vasukra Aindra
30-34	Kavasa Ailusa
35-36	Lusa Dhanaka
37	Abhitapa Saurya
38	Indra Muskavan
39-40	Ghosa Kaksivati
41	Suhastya Ghauseya
42-44	Krsna Angiras
45-46	Vatsapri Bhalandana
47	Saptagu Angiras
48-50	Indra Vaikuntha
51-53	Agni Saucika
54-56	Brhaduktha Vamadeva
57-60	Bandhu, Subandhu, Srutabandhu, Viprabandhu (Gaupayanas)
61-62	Nabhanedistha Manava
63-64	Gaya Plata

65-66	Vasukarna Vasukra
67-68	Ayasya Angiras
69-70	Sumitra Vadhryasva
71-72	Brhaspati Angiras
73-74	Gauriviti Saktya
75	Sindhuksit Praiyamedha
76	Jaratkarna Sarpa Airavata
77-78	Syumarasmi Bhargava
79-80	Agni Saucika or Sapti Vajambhara
81-82	Vishvamitra Bhauvana
83-84	Manyu Tapasa
85	Surya Savitri
86	Vrsakapi Aindra, Indra, Indrani
87	Payu Bharadvaja
88	Murdhanvan Vamadeva
89	Renu Vishvamitra
90	Narayana
91	Aruna Vaitahavya
92	Saryata Manava
93	Tanva Parthya
94	Arbuda Kadraveya Sarpa
95	Pururavas Aila, Urvasi
96	Baru Angiras, Sarvahari Aindra
97	Bhisag Atharvana
98	Devapi Arstisena
99	Vamra Vaikhanasa
100	Duvasyu Vandana
101	Budha Saumya
102	Mudgala Bharmyasva
103	Apratiratha Aindra
104	Astaka Vishvamitra

105 Sumitra Kautsa, Durmitra Kautsa
106 Bhutamsa Kasyapa
107 Divya Angiras, Daksina Prajapatya
108 Sarama, Panis
109 Juhu Brahmajaya
110 Rama Jamadagnya, Jamadagni Bhargava
111 Astadamstra Vairupa
112 Nabhahprabhedana Vairupa
113 Sataprabhedana Vairupa
114 Sadhri Vairupa
115 Upastuta Varstihavya
116 Agniyuta Sthaura
117 Bhiksu Angiras
118 Uruksaya Angiras
119 Laba Aindra
120 Brhaddiva Atharvana
121 Hiranyagarbha Prajapatya
122 Citramaha Vasishtha
123 Vena Bhargava
124 Agni, Varuna, Soma
125 Vak Ambhrni
126 Amhomuk Vamadeva
127 Kusika Saubhara, Ratri Bharadvaji
128 Vihavya Angiras
129 Prajapati Paramesthin
130 Yajna Prajapatya
131 Sukirti Kaksivata
132 Sakaputa Narmedha
133 Sudas Paijavana
134 Mandhata Yauvanasva
135 Kumara Yamayana

136 Juti, Vatajuti, Viprajuti, Vrsanaka, Karikrata, Etasa, Rsyasrnga (Vatarasanas)

137 Saptarsis

138 Anga Aurava

139 Visvavasu Devagandharva

140 Agni, Pavaka

141 Agni Trpasa

142 Sarnga, Jaritr, Drona, Sarisrkva, Stambhamitra Atri Sankhya

143 Urdhvasadman Yamayana

144 Indrani

145 Devamuni Airammada

146 Suvedas Sairisi

147 Prthu Vainya

148 Arcan Hairanyastupa

149 Mrlika Vasishtha

150 Sraddha Kamayani

151 Sasa Bharadvaja

152 Indramatara Devajamaya

153 Yami Vaivasvati

154 Sirimbitha Bharadvaja

155 Ketu Agneya

156 Bhuvana Aptya, Sadhana Aptya

157 Caksu Saurya

158 Saci Paulomi

159 Purana Vishvamitra

160 Yaksmanasana Prajapatya

161 Raksoha Brahma

162 Vivrha Kasyapa

163 Pracetas Angiras

164 Kapota Nairrta

165	Rsabha Vairaja Sakvara
166	Vishvamitra, Jamadagni
167	Anila Vatayana
168	Sabara Kaksivata
169	Vibhrat Saurya
170	Ita Bhargava
171	Samvarta Angiras
172	Dhruva Angiras
173	Abhivarta Angiras
174	Urdhvagrava Arbuda
175	Sunu Arbhava
176	Patanga Prajapatya
177	Aristanemi Tarksya
178	Sibi Ausinara, Pratardana Kasiraja, Vasumanas
179	Rauhidasva Jaya Aindra
180	Pratha Vasishtha, Sapratha Bharadvaja,
181	Gharma Saurya Tapurmurdhan Barhaspatya
182	Prajavan Prajapatya
183	Visnu Prajapatya
184	Satyadhrti Varuni
185	Ula Vatayana
186	Vatsa Agneya
187	Syena Agneya
188	Sarparajni
189	Aghamarsana Madhucchandas
190	Samvanana Angiras
191	

There are obviously corruptions in the Anukramanis in the form of ascriptions to fictitious composers. This is particularly the case in Mandala X, where a large number of hymns are ascribed to composers whose names, or patronyms/epithets, or both, are fictitious.

However, in the first eight Mandala, except in the case of one single hymn (VIII.47), it is very easy to identify the actual composer (by which we mean the Rishi who actually composed the hymn, or his eponymous ancestor to whose name the hymn is to be credited as per the system followed in the particular Mandala) of a hymn ascribed to a fictitious composer.

Hence, in our listing of the composers of the first eight Mandalas, we have replaced the fictitious names in the Anukramanis with the names of the actual composers, whose identity is clear from those same Anukramanis. In all these cases, the actual composer is the Rishi of the hymn or the Rishi of the Mandala. The hymns in question are:

(1) Hymns where the entire hymn, or verses therein, are ascribed solely (in III.23 and IV.42) or alternatively (in the others) to Rishis or kings who are referred to within the hymns by the actual composer:

Hymn	*Fictitious Composers*	*Actual Composer*
I.100	Ambarisa, Sahadeva, Bhayamana, Suradhas	Rjrasva
I.105	Trita Aptya	Kutsa
I.126	Bhavayavya, Romasa	Kaksivan
III.23	Devasravas, Devavata	Vishvamitra
IV.42	Trasadasyu Paurukutsa	Vamadeva
V.27	Trasadasyu, Tryaruna, Asvamedha	Atri
VI.15	Vitahavya	Bharadvaja
VIII.1	Asanga, Sasvati	Medhatithi
VIII.34	Vasurocis	Nipatithi

(2) Dialogue hymns, in some of which verses are ascribed to Gods and even rivers:

Hymn	*Fictitious Composers*	*Actual Composer*
I.165	Indra, Maruts, (epon.) Agastya	Agastya
I.170	Indra, (epon.) Agastya	Agastya
I.179	(epon.) Agastya, Lopamudra, a pupil	Agastya
III.33	(epon.) Vishvamitra, Rivers	Vishvamitra
IV.18	(epon.) Vamadeva, Indra, Aditi	Vishvamitra

(3) Hymns which are ascribed alternatively to the actual composers and to their remote ancestors:

Hymn	*Fictitious Composers*	*Actual Composer*
III.31	Kusika Aisirathi	Vishvamitra Gathina
VIII.27-31	Manu Vaivasvata	Kasyapa Marica
VIII.71	Purumilha Angiras	Suditi Purumilha

3

The Rigveda

The composers of the Rigveda are divided into ten families. These ten families are identified on the basis of the fact that each family has its own Apri-sukta. An Apri-sukta is a particular type of ritual hymn "consisting of invocations to a series of deified objects, and said to be introductory to the animal sacrifice".

The ten Apri-suktas, and the ten families of composers to whom they belong, are:

1. I.13 Kanvas (Kevala-Angirases)
2. I.142 Angirases
3. I.188 Agastyas
4. II.3 Grtsamadas (Kevala-Bhrgus)
5. III.4 Vishvamitra
6. V.5 Atris
7. VII.2 Vasishtha
8. IX.5 Kasyapas
9. X.70 Bharatas
10. X.110 Bhrgus

    In addition to hymns and verses composed by members of these ten families, we also have the two following categories of hymns and verses:

11. Those composed *jointly* by members of different families.
12. Those composed by Rishis whose family identity is *unknown* or unidentifiable.

The family-wise distribution of the hymns in each Mandala is as follows:

Mandala I (191 hymns, 2006 verses)

1 *KANVAS* (27 hymns, 321 verses): 12-23, 36-50

2. *ANGIRASES* (96 hymns, 1047 verses): 31-35, 51-64, 74-98, 100-126, 140-164

3. *AGASTYAS* (27 hymns, 239 verses): 165-191

5. *Vishvamitra* (18 hymns, 207 verses): 1-11, 24-30

7. *Vasishtha* (9 hymns, 91 verses): 65-73

8. *Kasyapas* (1 hymn, 1 verse): 99

9. *Bharatas* (13 hymns, 100 verses): 127-139

Mandala II (43 hymns, 429 verses)

4. *GRTSAMADAS* (39 hymns, 398 verses): 1-3, 8-43

10. *BHRGUS* (4 hymns, 31 verses): 4-7

Mandala III (62 hymns, 617 verses)

5. *Vishvamitra* (60 hymns, 588 verses): 1-35, 37-61

11. *Joint* (2 hymns, 29 verses): 36, 62

    2. *Angirases* (1 verse): 36.10

    5. *Vishvamitra* (25 verses): 36.1-9, 11; 62.1-15

    11. *Joint Vishvamitra and Bhrgus* (3 verses): 62.16-18

Mandala IV (58 hymns, 589 verses)

2. *Angirases* (58 hymns, 589 verses): 1-58

Mandala V (87 hymns, 727 verses)

2. *Angirases* (3 hymns, 19 verses): 15, 35-36

3. *Agastyas* (1 hymn, 4 verses): 24

5. *Vishvamitra* (2 hymns, 19 verses): 33-34

6. *Atris* (79 hymns, 655 verses): 1-14, 16-23, 25-28, 30-32, 37-43, 45-87

7. *Vasishtha* (1 hymn, 15 verses): 29

11. *Joint* (1 hymn, 15 verses): 44

    6. *Atris* (1 verse) 44.13

    8. *Kasyapas* (11 verses): 44.1-9, 14-15

    11. *Joint Atris and Kasyapas* (3 verses): 44.10-12

Mandala VI (75 hymns, 765 verses)

2. *Angirases* (75 hymns, 765 verses): 1-75

Mandala VII (104 hymns, 841 verses)

7. *Vasishtha* (102 hymns, 832 verses): 1-100, 103-104
11. *Joint* (2 hymns, 9 verses): 101-102
    11. *Joint Angirases and Vasishtha* (2 hymns, 9 verses): 101-102

Mandala VIII (103 hymns, 1716 verses)

1. *Kanvas* (55 hymns, 933 verses): 1, 3-22, 32-34, 39-41, 45, 48-66, 72, 76-78, 81-83, 103
2. *Angirases* (25 hymns, 460 verses): 23-26, 43-44, 46, 68-71, 75, 80, 85-86, 88-90, 92-96, 98-99
3. *Agastyas* (1 hymn, 21 verses): 67
6. *Atris* (7 hymns, 88 verses): 35-38, 73-74, 91
8. *Kasyapas* (6 hymns, 74 verses): 27-31, 97
10. *Bhrgus* (4 hymns, 46 verses): 79, 84, 100-101
11. *Joint* (4 hymns, 76 verses): 2, 42, 87, 102
    1. *Kanvas* (2 verses): 2.41-42
    11. *Joint Kanvas and Angirases* (40 verses): 2.1-40
        Joint Kanvas and Atris (1 hymn, 6 verses): 42
        Joint Angirases and Vasishtha (1 hymn, 6 verses): 87
        Joint Angirases and Bhrgus (1 hymn, 22 verses): 102

Mandala IX (114 hymns, 1108 verses)

1. *Kanvas* (8 hymns, 50 verses): 2, 41-43, 94-95, 104-105
2. *Angirases* (30 hymns, 217 verses): 4,27-31, 35-40, 44-46, 50-52, 61, 69, 72-74, 80-83, 93, 98, 112
3. *Agastyas* (2 hymns, 12 verses): 25-26
5. *Vishvamitras* (5 hymns, 44 verses): 1, 3, 70-71, 84
6. *Atris* (2 hymns, 16 verses): 32, 68
7. *Vasishtha* (1 hymn, 6 verses): 90

8. *Kasyapas* (36 hymns, 300 verses): 5-24, 53-60, 63-64, 91-92, 99-100, 113-114
9. *Bharatas* (2 hymns, 27 verses): 96, 111
10. *Bhrgus* (14 hymns, 136 verses): 47-49, 62, 65, 75-79, 85, 87-89
11. *Joint* (6 hymns, 196 verses): 67, 86, 97, 101, 107-108
    2. *Angirases* (32 verses): 67.1-3, 7-9; 97. 45-48; 107.1, 3; 108.4-13
    4. *Grtsamadas* (3 verses): 86.46-48
    5. *Vishvamitra* (8 verses): 67.13-15; 101. 13-16; 107.5
    6. *Atris* (12 verses): 67.10-12; 86.41-45; 101.1-3; 107.4
    7. *Vasishtha* (54 verses): 67. 19-21; 97.1-44; 107.7; 108.1-3, 14-16
    8. *Kasyapas* (4 verses): 67.4-6; 107.2
    10. *Bhrgus* (4 verses): 67.16-18; 107.6
    11. *Joint Angirases and Vasishtha* (11 verses): 67.22-32
        Joint Saptarsis (19 verses): 107. 8-26
    12. *Unknown* (8 hymns, 104 verses): 33-34, 66, 102-103, 106, 109-110

Mandala X (191 hymns, 1754 verses)

1. *Kanvas* (1 hymn, 9 verses): 115
2. *Angirases* (58 hymns, 485 verses); 11-12, 37, 39-44, 47-56, 67-68, 71-72, 75, 79-80, 87-88, 100, 105, 111-114, 117-118, 126, 128, 131-132, 134, 138, 149, 152, 155-156, 158, 164, 169-170, 172-174, 178, 182, 187-188, 191.
3. *Agastyas* (4 hymns, 40 verses): 57-60
5. *Vishvamitra* (12 hymns, 91 verses): 89-90, 104, 121, 129-130, 160-161, 177, 183-184, 190
6. *Atris* (8 hymns, 112 verses): 45-46, 61-64, 101, 143

7. *Vasishtha* (26 hymns, 276 verses): 20-29, 38, 65-66, 73-74, 83-84, 86, 95, 99, 103, 119, 122, 147, 150, 180
8. *Kasyapas* (3 hymns, 24 verses): 106, 136, 163
9. *Bharatas* (4 hymns, 42 verses): 69-70, 102, 133
10. *Bhargus* (24 hymns, 255 verses): 10, 13-19, 77-78, 91-93, 97-98, 110, 120, 123, 135, 144, 148, 154, 165, 171
11. *Joint* (7 hymns, 49 verses): 96, 107, 127, 137, 167, 179, 181
    2. *Angirases* (4 verses): 137.1,3; 181. 2-3
    5. *Vishvamitra* (1 verse): 137.5
    6. *Atris* (1 verse): 137.4
    7. *Vasishtha* (2 verses): 137.7; 181.1
    8. *Kasyapas* (1 verse): 137.2
    9. *Bharatas* (1 verse): 179.2
    10. *Bhrgus* (1 verse): 137.6
    11. *Joint Kanvas and Angirases* (1 hymn, 8 verses): 127
        Joint Angirases and Vishvamitra (1 hymn, 11 verses): 107
        Joint Angirases and Vasishtha (1 hymn, 13 verses): 96
        Joint Vishvamitra and Bhrgus (1 hymn, 4 verses): 167
    12. *Unknown* (2 verses): 179.1,3
12. *Unknown* (44 hymns, 371 verses): 1-9, 30-36, 76, 81-82, 85, 94, 108-109, 116, 124-125, 139-142, 145-146, 151, 153, 157, 159, 162, 166, 168, 175-176, 185-186, 189

Clarifications regarding Mandala X: Mandala X is a very late Mandala, and stands out from the other nine Mandalas in many respects. One of these is the general ambiguity in the ascriptions of the hymns to their composers. In respect of 44 hymns, and 2 other verses, it is virtually impossible even to identify the family of the composer.

In respect of many other hymns and verses, where we have identified the family affiliations of the composers, the following clarifications are in order:

Family 1: KANVAS (1 hymn)

1. *Upastuta Varstihavya* (1 hymn): X.115
   a. This Rishi practically identifies himself as a Kanva in verse 5 of the hymn.
   b. Outside this hymn, three out of four references to Upastuta are by Kanvas (I.36.10, 17; VIII.5.25; 103. 8), and in the fourth reference, Upastuta is named along-with Kali (another Kanva Rishi, composer of VIII.66).

Family 2: ANGIRASES (19 hymns)

1. *Indra Vaikuntha* (3 hymns): X.48-50

   Saptagu Angiras, the composer of X.47, is clearly the composer of these three hymns, which constitute a continuation of the theme in hymn 47. Hymn 47 is addressed to Indra as Indra Vaikuntha, and these three hymns, in the manner of a dialogue-hymn, constitute Indra's "reply" to Saptagu.

2. *Agneyas* (8 hymns): X.51-53, 79-80, 156, 187-188

   Agni Saucika/Sapti Vajambhara: X.51-53, 79,-80

   Ketu Agneya: X.156

   Vatsa Agneya: X.187

   Syena Agneya: X.188

   a. Agni Saucika is identifiable with the Bharadvaja Rishi Agni Barhaspatya (joint composer of VIII. 102).
   b. Suci is a Bharadvaja gotra.
   c. The word Vajambhara is found in only two verses outside this hymn, both by Angirases:
      I. 60. 6; IV.1.4.
   d. Vaja-m-bhara is clearly an inverted form of Bhara-d-Vaja.
   e. The only gotras with Agni are Bharadvaja and Kasyapa gotras.

3. *Sauryas* (4 hymns): X.37, 158, 170, 181 (joint)

   Abhitapa Saurya: X.37

   Caksu Saurya: X.158

   Vibhrat Saurya: X.170

   Gharma Saurya:X.181 (joint)

   a. The only gotras with *Surya* are Bharadvaja and Vishvamitra gotras.
   b. The only other hymns to Surya are by g Bharadvaja (I.115) and a Kanva (I. 50).
   c. The joint hymn by Gharma Saurya is with a Bharadvaja and a Vasishtha.
   d. A word meaning asura-slayer, *asurahan/asuraghna*, occurring in X.170. 2, is found elsewhere only in hymns by a Bharadvaja (VI. 22. 4) and a Vasishtha (VII.13.1).
   e. The three above hymns by Saurya Rishis have repetitions in common only with hymns by Angirases and by Gartsamada (a descendant of Bharadvaja):

      X.37.4: X.127.2 (Ratri Bhdradvaji)

      Jyotisa badhase tamo.

      X.37.10: II.23.15 (Gartsamada Saunahotra)

      Dravinam dhehi citram.

      X.158.5: I.82.3 (Gautama Rahugana)

      Susandrsam tva vayam.

      X.170.4: VIII.98.3 (Nrmedha Angiras)

      Vibhrajanjyotisa svaragaccho rocanam divah.

4. *Auravas* (3 hymns): X.11-12, 138

   Anga Aurava: X.138

   Havirdhana Angi: X.11-12

   The patronymics of these Rishis show them to be descendants of Uru Angiras (joint composer of IX.108).

5. *Aristanemi Tarksya* (1 hymn): X.178.

   a. The only other hymns to horses are by Angirases (I.162-163; IV. 38-40) and a Vasishtha (VII. 44).

b. The word Tarksya, outside this hymn, is found only in one verse by an Angiras, Gautama Rahugana (1.89.6).

c. The only hymns which have repetitions in common with X.178 are by Vamadeva Gautama:

X.178.2: IV.23.10 Prthvi bahule gabhire

X.178.3: IV.38.10

SavasA panca krstih Surya iva jyotisapastatana.

Family 5: Vishvamitra (9 hymns)

1. *Prajapatyas* (9 hymns): 90, 107 (joint), 121, 129-130, 161, 177, 183-184

Narayana: X.90

Daksina Prajapatya: X.107 (joint)

Hiranyagarbha Prajapatya: X.121

Prajapati Paramesthin: X.129

Yajna Prajapatya: X.130

Yaksmanasana Prajapatya: X.161

Patanga Prajapatya: X.177

Prajavan Prajapatya: X.183

Visnu Prajapatya: X.184

a. Prajapati Paramesthin, clearly the patriarch of this group of Rishis, is identifiable with Prajapati Vishvamitra (composer of III.54-56).

b. The only hymn which has a repetition in common with X.129 (by Prajapati Paramesthin) is III.54 (by Prajapati Vishvamitra):

X. 129.6: III.54.5

Ko addha veda ka iha pra vocat.

c. All the above hymns deal with the subject of creation. The only other hymn dealing with this subject is X.190, composed by Aghamarsana Vishvamitra; and the only other verse to which the Anukramanis assign the same subject is I.24.1, composed by Sunahsepa Ajigarti (Vishvamitra).

d. Vishvamitra is traditionally associated with creation. The epics relate the story of Trisanku, in which Vishvamitra sets out to teach the Gods a lesson by creating a parallel universe. He finally desists only when the Gods plead with him and accede to his demand. But, even today, "duplicate" objects in nature are called *Vishvamitra-srsti* or Vishvamitra's creations.

e. Narayana is a Vishvamitra gotra; and the hymn by Narayana a, who is not given any patronymic, is placed immediately after a hymn by a Vishvamitra: Renu Vishvamitra (X.89).

Family 7: Vasishtha (23 hymns)

1. *Suvedas Sairisi* (1 hymn): X. 147 Sairisi is a Vasishtha gotra.
2. *Vamra Vaikhanasa* (1 hymn): X.99
   a. The word *Sisnadeva* (X.99.3) is found only once outside this hymn in VII.21.5, composed by Vasishtha Maitravaruni. The word *Sisna* by itself occurs only thrice in the Rigveda, once in a hymn by a Vasishtha, Vasukra Aindra (X.27.19), and once in a hymn by a Vasishtha associate, Kutsa Angiras (1.105.8). The third occurrence, in X.33.3, is in a hymn by a Rishi whose family cannot be identified.
   b. The only hymn which has a repetition in common with this hymn is X.20, composed by a Vasishtha, Vimada Aindra: X.99.12: X.20.10 Isamurjam suksitim visvamabhah.
3. *Manyu Tapasa* (2 hymns): X.83-84
   a. Manyu Tapasa is identifiable with Manyu Vasishtha (joint composer of IX.97).
   b. Tapasa, an epithet signifying heat or passion, has an added symbolic significance in this case: Tapa is a Vasishtha gotra.
   c. The word Manyu is translated, by Griffith, as a name in only one other hymn, X.73.10, composed by Gauriviti Saktya, a Vasishtha.
4. *Pururavas Aila and Urvasi* (1 hymn): X.95.
   a. Verse 17 of the hymn clearly declares: "I, Vasishtha,

call Urvasi to meet me." The name Vasishtha is translated by Griffith as "her best love".

b. Outside this hymn, the word Urvasi occurs only twice throughout the Rigveda: once in a hymn by an Atri (V.41.19), where it is an epithet for a deified river; and once in a hymn by a Vasishtha (VII.33.11) where Urvasi is referred to as the mother of Vasishtha.

5. *Aindras* (18 hymns): X.20-29, 38, 65-66, 86, 96 (joint), 103, 119, 180

Vimada Aindra and Vasukrta Vasukra: X.20-26

Vasukra Aindra: X.27-29

Indra Muskavan: X.38

Vasukarna Vasukra: X.65-66

Vrsakapi Aindra: X.86

Sarvahari Aindra: X.96 (joint)

Apratiratha Aindra: X.103

Laba Aindra: X. 119

Jaya Aindra: X.180

a. The only hymns, other than X.38, in which Indra is named as composer, are hymns in which the God Indra is depicted as speaking in the first person. But X.38 does not depict Indra speaking in the first person, and it is clear that Indra here is the name of the composer, who is the patriarch of the Aindra group of Rishis in Mandala X.

b. Indra is a Vasishtha gotra.

c. Indra Muskavan is identifiable with Indrapramati Vasishtha (joint composer of IX.97).

d. The word *muska* (X.38.5), which gives the Rishi his epithet Muskavan, is found only once outside this hymn, in X. 102.4, composed by a Bharata. The Bharatas are very closely associated with the Angirases and Vasishtha.

e. X.38.5 refers to the Rishi Kutsa. The Kutsas are very close associates of the Vasishtha: the only reference to Kutsas by non-Kutsas are in hymns by Vasishtha

(VII.25.5; X.29.2); the only references to Vasishtha by a non-Vasishtha is in a hymn by a Kutsa (I.112.9); and the only hymn in which a Kutsa figures as a joint composer is IX.97, which is jointly attributed to eleven Vasishtha Rishis (including Indrapramati) and a Kutsa.

f. Vasukra Aindra is identifiable with Vasukri Vasishtha (joint composer of IX.97).

g. Vasukarna Vasukra calls himself a Vasishtha (in X.65.15), and, in verse 12 of the same hymn, he refers to Vimada (Aindra).

h. Jaya is a Vasishtha gotra

i. All the four other hymns (including the joint hymn) have repetitions in common with Vasishtha or their associates:

X.86.5: VII.104.7 (Vasishtha Maitravaruni)

X.103.4: VII.32.11 (Vasishtha Maitravaruni)

X. 119.13: X. 150.1 (Mrlika Vasishtha): III.9.6. (Vishvamitra Gathina).

X.96.13: I.104.9 (Kutsa Angiras)

X.96.2: I.9.10 (Madhucchandas Vishvamitra):

X.133.1 (Sudas Paijavana).

Apart from these, the four hymns have only two other repetitions (one of which is in common with a Vishvamitra).

Family 10: Bhrgus (11 hymns)

1. *Yamayanas* (11 hymns): X.10, 13-19, 135, 144, 154

Yama Vaivasvata and Yami Vaivasvati: X.10

Vivasvan Aditya: X.13

Yama Vaivasvata: X.14

Sankha Yamayana: X.15

Damana Yamayana: X.16

Devasravas Yamayana: X. 17

Sankhasuka Yamayana: X.18

Mathita Yamayana: X.19

Kumara Yamayana: X.135

Urdhvakrsana Yamayana: X.144

Yami Vaivasvati: X.154

a. Yamayana or Yamyayana is a Bhrgu gotra.

b. Mathita is also a Bhrgu gotra.

c. The alternative names given in the Anukramanis for the composer of X.19, Mathita Yamayana, are Bhrgu or Cyavana Bhargava.

d. Yama is mentioned alongwith ancient, mythical Bhrgu Rishis, Atharvana and Usana Kavya in I.83.5.

e. Hymn X.14.5 states: "Our fathers are Angirases, Navagvas, Atharvanas, Bhrgus." Bhrgu hymns in Mandalas IX and X often identify with both Angirases and Bhrgus (see, for example, IX. 62.9, and the comment on it in Griffith's footnotes).

f. All the above hymns deal with the topics of funerals and death. Tradition ascribes the initiation of funeral rites and ceremonies to Jamadagni Bhargava.

The family identities of the other composers of Mandala X are either obvious from their patronymics, or known from the gotra lists, or else unidentifiable.

All this information is summarized in the two following tables:

The Chronological Order of the Rigveda

The first step in any historical analysis of the Rigveda is the establishment of the *internal* chronology of the text.

The Rigveda consists of ten Mandalas or Books. And, excepting likely interpolations, these Mandalas represent different epochs of history. The arrangement of these Mandalas in their chronological order is the first step towards an understanding of Rigvedic history. Regarding the chronology of these Mandalas, only two facts are generally recognised:

1. The six Family Mandalas II-VII form the oldest core of the Rigveda.
2. The two serially last Mandalas of the Rigveda, IX and X, are also the chronologically last Mandalas in that order.

In this chapter, we will establish a more precise chronological arrangement of the Mandalas based on a detailed analysis of evidence within the text. However, the precise position of the last two Mandalas does not require much analysis:

1. Mandala X is undoubtedly the chronologically last Mandala of the Rigveda.

As B.K. Ghosh puts it: "On the whole... the language of the first nine Mandalas must be regarded as homogeneous, in spite of traces of previous dialectal differences... With the tenth Mandala it is a different story. The language here has definitely changed."

He proceeds to elaborate on this point: "The language of the tenth Mandala represents a distinctly later stage of the Rigvedic language. Hiatus, which is frequent in the earlier Rigveda, is already in process of elimination here. Stressed *i.e.* cannot in sandhi be changed into *y w* in the earlier parts, but in the tenth Mandala they can.

The ending-*Asas* in nominative plural is half as frequent as-*As* in the *Rigveda* taken as a whole, but its number of occurrences is disproportionately small in the tenth Mandala. Absolutives in-*tvaya* occur only here.

The stem *rai*-is inflected in one way in the first nine Mandalas, and in another in the tenth; and in the inflexion of *dyau-*, too, the distribution of strong and weak forms is much more regular in the earlier Mandalas. The Prakritic verbal *kuru*-appears only in the tenth Mandala for the earlier *krinu.* Many words appear for the first time in the tenth Mandala.

The old locative form *pritsu,* adjectives like *girvanas* and vicarsani, and the substantive *viti* do not occur at all in the tenth Mandala, though in the earlier Mandalas they are quite common. The particle *sim* which is unknown in the Atharvaveda, occurs fifty times in the first nine Mandalas, but only once in the tenth. Words like *ajya, kala, lohita, vijaya,* etc. occur for the first time in the tenth Mandala, as also the root *labh-*."

In fact, strikingly different as the language of the tenth Mandala is from that of the other nine, it would in the natural course of events have been even more so: "The difference in language between the earlier Mandalas and the tenth would have appeared in its true proportions if the texts concerned had been written down at the time they were composed and handed down to us in that written form.

The fact, however, is that the text tradition of the *Rigveda* was stabilized at a comparatively late date, and fixed in writing at a much later epoch. The result has been not unlike what would have happened if the works of Chaucer and Shakespeare were put in writing and printed for the first time in the twentieth century... (this) to some extent also screens the differences that mark off the languages of the earlier Mandalas from that of the tenth."

So much for the tenth Mandala:

2. The chronological position of Mandala IX is equally beyond doubt: it is definitely much earlier than Mandala X, but equally definitely later than the other eight Mandalas.

Mandala IX was meant to be a kind of appendix in which hymns to Soma, ascribed to Rishis belonging to all the ten families, were brought together.

An examination of the Mandala shows that it was compiled at a point, of time when a Rigveda of eight Mandalas was already in existence as one unit with the eight Mandalas arranged in their present order: it is significant that the first four Rishis of both Mandala I as well as Mandala IX are, in the same order, Madhucchandas (with his son Jeta in Mandala I), Medhatithi, Sunahsepa and Hairanyastupa.

Hence, while we will touch occasionally upon Mandalas IX and X, our analysis will concentrate mainly on Mandalas I-VIII.

The main criteria which will help us in establishing the chronological order of the Mandalas are:

1. The inter-relationships among the composers of the hymns.
2. The internal references to composers in other Mandalas.
3. The internal references to kings and Rishis in the hymns. We will examine the whole subject under the following heads:

I. Inter-relationships among Composers.

II. Family Structure and the System of Ascriptions.

III. References to Composers.

IV. References to Kings and Rishis

V. The Structure and Formation of the Rigveda.

Appendix: Misinterpreted Words in the Rigveda.

Composers Inter-relationships

The inter-relationships among the composers of the hymns provide us with a very clear and precise picture.

We will examine the subject as follows:

A. The Family Mandalas II-VII.

B. Mandala I.

C. Mandala VIII.

D. Mandala I Detail.

E. Mandala IX.

F. Mandala X.

The Family Mandalas II-VII.

We get the following direct relationships among the composers of the Family Mandalas:

Prima facie, we get the following equations:

1. The family Mandalas can be divided into Early Family Mandalas (VI, III, VII) and Later Family Mandalas (IV, II, V)

   The Later Family Mandalas have full hymns composed by direct descendants of Rishis from the Early Family Mandalas.

2. Mandala VI is the *oldest* of the Early Family Mandalas, since descendants of its Rishis are composers in *two* of the Later Family Mandalas: IV and II.

3. Mandala V is the *latest* of the Later Family Mandalas, since it has hymns by descendants of Rishis from two of the Early Family Mandalas: III and VII.

4. Mandala VII is the latest of the Early Family Mandalas since (unlike Mandalas VI and III which do not have a *single* hymn composed by any descendant of any Rishi from any other Mandala) there are two joint hymns (VII.101-102) which are jointly composed by Vasishtha and Kumara Agneya (a member of the Agneya group of Bharadvaja Rishis), a descendant of Bharadvaja of Mandala VI.

5. Mandala IV is older than Mandala II because:

a. It has only two hymns composed by descendants of *Rishis from Mandala VI, while the whole of Mandala II* except for four hymns is composed by descendants of Rishis from Mandala VI.

b. Mandala II goes one generation further down than Mandala IV.

6. Mandala V, as we saw, has hymns by descendants of Rishis from *two* of the Early Family Mandalas: III and VII.

In addition, it also has a hymn by descendants of a Rishi who (although not himself a composer) is contemporaneous with Mandala VII: hymn V.24 is composed by the Gaupayanas who are descendants of Agastya, the brother of Vasishtha of Mandala VII.

Conclusion: We get the following chronological order:

Mandala I

We get the following relationships between the composers of Mandala I and the Family Mandalas:

1. Mandala I has full hymns composed by direct descendants of Rishis from the Early Family Mandalas. 54 of the hymns in Mandala I fall into this category.
2. In addition, it also has full hymns composed by descendants of Rishis who (although not themselves composers) are contemporaneous with the Early Family Mandalas. 61 of the hymns in Mandala I fall into this category.
3. Mandala I does not have a *single hymn*, full or joint, composed by any *ancestor* of any Rishi from the Early Family Mandalas.
4. On the other hand, Mandala I has full hymns composed by *ancestors* of Rishis from the Later Family Mandalas. 21 of the hymns in Mandala I fall into this category:
5. The above hymns, it must be noted, include full hymns by *contemporaries* of Rishis from the Later Family Mandalas, who are also, at the same time, *descendants* of Rishis from the Early Family Mandalas or from Mandala I itself:
6. Mandala I does not have a *single hymn*, full or joint, composed by any *descendant* of any Rishi from the Later Family Mandalas.

Conclusion: Mandala I is *later* than the Early Family Mandalas, but both *earlier* than as well as *contemporary* to the Later Family Mandalas: Hence, we get the following chronological order:

Mandala VIII

We get the following relationships between the composers of Mandala VIII and those of the other seven Mandalas:

1. There are only two direct relationships between the composers of Mandala VIII, and the composers of the Early Family Mandalas (VI, III, VII) and the two older of the Later Family Mandalas (IV, II):

   All other relationships, if any, are through composers from Mandalas I and V.

2. On the other hand, not only are there close relationships between the composers of Mandala VIII, and the composers from Mandalas I and V, but there are also many composers in common:

Note: The Bhrgu hymns in Mandala VIII constitute a SPECIAL CATEGORY of hymns which stand out from the rest. These five hymns (VIII.79,84,100-102) are ascribed to ancient Bhrgu Rishis of the oldest period. Unlike in the case of Mandala X, ascriptions in Mandala VIII have to be taken seriously; and therefore the ascription of the above hymns to ancient Bhrgu Rishis is to be treated, in general, as valid (*in general,* in the sense that while hymns ascribed to, say, Usana Kavya, who is already a mythical figure even in the oldest Mandalas, may not have been composed *by him, they must at least have been composed by some ancient* Bhrgu Rishi).

The historical reasons for the non-inclusion of these hymns in the Family Mandalas, or even in Mandala I, and for their late introduction into the Rigveda in Mandala VIII, will be discussed in our chapter on the Indo-Iranian Homeland.

Mandala I Detail.

Mandala I consists of fifteen upa-mandalas. On the basis of the inter-relationships between the composers, we can classify these upa-mandalas into four groups:

Early upa-mandalas: The upa-mandalas which can be definitely designated as early upa-mandalas are those which are ascribed to direct descendants of composers from the Early Family Mandalas:

Madhucchandas	upa-mandala: I.1-11.
Sunahsepa	upa-mandala: I.24-30.
Parasara	upa-mandala: I.65-73.

Middle upa-mandalas: The upa-mandalas which can be designated as middle upa-mandalas are those ascribed to ancestors or contemporaries of composers from the earliest of the Later Family Mandalas:

Nodhas	upa-mandala: I.58-64.
Gautama	upa-mandala: I.74-93.

Late upa-mandalas: The upa-mandalas which can be designated as late upa-mandalas are those ascribed to ancestors or contemporaries of composers from Mandala VIII:

Medhatithi	upa-mandala: I.12-23.
Kanva	upa-mandala: I.36-43.
Praskanva	upa-mandala: I.44-50.

General upa-mandalas: Those upa-mandalas which cannot be definitely designated as either early or late upa-mandalas on the basis of inter-relationships must be designated as general upa-mandalas. These include:

a. Those ascribed to independent Rishis not directly connected with specific groups of composers in other Mandalas:

Hairanyastupa	upa-mandala: I.31-35.
Savya	upa-mandala: I.51-57.
Kaksivan	upa-mandala: I.116-126.
Dirghatamas	upa-mandala: I.140-164.

b. Those ascribed to descendants of persons (kings or Rishis) contemporaneous with the composers of the Early Family Mandalas, but not themselves composers of hymns either in the Early Family Mandalas or in Mandala I:

Kutsa	upa-mandala: I.94-115.
Parucchepa	upa-mandala: I.127-139.
Agastya	upa-mandala: I.165-191.

The Kutsa and Agastya upa-mandalas are ascribed to the eponymous Rishis Kutsa and Agastya themselves, but they are obviously late upa-mandalas composed by their remote descendants. Among other things, the *only* references to these eponymous Rishis within the hymns prove this:

The composers in the Kutsa upa-mandala refer to the Rishi Kutsa as a mythical figure from the past: I.106.6;112.9.

The composers in the Agastya upa-mandala repeatedly describe themselves as descendants of Mana (Agastya): I. 165.14,15; 166.15; 167.11; 169.10; 169.8; 177.5; 182.8; 184.4, 5; 189.8.

Mandala IX

As we saw, the chronological position of Mandala IX *after* the eight earlier Mandalas is beyond doubt. But Mandala IX ascribes many hymns to Rishis from the earlier Mandalas. According to some scholars, this indicates that while Mandala IX came into existence as a separate Mandala after the first eight Mandalas, many of the individual hymns to Soma were already in existence, and were originally included in the other Mandalas. Later they were "combed out of the other Mandalas" and compiled into a separate Mandala dedicated solely to Soma hymns.

This would appear to imply that the period of Mandala IX (like that of Mandala I) should be stretched out alongside the Periods of all the other Mandalas.

However, the contention that the hymns in Mandala IX could be "combed out of" the other Mandalas is not quite correct. Any "combing out" would be relevant only in the case of the five older Mandalas (VI, III, VII, IV, II); since the other three Mandalas (I, V and VIII) were finalised just before Mandala IX, and Soma hymns which should have been included in these Mandalas could just as well have been left out of the Mandalas even before their finalisation, as the idea of a separate Soma Mandala may already have fructified by then. And an examination of Mandala IX shows that it is a late Mandala. Mandala IX has 114 hymns. If we exclude the fourteen Bhrgu hymns, which we will refer to again in our chapter on the Geography of the Rigveda, the following is the chronological distribution of the hymns:

1. Forty-nine of the hymns are ascribed to Rishis belonging to the period of Mandala IX (*i.e.* new Rishis not found in

earlier Mandalas) or the period of Mandala X (*i.e.* R is with strange names and of unknown family identity):

Mandala IX: IX.5-26, 39-40, 44-46, 61, 63, 68, 70, 72-73, 80-83, 99-100, 111-112.

Mandala X: IX.33-34, 66, 102-103, 106, 109-110.

2. Forty hymns are ascribed to Rishis belonging to the last *layer of Mandalas to be finalised before Mandala IX (i.e.* Mandalas V, VIII and I):

   Mandala V: IX.32, 35-36, 53-60.

   Mandala VIII: IX.27-30. 41-43, 95, 104-105.

   Mandala I: IX.1-4, 31, 37-38, 50-52, 64, 69, 74, 91-94, 113-114.

3. Only *eleven* hymns can even be alleged to have been composed by Rishis belonging to the five earlier Family *Mandalas (VI, III, VII, IV and II), if one takes the ascriptions* at face value.

   But, in the case of at least nine of these hymns, it is clear, *on the basis of evidence within the Anukramanis themselves,* that these ascriptions are fictitious, and that the hymns are not composed by the early Rishis belonging to these five Family Mandalas, but by late Rishis belonging to the period of Mandalas IX and X.

   These nine hymns are: IX. 67, 84, 86, 96-98, 101, 107-108.

   An examination of the ascriptions in these nine hymns establishes their lateness:

   a. IX.67 and IX.107 are artificial hymns ascribed to the Saptarsi or Seven Rishis: Bharadvaja, Vishvamitra, Jamadagni, Vasishtha, Gautama, Kasyapa and Atri. (Incidentally, no other hymn is ascribed to Bharadvaja or Vishvamitra, and of the two other hymns ascribed to Vasishtha, one ascription is clearly fictitious.)

      It is clear that these Rishis belonged to different periods and could not have been joint composers in any hymn. The hymns are clearly composed by their descendants, or perhaps even by some single Rishis in their many names. In the case of IX.67, Pavitra Angiras (a Rishi who clearly belongs to the period of Mandala IX itself, being a new Rishi and also the composer of IX. 73 and 83) is named as a joint composer with the Saptarsi, and he is probably the composer even of the entire hymn.

b. IX.84 and IX.101 are ascribed to Prajapati Vacya (Vishvamitra), but this is clearly not the Prajapati Vacya (Vishvamitra) of Mandala III. He is clearly a Rishi belonging to the late period, identifiable as one of the Prajapatya group of Rishis whose hymns appear only in the late Mandalas (V.33-34, X.90, 107, 121, 129-130, 161, 177, 183-184).

   In IX.101, this Prajapati is a joint composer with Andhigu Syavasvi (who is clearly a late Rishi belonging to the period of Mandala IX, itself, being a descendant of Syavasvi Atreya of Mandalas V and VIII) and with various Rishis of unknown family identity (a circumstance which places them in the late period of Mandalas IX-X).

c. IX.86. is ascribed jointly to Atri and Gartsamada, and not only do these Rishis belong to different periods, but they are joint composers with various Rishis with strange names and of unknown family identity, which places the provenance of this hymn in the late period of Mandalas ix-x.

d. IX.96 is ascribed to Pratardana Daivodasi, but this Rishi is clearly the same late Bharata Rishi (descendant of the actual Pratardana) who is also a composer in the late Mandala X (*i.e.* X. 179.2).

e. IX.97 is ascribed jointly to Vasishtha, Kutsa, and various descendants of Vasishtha. This hymn clearly belongs to the late period, since three of its composers are also composers in Mandala X: Mrlika (X. 150), Manyu (X.83-84) and Vasukra. (X.27-29).

f. IX.98 and IX.108 are ascribed to Rjisvan Angiras or Bharadvaja. But this is clearly not the Rjisvan of Mandala VI:

In the case of IX.98, the name Rjisvan is clearly a confusion for the name Rjrasva Varsagira, since the hymn is jointly ascribed to Rjisvan and Ambarisa Varsagira (of 1.100).

In the case of IX. 108, this Rjisvan is joint composer with Gauriviti Saktya (composer of V.29), Rnancaya (patron of the composer of V.30), and various Rishis of unknown family identity (whose provenance is clearly in the late period of Mandalas IX-X).

In short, these nine hymns are clearly composed by Rishis belonging to the late period of Mandalas I-V-VIII-IX-X, and not the period of the five earlier Family Mandalas.

4. Ultimately, the only two hymns which can be ascribed to *Rishis belonging to the five earlier Family Mandalas, and* only for want of clear contrary evidence, are:

   IX.71 (ascribed to Rsabha Vaishvamitra of Mandala III)

   IX.90 (ascribed to Vasishtha Maitravaruni of Mandala VII)

   It is therefore clear that Mandala IX is a late Mandala, and that there was not much of "combing out" of hymns to Soma from earlier Mandalas in the process of its compilation.

   The chronological position of Mandala IX after the eight earlier Mandalas is therefore certain.

Mandala X

Mandala X, as we saw, was composed after the other nine Mandalas, and compiled *so long* after them that its *language alone,* in spite of attempts at standardisation, is sufficient to establish its late position.

The ascription of hymns in this Mandala is so chaotic that in most of the hymns the names, or the patronymics/epithets, or both, of the composers, are fictitious; to the extent that, in 44 hymns out of 191, and in parts of one more, the family identity of the composers is a total mystery.

In many other hymns, the family identity, but *not* the actual identity of the composers, is clear or can be deduced: the hymns are ascribed to remote ancestors, or even to mythical ancestors not known to have composed any hymns in earlier Mandalas.

Chronologically, the hymns in Mandala X fall in three categories:

a. Hymns composed in the final period of the Rigveda, long after the period of the other nine Mandalas.

b. Hymns composed in the period of Mandala IX, *after* the eight earlier Mandalas were finalised, by composers whose Soma hymns find a place in Mandala IX.

c. Hymns composed in the late period of Mandala VIII, which somehow missed inclusion in that Mandala.

The hymns of the second and third category were kept aside, and later included, *in changed linguistic form*, in Mandala X.

To round off our examination of the inter-relationships among the composers, we may note the following instances of composers in Mandala X who are descendants of Rishis from the latest Mandala VIII and IX:

In conclusion, we can classify the periods of the Mandalas into the following major periods:

1. *The Early Period*: The period of Mandalas VI, III, VII and the early upa-mandalas of Mandala 1.
2. *The Middle Period*: The period of Mandalas IV and II and the middle upa-mandalas of Mandala I; as also the earlier part of the general upa-mandalas of Mandala I.
3. *The Late Period*:
   a. The period of Mandalas V and VIII and the late upa-mandalas of Mandala I; as also the later part of the general upa-mandalas of Mandala I.
   b. The period of Mandala IX.
4. *The Final Period*: The period of Mandala X.

Family Structure and the Ascriptions System

The Mandalas of the Rigveda, as we have seen, can be arranged in a definite chronological order on the basis of the inter-relationships among the composers of the hymns. This chronological order is confirmed by a consideration of

A. The Family Structure of the Mandalas.

B. The System of Ascriptions.

The Family Structure of the Mandalas: If the Mandalas of the *Rigveda are arranged in order of gradation in family structure (i.e.* from the purest family structure to the least pure one), the arrangement tallies perfectly with our chronological order:

Firstly, the Family Mandalas:

1. The Bharadvaja Mandala (VI) has Bharadvajas as composers in every single hymn and verse. Non-Bharadvajas are *totally* absent in this Mandala.
2. The Vishvamitra Mandala (III) has Vishvamitra as composers in every single hymn; but non-Vishvamitra are present as *junior partners* with the Vishvamitra in two hymns (1 out of 11 verses in hymn 36; and 3 out of 18 verses in hymn 62).
3. The Vasishtha Mandala (VII) has Vasishtha as composers in every single hymn; but non-Vasishtha are present as *equal partners* with the Vasishtha in two hymns (101-102)
4. *The Vamadeva Mandala (IV) has non-Vamadevas as sole* composers in two hymns (43-44).

   These non-Vamadevas, however, belong to the same Angiras family as the Vamadevas, and share the same Apri Sukta.
5. *The Gartsamada Mandala (II) has non-Grtsamadas as sole* composers in four hymns (4-7).

   These non-Grtsamadas belong to a family *related* to the Grtsamadas (being Bhrgus while the Grtsamadas are Kevala-Bhrgus) *but having different Apri-suktas.*
6. The Atri Mandala (V) has non-Atris as *sole composers* in seven hymns (15, 24, 29, 33-36).

These non-Atris belong to four different families *not related* to the Atris, and having different Apri-suktas.

Then, the non-family Mandalas:

1. Mandala I is a collection of small family upa-mandalas.
2. Mandala VIII is not a Family Mandala; but one family, the Kanvas, still dominate the Mandala by a slight edge, with 55 hymns out of 103.

   There is, for the first time, a hymn (47) by a Rishi of unknown family identity.
3. Mandala IX is definitely not a family Mandala, having hymns or verses composed by every single one of the ten families. The dominant family, the Kasyapas, are the composers of only 36 hymns out of 114.

There are now eight full hymns (33-34, 66, 102-103, 106, 109-110) and parts of two others (86.1-40; 101.4-12) by Rishis of unknown family identity.

4. Mandala X, the latest Mandala by any standard, is not associated with any particular family.

There are 44 hymns by Rishis of unknown family identity.

Clearly, the older the Mandala, the purer its family structure.

The System of Ascriptions: There are basically two systems of ascription of compositions of the hymns, followed in the ten Mandalas of the Rigveda:

1. In the older system, the hymns composed by an eponymous Rishi as well as those composed by his descendants, are ascribed solely to the eponymous Rishi himself

   It is only when a particular descendant is important enough, or independent enough, that hymns composed by him (and, consequently, by *his* descendants) are ascribed to him.

   This system is followed in the first five Family Mandalas (VI, III, VII, IV, II) and also in Mandala I.

2. In the newer system, the ascription of hymns is more individualistic, and hymns are generally ascribed to the names of individual composers, except in cases where the composer himself chooses to have hymns composed by him ascribed to an ancestor.

This system is followed in Mandalas V, VIII, IX and X.

The dichotomy between the two systems will be clear from the following table: What is significant is that Mandala V *alone,* among the Family Mandalas, falls in the same class as the non-family Mandalas, thereby confirming that it is a late Mandala and the last of the Family Mandalas. Likewise, Mandala I falls in the same class as the other (than Mandala V) Family Mandalas, thereby confirming that it is, for the most part, earlier than Mandala V.

References to Composers

On the basis of one fundamental criterion (the inter-relationships among the composers) we have obtained a very clear and unambiguous picture of the chronological order of the

Mandalas. Now we will examine this chronological order of the Mandalas on the basis of a second fundamental criterion: the references to composers within the hymns.

The logic is simple: if a hymn in Mandala B refers to a composer from Mandala A as a figure from the past, this indicates that Mandala A is older than Mandala B.

This naturally does not include the following references, which are of zero-value for this purpose:

1. References to a Rishi by his descendants.
2. References to ancient Angiras and Bhrgu Rishis (eg. Brhaspati, Atharvana, Usana) who are mythical figures in the whole of the Rigveda, but to whom hymns are ascribed in Mandalas X or IX, or even VIII.
3. References to Kings from the ancient period (eg. Pratardana, Sudas) to whom hymns are ascribed in Mandala X or IX.

We will examine the references as follows:

A. The Early Mandalas and upa-mandalas.

B. The Middle Mandalas and upa-mandalas.

C. The Late Mandalas and upa-mandalas.

D. Mandala IX.

The Early Mandalas and upa-mandalas: The following is the situation in the Mandalas and upa-mandalas which we have classified as belonging to the Early Period:

1. *The two oldest Mandalas VI and III do not refer to a single composer from any other Mandala.*
2. The third oldest Mandala VII refers to one composer from the older Mandala III: Jamadagni (VII.96.3)

Mandala VII is also unique in its reference to three contemporary Rishis to whom upa-mandalas are ascribed in Mandala I:

Agastya (VII.33.10,13)

Kutsa (VII.25.5)

Parasara (VII.18.21)

However, all these references make it very clear that these Rishis are *contemporaries* of Vasishtha and not figures from the past:

a. Agastya is Vasishtha's brother.

b. The Kutsas are junior associates of the Vasishtha.

c. Parasara is Vasishtha's grandson.

The upa-mandalas ascribed to Agastya and Kutsa, as we have already seen, consist of hymns composed by their descendants, while Parasara is himself a descendant of Vasishtha.

Therefore, the references to these Rishis in Mandala VII not only do not show that Mandala I is older than Mandala VII, they in fact confirm that Mandala VII is older than Mandala I.

3. The early upa-mandalas of Mandala I (*i.e.* the Madhucchandas, Sunahsepa and Parasara upa-mandalas) do not refer to any composer from any other Mandala.

Thus the three oldest Mandalas and the three early upa-mandalas are completely devoid of references to composers from the periods of any of the other Mandalas, thereby firmly establishing their early position and their chronological isolation from the other Mandalas.

The Middle Mandalas and upa-mandalas: The Middle Mandalas, and upa-mandalas, as per our chronology, follow the Early Mandalas and upa-mandalas, and are contemporaneous with the early parts of the general upa-mandalas of Mandala I.

The following is the situation in these Mandalas and upa-mandalas belonging to the Middle Period:

1. Mandala IV refers to one composer from the older Mandala VI: Rjisvan (IV.16.13).

It also refers to two composers from the early part of the general upa-mandalas of Mandala I:

Mamateya (Dirghatamas) (IV.4.13)

Kaksiyan (IV.26.1)

This is matched by a cross-reference in the Dirghatamas upa-mandala by way of a reference to a composer from Mandala IV: Purumilha (I.151.2)

There is no reference in Mandala IV to any composer from any Mandala which follows it as per our chronology.

2. Mandala II does not refer to any composer from any other Mandala, earlier or later. And, for that matter, no other

composer from any other Mandala refers to the Grtsamadas of Mandala II.

3. The middle upa-mandalas of Mandala I (*i.e.* the Gautama and Nodhas upa-mandalas) refer to one composer from the older Mandala VI: Bharadvaja (I.59.7).

There is no reference in any of these Mandalas or upa-mandalas to any composer from the Late Mandalas and upa-mandalas.

The Late Mandalas and upa-mandalas: In sharp contrast to the meagre references in earlier Mandalas to composers from other Mandalas, we find an abundance of such references in the Late Mandalas and upa-mandalas (*i.e.* Mandalas V and VIII, and the general and the late upa-mandalas of Mandala I):

1. These Mandalas and upa-mandalas refer to the following composers from earlier Mandalas and upa-mandalas:

   Bharadvaja (I.116.8) from Mandala VI.

   Rjisvan (I.51.5; 53.8;101.1;V.29.11;VIII. 49.10; 50.10) from Mandala VI.

   Vasishtha (I.112.9) from Mandala VII.

   Agastya (I.117.11; VIII.5.26) from the period of Mandala VII.

   Sunahsepa (V.2.7) from the early upa-mandalas.

   Purumilha (I.151.2;183.5;VIII.71.14) from Mandala IV.

2. Mandala V refers to one composer from the late upa-mandalas: Kanva (V. 41. 4).

   This is matched by cross-references in the general and late upa-mandalas to a composer from Mandala V: Atri (I.45.3; 51.3; 139.9; 183.5).

3. Mandala VIII refers to the following composers from Mandala V:

   Babhru (VIII.22.10)

   Paura (VIII.3.12)

   Saptavadhri (VIII.73.9)

4. Mandala VIII refers to the following composers from the general upa-mandalas:

   Dirghatamas (VIII.9.10)

   Kaksivan (VIII.9.10)

This is matched by a number of cross-references in Mandala I to composers from Mandala VIII:

Priyamedha (I.45.3; 139.9)

Vyasva (I.112.15)

Trisoka (1.112.12)

Kali (I.112.15)

Rebha (I.112.5; 116.24; 117.4; 118.6; 119.6)

Visvaka (I.116.23; 117.7)

Krsna (I.116.23; 117.7)

Vasa (I.112.10; 116.21)

5. The general and late upa-mandalas refer to composers from other upa-mandalas:
   a. The Savya upa-mandala refers to Kaksivan (I.51.13)
   b. The Agastya upa-mandala refers to Gautama (I.183.5)
   c. The Medhatithi upa-mandala refers to Kaksivan (I.18.1)
   d. The Parucchepa upa-mandala refers to Kanva (I.139.9)
   e. The Kutsa upa-mandala refers to Kaksivan (I.112.11) and Kanva (I.112.5).
   f. The Kaksivan upa-mandala refers to Rjrasva (I.116.16; 117.17, 18), Gautama (I.116.9) and Kanva (I.117.8; 118.7).
6. Finally, the late Mandalas and upa-mandalas even refer to the following composers from Mandala X:

Brhaduktha (V.19.5)

Syumarasmi (I.112.16: VIII.52.2)

Vamra (I.51.9; 112.15)

Vandana (I.112.5; 116.11; 117.5; 118.6; 119.6)

Vimada (I.51.3; 112.19; 116.1; 117.20; VIII.9.15)

Upastuta (I.36.17; 112.15; VIII.5.25)

Ghosa (I.117.7: 120.5; 122.5)

It appears incredible, on the face of it, that composers from the very Late Mandala X should be named in earlier Mandalas. However, it fits in with our chronology: as we have seen, the hymns in Mandala X include hymns composed in the Late Period of Mandala VIII which somehow missed inclusion in that Mandala. They could not be included in the next Mandala IX since that Mandala contained only hymns to Soma. These hymns were therefore kept aside, and, not being canonised by inclusion in the text, they suffered linguistic changes, and were subsequently included in Mandala X in a language common to that Mandala.

However, these Rishis, belonging as they did to the period of Mandala VIII, happened to be named in incidental references in late hymns in the Late Mandalas and upa-mandalas.

Incidentally, Brhaduktha, named in V.19.5, has the patronymic Vamadeva, indicating that he is a descendant of Vamadeva of Mandala IV, thus again confirming our chronology.

Mandala IX: Mandala IX is a ritual Mandala devoted to Soma hymns, and references to Rishis, strictly speaking, have no place in it.

Nevertheless, we do find references to the following composers:

Jamadagni (IX.97.51) from the period of the Early Mandala III.

Kaksivan (IX.74.8) from the general Mandala I.

Vyasva (IX.65.7) from the Late Mandala VIII.

These references clearly prove the late provenance of Mandala IX.

The final picture that emerges from our analysis of the references to composers is exactly the same as the chronological picture obtained from our analysis of the inter-relationships among the composers.

In respect of Mandala I, it is now clear that the early upa-mandalas are definitely very early; and the late parts of the general and late upa-mandalas coincide with the closing period of Mandala VIII.

References to Kings and Rishis

It is not only composers who are referred to within the hymns: there are also references to Kings and Rishis (other than composers); and an examination of these references can help in throwing more light on the chronology of the Mandalas.

We will examine these references as follows:

A. The Bharata Dynasty.

B. Minor Kings and Rishis.

C. The Trksi Dynasty.

The Bharata Dynasty: The Bharata Dynasty is the predominant dynasty in the Rigveda. Eleven Kings of this dynasty are referred to in the Rigveda:

1. *Bharata:* VI.16.4;
2. *Devavata:* III.23.2, 3; IV.15.4; VI.27.7; VII. 18.22.
3. *Srnjaya:* IV.15.4; VI.27.7; 47.25.
4. *Vadhryasva:* VI. 61.1; X. 69.1, 2, 4, 5, 9-12;
5. *Divodasa:* I. 112.14; 116.18; 119. 4; 130.7, 10; II. 19.6. IV. 26.3; 30.20; VI. 16. 5, 19; 26.5; 31.4; 43.1; 47.22, 23; 61.1; VII. 18.25; VIII. 103.2; IX. 61.2.
6. *Pratardana:* VI.26.8; VII.33.14.
7. *Pijavana:* VII.18.22-23, 25.

8\. a. *Devasravas:* III.23.2, 3. b. Sudas: I.47.6; 63.7; 112.19; III.53.9, 11; V.53.2; VII. 18.5, 9, 15, 17, 22, 23, 25; 19.3, 6; 20.2; 25.3; 32.10; 33.3; 53.3; 60.8, 9; 64.3; 83.1, 4, 6-8.

9. *Sahadeva:* I. 100.17; IV. 15.7-10.
10. *Somaka:* IV. 15.9.

The names of these Kings are given above in order of their relative positions in the dynastic list (not necessarily in succeeding generations, since it is possible that there are many intervening generations of Kings who are not named in the Rigveda).

Their relative positions are based on information within the hymns:

1. Bharata is the eponymous ancestor of this dynasty.
2. Devavata is referred to as an ancestor of Srnjaya (IV. 15.4; VI.27.7), Devasravas (III.23.2, 3) and Sudas (VII.18.22).
3. Srnjaya is referred to as a descendant of Devavata (IV. 15.4; VI.27.7), and ancestor of Divodasa (VI.47.25).
4. Vadhryasva is referred to as the father of Divodasa (VI.61.1).
5. Divodasa is referred to as a descendant of Srnjaya (VI.47.25), a son of Vadhryasva (VI.61.1) and an ancestor of Sudas (VII.18.25).
6. Pratardana is referred to as a descendant of Divodasa

(Anukramanis of IX.96), the father of an unnamed King (VI.26.8), and ancestor of Sudas (VII.33.14).

7. Pijavana is referred to as an ancestor of Sudas (VII.18.22, 23, 25).

8 a. Devasravas is referred to as a descendant of Devavata (III.23.2, 3). b. Sudas is referred to as a descendant of Divodasa (VII.18.25), Pratardana (VII.33.14) and Pijavana (VII.18.22, 23, 25).

9. Sahadeva is referred to as the father of Somaka (IV.15.7-10).

10. Somaka is referred to as the son of Sahadeva (IV.15.7-10). (Srnjaya and Devavata are referred to in verse 4 of the hymn.)

As we can see, the relative positions of all these Kings are clear from the references. It is only in the case of Devasravas (about whom the only information we have is that he is a descendant of Devavata) that a word of clarification becomes necessary:

Hymn 23 refers to two Kings, Devavata and Devasravas; and *(as in the case of IV.42; V.27; VI.15) these Kings, who are referred* to in the hymn are named as the composers of the hymn in the Anukramanis.

Most scholars, ancient and modern, assume from this that while Devavata and Devasravas may or may not be composers of the hymn, they are at least contemporaries and possibly brothers.

It is, however, very clear from the hymn that they are neither composers nor contemporaries: the composer is Vishvamitra, while Devasravas is the King who is being addressed by the composer, and Devavata is a King from the remote past, an ancestor of Devasravas, who is being invoked and whom Devasravas is being asked to remember and emulate.

While this makes it clear that Devasravas is a descendant of Devavata, his exact position in the dynastic list is not immediately clear. However, the fact that Mandala III is contemporaneous with the period of Sudas gives us the following options:

a. Devasravas is a contemporary clansman (brother/cousin/uncle) of Sudas.

b. Devasravas is another name for Sudas himself.

The two main heroes of the dynasty are Divodasa and Sudas:

Divodasa is referred to as a contemporary only in Mandala VI (VI.16.5; 31.4; 47.22, 23). In all other references to him, he is a figure from the past.

Sudas is referred to as a contemporary only in Mandalas III and VII (III.53.9, 11; VII. 18.22, 23; 25.3; 53.3; 60.8, 9; 64.3). In all other references to him, he is a figure from the past.

Between them, Divodasa and Sudas are referred to in every single Mandala of the Rigveda except in Mandala X.

From this, we get a clear chronological picture:

Mandala VI	-Divodasa
Mandala III	-Sudas
Mandala VII	-Sudas
All other Mandalas	-post-Sudas

(Mandala III is placed before Mandala VII because the hymns make it clear, and almost every single authority, ancient and modern, is unanimous, that Vishvamitra was the earlier priest of Sudas and Vasishtha the later one.)

Further: Sahadeva, a descendant of Sudas (as per all traditional information) is referred to as a contemporary in hymn I.100; while his son Somaka is referred to as a contemporary in IV.15.

Hymn I.100 is ascribed to Rjrasva and the Varsagiras; but the hymn is clearly composed by a Kutsa Rishi, as it is included in the Kutsa upa-mandalas. In general, the hymns in this upa-mandalas are late ones, and include, in its Asvin-hymns, some of the latest hymns in Mandala I. But this particular hymn, I.100, appears to be the oldest hymn in this upa-mandala, and perhaps constituted the nucleus around which Kutsas of a later period formed their upa-mandalas.

The chronological picture we get for the Bharatas, consequently, is as follows:

> *The above order tallies exactly with the order of the earliest Mandalas in our chronology. Incidentally, the earliest historically relevant King of this dynasty in the Rigveda, Devavata, is referred to only in the four Mandalas (VI, III, VII, IV), which clearly represent the heyday of the Bharata dynasty.*

Minor Kings and Rishis: A great number of minor Kings and Rishis are named in references throughout the Rigveda. However, most of them are irrelevant to our chronological analysis, since they do not provide any information which could be useful in arranging the Mandalas in their chronological order.

Such include:

a. Those who are mythical or ancestral figures in all the Mandalas which refer to them.

b. Those who are *not* referred to in more than one Mandala- (unless they can be logically and chronologically connected with other Kings or Rishis in other Mandalas).

c. Those who are referred to only in two Mandalas, and one of these two is Mandala X.

References which *are* relevant to our analysis are references to Kings and Rishis who are contemporary in one or more Mandalas, and figures from the past in others. Unfortunately, unlike the Bharata Kings, none of the minor Kings and Rishis fulfil this criterion. Hence, rather than using these references to clarify our already established chronological picture, we can, in effect, use our already established chronological picture to clarify the chronological position of these Kings and Rishis. Thus:

a. In one case, we can conclude that, of the two following Kings (each of whom is referred to as a contemporary in the respective reference) the first is probably an ancestor of the second: Abhyavartin Cayamana: VI.27.5, 8. Kavi Cayamana: VII.18.8

b. We can conclude that the following Kings or Rishis (none of whom is referred to as a contemporary in any reference) probably belong to the early period:

   Dabhiti: I. 112.23; II. 13.9; 15.4, 9; IV. 30.21; VI. 20.13; 26.6; VII. 19.4; X. 113.9.

   Saryata/Saryata:I. 51.12; 112.17; III. 51.7.

   Dasadyu: I. 33.14; VI. 26.4.

   Turvayana: I. 53.10; 174.3; VI. 18.13; X. 61.2.

c. We can, likewise, conclude that the following kings (who are also not referred to as contemporaries) probably belong to the middle period:

Vayya: I. 54.6; 112.6; II. 3.6; 13.12; IV. 19.6; V. 79.1-3; IX. 68.8.

Turviti: I. 36.18; 54.6; 61.11; 112.23; II. 13.12; IV. 19.6.

However, the references to some minor Kings do help to confirm our chronological order in respect of our classification of certain Mandalas (V, VIII and the general and late upa-mandalas of Mandala I) as late ones:

a. These Kings are referred to as contemporaries (being, in fact, patrons of the composers) in most of the references.

b. They are not referred to in any of the earlier Mandalas.

c. They are referred to in more than one of these Late Mandalas. These Kings are:

   a. Asvamedha: V. 27.4-6 (patron). VIII. 68.15-17 (patron).

   b. Narya/Narya: I. 54.6; 112.9; VIII. 24.29 (patron).

   c. Dhvasra/Dhvasanti and Purusanti: I. 112.23; IX. 58.3 (patron).

      (The composer of IX.58 is Avatsara Kasyapa, who is also the composer of V.44.1-9, 14-15.)

   d. Rusama: V. 30.12-15 (patron). VIII. 3.12; 4.2; 51.9.

   e. Srutaratha: I. 122.7; V.36.6.

   f. Prthusravas: I. 116.21; VIII. 46.24 (patron).

   g. Svitrya: I. 33.14-15; V. 19.3 (patron).

   h. Adhrigu: I. 112.20; VIII. 12.2; 22.10.

The Trksi Dynasty: Three Kings of the Trksi dynasty (apparently corresponding to the Iksvaku dynasty of the Puranas) are referred to in the Rigveda.

We are taking up the references to these Kings last of all because these references *alone* among all the references to Kings and Rishis in the Rigveda, *appear* to fail to fit into our chronology of the Rigveda.

These Kings are:

a. Mandhata: I. 112.13; VIII. 39.8; 40.12.

b. Purukutsa: I. 63.7; 112.7; 174.2; VI. 20.10.

c. Trasadasyu: I.112.14; IV. 38.1; 42.8; V. 27.3; VIII. 8.21; 19.32; 36.7; 37.7; 49.10; X. 33.4; 150.5.

Trasadasyu Paurukutsa: IV. 42.9; V. 33.8; VII. 19.3; VIII. 19.36.

d. Trasadasyava: VIII. 22.7.

Trasadasyu is clearly the most important of these Kings, and he and Purukutsa belong to the same period (since the reference in IV.42.8-9 makes it clear that Purukutsa is the actual father, and not some remote ancestor, of Trasadasyu).

And equally clearly, this period is the *late* period:

a. Trasadasyu's name occurs the greatest number of times in Mandala VIII (as Divodasa's name does in Mandala VI, and Sudas' in Mandala VII).
b. Trasadasyu's son (referred to only as Trasadasyava) also clearly belongs to the period of Mandala VIII.
c. Trasadasyu is referred to as a patron, and therefore a contemporary, only in Mandalas V and VIII (V.27.3; 33.8; VIII.19.32, 36).

And yet, we find four references to Purukutsa and Trasadasyu in the *older* Mandalas (VI.20.10; VII.19.3; IV.38.1; 42.8-9), and one in the middle upa-mandalas (I.63.7).

This raises a piquant question: is there something wrong with our chronology of the Rigveda, or is there something incongruous about these five references in the older Mandalas?

There is clearly nothing wrong with our chronology of the Rigveda:

1. Our chronology is based on detailed analyses of totally independent factors, each of which gives us exactly the *same* clear and integrated picture of the chronological order of the Mandalas. This picture cannot be invalidated or questioned on the basis of five references to one pair of kings.
2. And, in fact, an examination of the contemporary references to Trasadasyu confirms rather than contradicts our chronology:

Trasadasyu is referred to as a patron and contemporary by only three Rishis:

Atri Bhauma (V.27.3)

Samvarana Prajapatya (V.33.8)

Sobhari Kanva (VIII.19.32)

Using Vishvamitra and Mandala III as a base, we get the following chronological equations:

a. Sudas is many generations prior to Trasadasyu, since Sudas is contemporaneous with Vishvamitra, while Trasadasyu is contemporaneous with Vishvamitra's remote descendent Samvarana.

b. Sudas is many generations prior to Trasadasyu, since Sudas is contemporaneous with Vishvamitra, whose junior associate is Ghora Angiras, while Trasadasyu is contemporaneous with Ghora's remote descendant Sobhari.

c. Mandala III is much older than Mandala V, since Vishvamitra is the Rishi of Mandala III, while his remote descendant Samvarana is a Rishi in Mandala V.

d. Mandala III is much older than Mandala VIII, since Ghora is a junior associate of Vishvamitra (the Rishi of Mandala III), while his remote descendants are Rishis in Mandala VIII.

e. Mandala VII, which is also contemporaneous with Sudas, is also therefore much older than Mandalas V and VIII.

Thus, the very fact that Samvarana Prajapatya is one of the Rishis contemporaneous with Trasadasyu is proof of the validity of our chronology.

But this brings us to the second part of the question: is there something incongruous about the five references to Purukutsa and Trasadasyu in the older Mandalas?

And the only answer can be: these five references must be, *have* to be, interpolations or late additions into the older Mandalas.

If so, this is a unique and special circumstance in the Rigveda. There are other actual or alleged cases of interpolations in the Rigveda (all interpolations made during different stages of compilation of the Rigveda before the ten-Mandala Rigveda was finalized), but *all* of them are incidental ones pertaining to ritual hymns or verses. But these, if they are interpolations, are deliberate interpolations of a political nature, since only one father-and-son pair of Kings forms the subject of the interpolated references. And only some unique circumstance could have been responsible for this.

The nature of this unique circumstance can only be elucidated by an examination of the nature of the references themselves.

And, on examination, we get the following picture: the five references in the older Mandalas and upa-mandalas are laudatory and even adulatory references to Purukutsa and Trasadasyu. *Purukutsa and Trasadasyu, although they were not even Vedic Aryans* (as we shall see in our chapter on the identity of the Vedic Aryans) are accorded the highest praise in the Rigveda; and this high praise is on account of the fact that they were responsible for the *victory, perhaps the very survival as a nation, of the Purus (who* were the Vedic Aryans) in a vital struggle between the Purus and their enemies which must have taken place during the period of the Late Mandalas.

As a result, the extremely grateful Rishis belonging to the families intimately connected with the Bharatas (namely, the Angirases of both the Bharadvaja and Gautama groups, and the Vasishtha) recorded their tribute to Purukutsa and Trasadasyu in the form of verses. The case of Purukutsa and Trasadasyu was clearly such a special one in the eyes of these Rishis that in their case, *and only in their case in the whole of the Rigveda,* they made a point of breaking with orthodox tradition and interpolating these verses in their praise into the older Mandalas and upa-mandalas connected with their families.

The praise is equally special: in IV.42.8-9, Trasadasyu is twice referred to as a "demi-god", *ardhadeva,* a phrase which is not found again in the Rigveda; and even the circumstance of his birth is glorified. The seven Rishis are described as performing sacrifices, and Purukutsa's wife as giving oblations to Indra and Varuna, before the Gods are pleased to reward them with the birth of Trasadasyu, "the demi-god, the slayer of the foeman".

IV.38.1, likewise, thanks Mitra and Varuna for the services which Trasadasyu, "the winner of our fields and plough-lands, and the strong smiter who subdued the Dasyus", rendered to the Purus.

VI.20.10 refers to the Purus lauding Indra for the help rendered by him to Purukutsa (read: the help rendered by Purukutsa to the Purus) in a war against the Dasa tribes.

1.63.7 refers to Indra rendering military aid to the Purus, by way of Purukutsa and by way of Sudas.

VII.19.3 refers to Indra helping the Purus "in winning land and slaying foemen", once by way of Trasadasyu Paurukutsa and once by way of Sudas.

These five interpolated references in the older Mandalas stand out sharply from the other references in eleven hymns in the later Mandalas: those references do not *even once* refer to the Purus in connection with Purukutsa and Trasadasyu; and the only praise of these kings is found in the *danastutis* (V.33; VIII.19).

That the five references to Purukutsa and Trasadasyu in the older Mandalas and upa-mandalas are interpolations is, therefore, proved by:

1. Their violation of our chronology; and even of their own implied chronology.
2. Their special nature which makes them stand out sharply from the other references to these kings in later Mandalas.
3. The fact that in the case of at least two of these five references, even the Western scholars have noted that they are interpolations or late additions (which is a very high ratio, considering that such interpolations are not necessarily detectable):

In respect of IV.42.8-9, Griffith tells us that "Grassmann banishes stanzas 8, 9 and 10 to the appendix as late additions to the hymn".

In respect of VII.19, the entire hymn appears to be a late addition into Mandala VII. This Man ala is contemporaneous with the period of Sudas; and in his footnote to VII. 19.8, Griffith notes that the King referred to in the verse is "probably a descendant of Sudas, who must have lived long before the composition of this hymn, as the favour bestowed on him is referred to as old in stanza 6".

So much for these references, which, *alone* in the whole of the Rigveda, *appear* to stand out against our chronology of the Mandalas.

But, before concluding this section, we must also take note of the references to Mandhata: the only references to him in the Rigveda are in late Mandalas.

On the face of it, this would appear to fit in with the general picture: Purukutsa, Trasadasyu and Trasadasyava belong to the period of the late Mandalas, and their ancestor Mandhata also belongs to the same period. However, this runs in the face of the traditional picture of Mandhata: all tradition outside the Rigveda is unanimous in identifying him as a very early historical king.

Of course, when information outside the Rigveda is in contradiction to information in the Rigveda, the former is to be rejected. But is it really in contradiction in this case?

An examination shows that although the three references in the Rigveda occur in late Mandalas, they are unanimous (with each other and with traditional information outside the Rigveda) in identifying Mandhata as a King from the remote past:

a. Not one of the three references treats Mandhata as a contemporary person.

b. In fact, VIII.39.8 refers to him as one of the earliest performers of the sacrifice, *yajneSu purvyam*.

   Likewise, VIII.40.12 refers to Mandhata together with the ancient Angirases as "our ancestors".

c. The general period of Mandhata also appears to be indicated in two of the references:

VIII.40.12, as we saw, classifies Mandhata with the ancient Angirases.

I.112.13 is more specific: it names Mandhata in the same verse as Bharadvaja. (The other reference to Bharadvaja in this particular set of Asvin hymns, in I.116.18, likewise refers to Bharadvaja and Divodasa in the same verse.)

The inference is clear: Mandhata belongs to the earliest period of Mandala VI and beyond. The whole situation reeks of irony: the Trksi Kings Purukutsa and Trasadasyu belong to the period of the late Mandalas, but references (albeit interpolations) to them are found in the oldest Mandalas; whereas their ancestor Mandhata, who belongs to the oldest period, even preceding Mandala VI, is referred to only in the latest Mandalas.

As there is logic behind the first circumstance, there is logic behind the second one as well:

1. Mandhata is not referred to in the oldest Mandalas because his period preceded the period of these Mandalas; and he was a non-Puru King while these Mandalas are specifically Bharata (Puru) Mandalas.

2. He is referred to in the later Mandalas because:
   a. The composer who refers to him in VIII.39.8 and VIII.40.12 is Nabhaka Kanva. According to tradition, Nabhaka is a King from the Iksvaku (Trksi) dynasty who joined the Kanva family of Rishis. He is, therefore, a descendant of Mandhata, whom, indeed, he refers to as his ancestor.
   b. Hymn I.112 (like I.116) is a historiographical hymn, which refers to many historical characters. These historiographical hymns, incidentally and inadvertently, provide us with many historical clues. The reference to Mandhata is an example of this.

In conclusion, the references to Kings and Rishis in the Rigveda fully confirm and corroborate our chronology.

The Rigvedic Structure and Formation

The structure and formation of the Rigveda can be summarised from various angles:

A. The Order of the Mandalas.
B. The Formation of the Rigveda.
C. The Chronology of the Rishis.
D. The Chronology of the Mandalas.

The Order of the Mandalas: The chronological order of the Mandalas, as we saw, is: VI, III, VII, IV, II, V, VIII, IX, X, with the chronological period of Mandala I spread out over the periods of at least four other Mandalas (IV, II, V, VIII).

Needless to say, the chronological order of the ten Mandalas appears to bear no relationship to the serial order in which the Mandalas are arranged. But the matter becomes clearer when we examine the case of the Family Mandalas separately from the case of the non-family Mandalas.

There is a general consensus among the scholars that the six Family Mandalas, II-VII, formed the original core of the Rigveda, and the four non-family Mandalas, I and VIII-X, were added to the corpus later.

The serial order of the non-family Mandalas tallies with their chronological order. The only two problems are:

1. Why is Mandala I placed *before*, rather than after, the corpus of the Family Mandalas?
2. The Family Mandalas are *not* arranged in chronological order; so what is the criterion adopted in their arrangement?

These questions have remained unanswered. But actually the answers are clear from the evidence:

1. *Mandala I, unlike the other non-family Mandalas, is not* unambiguously later than the Family Mandalas in terms of composition and compilation: many upamandalas in this Mandala are contemporaneous with the Later Family Mandalas, and some even precede them.

   It is in recognition of this fact that the compilers of the Rigveda placed it before the Family Mandalas.
2. The Family Mandalas were formulated into a text before the addition of the non-family Mandalas, and the criterion for their arrangement was not chronology, but *size*: Mandala II is the smallest of the Family Mandalas with 429 verses, while Mandala VII is the biggest with 841 verses.

The number of verses in the six Family Mandalas is, respectively: 429, 617, 589, 727, 765, 841.

Clearly, there is a lacuna here: Mandala III (617 verses) has more verses than Mandala IV (589 verses).

The only logical explanation for this is that Mandala III originally, at the time of fixing of the arrangement of the Family Mandalas, had fewer verses than Mandala IV; but many verses were added to it at a later point of time, which upset the equation.

Surprisingly, this is not just a matter of logic: the fact is directly confirmed in the Aitareya Brahmana the Brahmana text which is connected with the Rigveda.

According to the Aitareya Brahmana (VI.18), six hymns (III.21, 30, 34, 36, 38-39) were "seen" (*i.e.* composed) by Vishvamitra at a later point of time to compensate certain other hymns which were "seen" by Vishvamitra but were misappropriated by Vamadeva.

That is: after the text of the Family Mandalas was fixed, a dispute arose with the Vishvamitra claiming that some of the hymns included in the Vamadeva Mandala were actually composed by Vishvamitra. The dispute was resolved by including some new hymns into Mandala III, by way of compensation, in lieu of the disputed hymns.

If these six hymns (III.21, 30, 34, 36, 38-39), which have a total of 68 verses, are excluded from the verse count of Mandala III, we get, more or less, the original verse count of the six Family Mandalas: 429, 549, 589, 737, 765, 841.

The Formation of the Rigveda: The process of formation of the Rigveda took place in four stages.

1. *The Six-Mandala Rigveda*: The Family Mandalas.
2. *The Eight-Mandala Rigveda*: Mandalas I-VIII.
    a. *Major interpolations*: III.21, 30, 34, 36, 38-39.
    b. *Minor interpolations*: References to Trksi Kings in older Mandalas.
    c. *Introductions*: Old Bhrgu hymns included in the Rigveda in Mandala VIII.
3. *The Nine-Mandala Rigveda*: Mandalas I-IX.
    Major interpolations: The Valakhilya hymns VIII. 49-59.
4. *The Ten Mandala Rigveda*: Mandalas 1-X.
    a. Minor interpolations: (not specifiable here)
    b. Minor adjustments: Splitting and combining of hymns to produce symmetrical numbers (191 hymns each in Mandalas I and X) or astronomically or ritually significant numbers and sequences (see papers by Subhash C. Kak, Prof. of Electrical and Computer Engineering, Louisiana State University, Baton Rouge, U.S.A.).

The completion of the fourth stage saw the full canonization of the Rigveda, and the text was frozen into a form which it has maintained to this day.

The Chronology of the Rishis: The chronological positions of some major Rishis are summarized in the following chart. Asterisks indicate the first Rishi from whom the family originated (chart on next page).

The chart is self-explanatory. However, the following points must be clarified, particularly in respect of the eponymous Rishis of the general upa-mandalas, whose period stretches across the periods of four Mandalas (IV, II, V, VIII):

a. Agastya and Kutsa are contemporaries of Vasishtha, but the upa-mandalas which bear their names were composed by their descendants, and therefore figure as general upa-mandalas which come later in time.

b. Kasyapa is later than Vamadeva, but he is also earlier than Atri (his descendant Avatsara Kasyapa being a senior Rishi in V.44), and he must therefore be placed in the period of Mandala I between the middle and late upa-mandalas.

c. Parucchepa's upa-mandala has been classified as a general upa-mandalas on the ground that there is no direct relationship between Parucchepa and the actual composers of either the Early, Middle or Late Mandalas. However, it is clear that the beginnings of the Parucchepa upa-mandala lie in the late rather than the middle period: unlike in the case of other Mandalas and upa-mandalas, the Parucchepa upa-mandala appears to be composed by a single composer rather than by a group of composers comprising many generations (the uniformity of style and content of the hymns certainly gives this impression), and this composer already names Atri, Kanva, and Priyamedha as senior Rishis (I.139.9).

The Chronology of the Mandalas: We are concerned, in this chapter and this book, with the internal chronology of the Rigveda rather than with its absolute chronology: that is, we are concerned with the chronological sequence of the different parts of the Rigveda, and not with the exact century BC to which a particular part belongs.

However, the absolute chronology of the text is ultimately bound to be a vital factor in our understanding of Vedic history; and, while we leave the subject for the present to other scholars, it will be pertinent to note here that our analysis of the internal chronology of the Rigveda does shed some light on an aspect which is important to any study of absolute chronology: namely, the duration of the period of composition of the Rigveda.

It is clear that the Rigveda was not composed in one sitting, or in a series of sittings, by a conference of Rishis: the text is clearly the result of many centuries of composition. The question is: just how many centuries? The Western scholars measure the periods of the various Mandalas in terms of decades, while some Indian scholars go to the other extreme and measure them in terms of millenniums and decamillenniums.

A more rational, but still conservative, estimate would be as follows:

1. There should be, at a very conservative estimate, a minimum of at least six centuries between the completion of the first nine Mandalas of the Rigveda and the completion of the tenth.
2. The period of the Late Mandalas and upa-mandalas (V, VIII, IX, and the corresponding parts of Mandala I) should together comprise a minimum of three to four centuries.
3. The period of the Middle Mandalas and upa-mandalas (IV, II, and the corresponding parts of Mandala I) and the gap which must have separated them from the period of the Late Mandalas, should likewise comprise a minimum of another three to four centuries.
4. The period of Mandalas III and VII and the early upa-mandalas of Mandala I, beginning around the period of Sudas, should comprise at least two centuries.
5. The period of Mandaḷa VI, from its beginnings in the remote past and covering its period of composition right upto the time of Sudas, must again cover a menimum of at least six centuries.

Thus, by a conservative estimate, the total period of composition of the Rigveda must have covered a period of at least two millenniums.

Incidentally, on all the charts shown by us so far, we have depicted all the Mandalas on a uniform scale. A more realistic depiction would be as follows:

Words Misinterpreted in the Rigveda

There are some words in the Rigveda which have been misinterpreted as names of Kings or Rishis (often because some of these words were also the names or epithets of Rishis in later parts of the text), thereby causing confusion in Rigvedic interpretation.

The exact nature of these words has, therefore, to be clarified. These words are:

A. Atri.

B. Kutsa.

C. Ausija.

D. Trksi.

E. Atithigva.

Atri: Atri is the name of a Rishi, the eponymous founder of the Atri family of Mandala V. His name is referred to in the following hymns (not counting references, to him, or to themselves, by the Atris):

I.45.3; 51.3; 139.9; 183.5; V.15.5; VIII.5.25; X.150.5

However, the word Atri existed *before* the period of this Rishi, *as a name or epithet of the Sun*, which was the original meaning of this word. The Rishi of this name came later.

We will be concerned here only with the references to this mythical Atri, the Sun. These references are found in 15 hymns:

I. 112.7, 16; 116.8; 117.3; 118.7; 119.6; 180.4; II. 8.5; V. 40.6-9; 78.4; VI. 50.10; VII. 68.5; 71.5; X. 39.9; 80.3; 143.1, 3.

The word in the above references is confused by scholars with the name of the Rishi Atri. However, it is clear that there is a mythical Atri in the Rigveda distinct from the historical Atri, and, for that matter, a mythical Kutsa distinct from the historical Kutsa: Macdonell, in his Vedic Mythology, classifies Atri and Kutsa alongwith "Mythical Priests and Heroes" like Manu, Bhrgu, Atharvana, Dadhyanc, ANgiras, Navagvas, Dasagvas and Usana, whom he distinguishes from "several other ancient seers of a historical or semi-historical character... such (as) Gautama, Vishvamitra, Vamadeva, Bharadvaja and Vasishtha".

That this mythical Atri is distinct from the historical Atri, and the myth existed long before the birth of this historical Rishis confirmed by an examination of the references: we find that these references undergo a complete transformation in Mandala V, affected by Rishis of the Atri family in a deliberate attempt to try and appropriate the myth for themselves by identifying the mythical Atri with the eponymous Atri, their ancestor.

This, on the one hand, shows up an interesting aspect of the family psychology of the Rishis, and, on the other, confirms our chronological order of the Mandalas.

The references fall into three categories:

1. References in older Mandalas (VI, VII, II) where Atri is a name of the Sun.
2. References in Mandala V where Atri the Sun is deliberately transformed into Atri the Rishi, as part of two new myths.
3. References in later Mandalas (I, X) where the Rishi Atri is fully identified with the mythical Atri in a transformed myth.

To elaborate:

1. VI.50.10 and VII.71.5 refer to the Asvins rescuing Atri from "great darkness". As Griffith points out in his footnote to VII.71.5: "The reappearance, heralded by the Asvins or Gods of Twilight, of the departed Sun, appears to be symbolised in all these legends."

   VII.68.5 also refers to the same natural phenomenon, the gradual appearance of the Sun at dawn, in a different way: it credits the Asvins with making Atri (the Sun) increasingly bright and glorious with food and nourishment from their rich store.

   II.8.5 does not refer to the Asvins. It uses the word Atri as an epithet for Agni (who is literally the earthly representative of the Sun). The epithet is clearly a repetition of a simile in the previous verse, II.8.4, where also Agni is likened to the Sun (Bhanu).

2. Two references by the Atris bifurcate the original myth into two distinct myths, both connected up with their eponymous ancestor.

   In the original myth, the Asvins rescue Atri, the Sun, from "great darkness".

   In the two transformed myths:

   a. The Asvins rescue Atri, the Rishi, from a pit or cavern: V.78.4.
   b. Atri, the Rishi, rescues the Sun from "great darkness": V.40.6-9.

In V.78.4, Atri, lying in a deep pit or cavern, calls out to the Asvins for help, and is rescued by them from his distress.

In V.40.6-9, the Sun has been pierced "through and through with darkness" by a demon called Svarbhanu (literally "sky-sun"), and all creatures stand bewildered and frightened by the sight. Atri, however, by his Brahmanic powers, "discovered Surya concealed in gloom", and, with the same powers, "established the eye of Surya in the heavens". The hymn smugly concludes: "The Atris found the Sun again... This none besides had power to do."

3. All the eleven references (in nine hymns) in the later Mandalas (*i.e.* in late upa-mandalas of Mandala I, and in Mandala X) reflect one of the two transformed versions of the myth:

   They refer to the Rishi Atri being rescued (X.143.1, 3) from a fiery, burning pit (I.112.7, 16; 116.8; 11 8.7; 119.6; 180.4; X.39.9; 80.3), or simply a pit (I.117.3), by the Asvins.

   The "fiery, burning pit" of the transformed myth is clearly incompatible with the "great darkness" of the original nature-myth.

Kutsa: Kutsa is the name of a Rishi, the eponymous ancestor of the Kutsa Rishis of Mandala I. His name is referred to in the following hymns: VII.25.5; X.29.2; 38.5.

However, the word Kutsa existed before the period of this Rishi, *as a name or epithet of Vajra, the thunderbolt,* which was the original meaning of this word. The Rishi of this name came later.

We will, again, be concerned here only with the references to this mythical Kutsa, the thunderbolt. These references are found in 24 hymns:

I. 33.14; 51.6; 63.3; 106.6; 112.9, 23; 121.9; 174.5; 175.4;

II. 19.6;

IV. 16.10-12; 26.1; 30.4;

V. 29.9, 10; 31.8;

VI. 20.5; 26.3; 31.3;

VII. 19.2;

VIII. 1.11; 24.25;

X. 40.6; 49.3, 4; 99.9; 138.1.

The word in the above references is confused by the scholars with the name of the Rishi Kutsa.

It is true that, in this case, there is more of an excuse for this confusion: while the mythical Atri is not a very personalized or anthropomorphised figure in the early references (before the Atris play their sleight of hand), the mythical Kutsa is a highly anthropomorphised form of the thunderbolt from the very beginning.

However, the confusion has been only in the minds of the interpreters of the hymns. The composers were under no delusions about the identity of this mythical Kutsa, and the evidence identifying this Kutsa with the thunderbolt is overwhelming:

1. The Naighantuka (2.20) gives *Kutsa* as one of the synonyms of *Vajra* (the thunderbolt).
2. Kutsa is given the epithet Arjuneya in four of the above hymns (I.112.23; IV.26.1; VII. 19.2; VIII.1.11). This is wrongly interpreted as a patronymic of the Rishi Kutsa. Actually, this is an epithet signifying the white flash of the thunderbolt.

   In another verse, III.44.5 (which does not refer to Kutsa), *arjunam*, "the Bright", is given as a synonym of *vajram*.
3. All the references to the mythical Kutsa (except the two by the Kutsas themselves: I.106.6; 112.9, 23) refer directly or indirectly to a celestial battle between Indra, the thunder-god, and Susna, the demon of drought whose other epithet is *kuyava*, "bad grain". (Two of the verses, IV.26.1 and X.40.6, only *mention* Kutsa, and do not refer to this battle, but other factors show that it is the mythical Kutsa who is being referred to.)

   The place of Kutsa in these references can be understood only on the basis of his identity as the personified form of Indra's thunderbolt:

   a. In three references, Indra kills the demon *with* Kutsa (*kutsena*) as with a weapon: IV.16.11; V.29.9; VI.31.3.
   b. In most of the references, however, Indra is represented as doing the deed of killing the demon *for* Kutsa, or

in aid of Kutsa. There is, however, a coherent mythological explanation for the conversion of Kutsa from the *instrument* of the deed to its *beneficiary*:

Six of the above references refer to the chariot-wheel of the Sun: I.174.5; 175.4; IV.16.12; 30.4; V.29.9; VI.31.3. In his footnote to I.175.4, Griffith explains that "Indra is said to have taken the wheel of the chariot of the Sun, and to have cast it like a quoit against the demon of drought". This was done, as per IV.30.4, "for... Kutsa, as he battled" (against the demon of drought).

In another hymn (which does not refer to Kutsa), there is again a reference to this use of the chariot-wheel of the Sun. Here, in his footnote to I.130.9, Griffith provides the myth in greater detail, albeit in a later evolved form: *"He tore the Sun's wheel off*: according to Sayana, Brahma had promised the Asuras or fiends that Indra's thunderbolt should never destroy them. Indra, accordingly cast at them the wheel of the Sun's chariot and slew them therewith." In short: as the thunderbolt (Kutsa) was proving to be ineffectual as it battled against the demon of drought, Indra despatched the chariot-wheel of the Sun to its aid.

c. In two of the references, Kutsa is even referred to as the charioteer of Indra: II.19.6; VI.20.5.

The connotation of Indra's "chariot" is clear in the Rigveda: Indra's chariot is the thunderbolt on which he streaks across the sky. The Bhrgus are credited in the Rigveda with the manufacture of Indra's thunderbolt: in IV. 16.20, they are described as the manufacturers of Indra's chariot.

The sense of Kutsa being Indra's charioteer is therefore clear: the thunderbolt is Indra's chariot, and the anthropomorphised form of the thunderbolt is Indra's charioteer.

4. The identity between the mythical Kutsa and Indra's thunderbolt should have been clear to the scholars:

Griffith, for example, describes Kutsa in his various footnotes as "the particular friend of Indra" (I.33.14); "a favourite of Indra" (I.112.23); "favourite of Indra" (II.19.6);

"the favoured friend of Indra" (IV.16.10); "the special friend of Indra" (VI.31.3); "Indra's favourite companion" (X.29.2).

But, wherever there is a reference to Indra's "friend" within the hymns themselves, and no names are mentioned, Griffith, in his footnotes, has no doubt as to the identity of this friend: "*Thy friend*: probably the vajra or thunderbolt, which is Indra's inseparable associate and ally" (1.10.9); "*With thy friend*: the thunderbolt" (1.53.7); "*His friend*: his constant companion, the thunderbolt" (X.50.2).

Griffith's conclusion is based on a direct statement in VI.21.7: "With thy own ancient friend and companion, the thunderbolt..."

In the circumstance, it is strange that no scholar has seen fit to think twice before deciding that the Kutsa, who is Indra's favourite friend and companion, could be a human Rishi.

5. The *only* other name in the Rigveda identified by Griffith in his footnotes as that of a friend of Indra, in a similar manner, is that of Usana Kavya: "the especial friend of Indra" (I.51.10; IV.16.2); "Indra's special friend" (V.29.9); "a favoured friend and companion of Indra" (X.22.6); "Indra's friend" (X.49.3).

   What is significant is that Usana is referred to five times in the same verse as Kutsa (VI.26.1; V.29.9; 31.8; X.49.3; 99.9) and five times in the same hymn (Kutsa: I.51.6; 121.9; IV. 16. 10-12; VI.20.5; X.40.6; Usana: I.51.10-11; 121.12; IV.16.2; VI.20.11; X.40.7).

   When we consider that there are 1028 hymns and 10552 verses in the Rigveda, and that the mythical Kutsa and Usana are referred to in only 29 verses and 19 verses respectively, the number of hymns and verses they share in common is too significant to be coincidental. Clearly, Kutsa and Usana share a close and special relationship.

   And what is this close and special relationship? The Rigveda is very clear at least about the nature of the close and special relationship between Indra and Usana: Usana Kavya is mythically credited with being the (Bhrgu) person who manufactured the *Vajra* or thunderbolt, and gave it to Indra for his weapon (I.51.10; 121.12; V.34.2).

The nature of the close and special relationship between Usana, Indra and Kutsa is therefore clear: they are, respectively, the manufacturer, wielder, and personification of the thunderbolt.

6. Curiously, in a clear case of imitation of the Atris, we find here also a blatant attempt by the Kutsas to transform the myth so as to connect it up with their eponymous ancestor.

But while the transformation by the Atris is effected by bifurcating the original Atri myth into two different myths, the transformation by the Kutsas is effected by taking the original Kutsa myth, and the more successful of the two transformed Atri myths, grafting them together, and then bifurcating them into two different myths:

In the original Kutsa myth, Indra aids the mythical Kutsa in a celestial battle.

In the transformed Atri myth, the Asvins rescue the Rishi Atri from a pit.

In the two transformed Kutsa myths:

a. Indra rescues the Rishi Kutsa *from a pit*: I.106.6 (which is also the only hymn which emphatically calls Kutsa a "Rishi").

b. The Asvins aid the Rishi Kutsa (in a battle? But this is not specified. Note: this is the only hymn in which Indra is replaced by the Asvins): I.112.9, 23.

This transformation of the original myth by the Kutsas is too clumsy, and too late in the day, to influence other references in the Rigveda, unlike the transformation of the Atri myth by the Atris, where the transformed myth becomes the basis for all subsequent references.

And the objective behind this transformation is far more modest than the objective of the Atris: while the Atris seek to glorify their eponymous ancestor by usurping the original deed of the Asvins and crediting their ancestor with supernatural powers, the Kutsas seem content merely with identifying their eponymous ancestor with the mythical Kutsa of earlier references.

But the transformation serves to underline the fact that the original mythical Kutsa originally had nothing to do with the Rishi Kutsa.

Besides the Rishi Kutsa and the mythical Kutsa, there is a third Kutsa in the Rigveda who is referred to in four hymns: I.53.10; II.14.7; VI.18.13; X.83.5.

We will examine these references in the course of our examination of the word Atithigva.

Ausija: Ausija is an epithet of the Rishi Kaksivan, who is called Kaksivan *Ausija* Dairghatamas in the Anukramanis, and whose descendants are considered as forming a third major branch of the Angiras family (after the Bharadvajas and Gotamas), the Ausijas.

In the Rigveda, however, this is neither the exclusive nor the original meaning of the word. In its original meaning, Ausija is *a name of the Sun*.

The word is referred to in the following hymns:

> *I.18.1; 112.11; 119.9; 122.4, 5; IV.21.6, 7; V.41.5; VI.4.6; X.99.11;*

The references may be examined in three groups:

1. *The Family Mandalas:*
   a. VI.4.6: Agni is compared with the Sun. Agni spreads over both the worlds with splendour "like Surya with his fulgent rays", and dispels the darkness "like Ausija with clear flame swiftly flying".
   b. IV.21.6-8 (the word Ausija is not repeated in verse 8): Indra unbars the spaces of the mountains (*i.e.* the rain-clouds) and lets loose "his floods, the water-torrents" which are lying hidden in "Ausija's abode" (analogous to "Vivasvan's dwelling" in I.53.1; III.34.7; 51.3; X.75.1; aspecially X.75.1 which also refers to the Waters.)
   c. V.41.5: Atri is the priest of Ausija.

The meaning of Ausija is very clear from the above references. In the case of VI.4.6, Sayana recognizes Ausija as a name of the Sun. However, Griffith disagrees and feels instead that Ausija in VI.4.6 is "some contemporary priest who is regarded as bringing back the daylight by prayer and sacrifice". In the case of V.41.5, all scholars, from Sayana to Griffith, are in agreement that Atri is "the ministrant priest of Kaksivan, the son of Usij". According to these scholars, then, Ausija is a Rishi (Kaksivan) who dispels darkness with a clear flame flying in the sky, whose abode is the place (*i.e.* the sky) where rain-clouds store their water-torrents, and who has another Rishi, Atri, as his priest! The absurdity of the above ideas is self-evident. Clearly, it is the Sun being referred to in all the above references: V.40, as we have already seen, makes it very clear that the Atris consider themselves to be special priests of the Sun.

2. *Mandala I*

   All the references to Ausija in Mandala I are in the general and late upa-mandalas. Here, it is clear, the word is an epithet of Kaksivan: it is used in that sense in I.18.1; 119.9; 122.4, 5.

   In I.112.11, it is used as an epithet of Dirghasravas, who is referred to as a merchant. However, Kaksivan is also referred to in the same verse, and it is natural to assume that the epithet applies to both of them.

3. *Mandala X*

On the basis of the references in Mandala 1, the scholars erroneously assume that Ausija is a patronymic of Kaksivan, rather than an epithet. Hence they presume the existence of an ancestor named Usij.

The single occurrence of this word in Mandala X disproves this presumption: in X.99.11, Ausija is an epithet of Rjisvan, who belongs to the Bharadvaja branch of the Angiras family.

Even Griffith realizes that the explanation of Ausija as a patronymic does not fit the case here: "*Ausija*: son of Usij. But as this patronymic does not properly belong to Rjisvan, the word here may perhaps mean 'vehement' 'eagerly desirous'." What the scholars do not realize is that the explanation of Ausija as a patronymic does not fit the case anywhere: Ausija is the Sun in the Family Mandalas, and an epithet in later Mandalas: an epithet of Kaksivan in Mandala I and Rjisvan in (the single use of the word in) Mandala X.

Trksi: Trksi is the name of a tribe: the tribe to which Purukutsa and Trasadasyu belong, and hence equivalent to the Iksvakus of traditional history.

The word occurs only twice in the Rigveda: VI.46.8; VIII.22.7.

This name is wrongly interpreted as the name of a King on

the basis of VIII.22.7, which is translated as: "Come to us, Lords of ample wealth, by paths of everlasting Law; Whereby to high dominion ye with mighty strength raised Trksi, Trasadasyu's son."

However, VI.46.8 makes it very clear that Trksi is the name of a *tribe* and not a person. The following is a translation of VI.46.7-8: "All strength and valour that is found, Indra, in tribes of Nahusas, and all the splendid fame that the Five tribes enjoy, bring all manly powers, at once. Or, Maghavan, what vigorous strength in Trksi lay, in Druhyus or in Puru's folk, fully bestow on us that, in the conquering fray, we may subdue our foes in fight."

On Trksi, Griffith comments: "*Trksi*: a King so named, says Sayana." However, it is clear that it is only tribes who are being referred to: the idea that the name of one King could be included in a list of tribes is based purely on the interpretation of VIII.22.7.

However, the interpretation of VIII.22.7 is wrong the phrase "Trksim... Trasadasyavam" is to be translated, *not* as "Trksi, Trasadasyu's son", but as "*the* Trksi, Trasadasyu's son". The name of the son is not specified, and he is referred to only by his patronymic, as in the case of so many other references in the Rigveda: eg. Pratardani (V1.26.8, son of Pratardana), Saryata (I.51.12; III.51.3, son of Saryata) and so on.

Atithigva: The word Atithigva is found in thirteen hymns in the Rigveda: I. 51.6; 53.8, 10; 112.14; 130.7; II. 14.7; IV. 26.3; VI. 18.13; 26.3; 47.22; VII. 19.8; VIII. 53.2; 68.16, 17; X. 48.8.

There is no general misinterpretation as such of this word. However, a clarification of the different meanings of the word will be in order here:

1. Atithigva is an epithet of Divodasa in five hymns: I.112.14; 130.7; IV.26.3; VI.26.3 (Divodasa 26.5); 47.22.

   This is also likely to be the case in one more hymn: I.51.6, which refers to Sambara (who is associated in numerous other references, including in four of the above ones, with Divodasa).

2. *But in four hymns, Atithigva is an epithet of a descendant* of Sudas (while Divodasa is an *ancestor* of Sudas: VII.18.25): I.53.8; VII.19.8: VIII.68.16, 17; X.48.8.

   Hymn VII.19 is a late hymn interpolated into Mandala

VII, as we have seen in our earlier discussion on the Trksi interpolations, and it pertains to the late period of Mandala VIII. This hymn refers to Sudas as an ancient figure from the past, while it refers to the second Atithigva in the eighth verse as a contemporary figure. Griffith notes that this Atithigva is "probably a descendant of Sudas who must have lived long before the composition of this hymn".

In VIII.68.16, 17, as well, this Atithigva is a near contemporary figure: his son Indrota is the patron of the Rishi of this hymn.

I.53.8 and X.48.8 refer to the victory of this Atithigva over Karanja and Parnaya, who are not referred to elsewhere in the Rigveda.

The fact that Atithigva represents three different entities in the Rigveda is accepted by many scholars. Keith and Macdonell, in their *Vedic Index of Names and Subjects*, note that "Roth distinguishes three Atithigvas—the Atithigva Divodasa, the enemy of Parnaya and Karanja, and the enemy of Turvayana". Keith and Macdonell themselves appear to disagree: "But the various passages can be reconciled." However, actually, their own interpretation must also show three Atithigvas, since, even within the favourable references to Atithigva, they admit that while the word refers "in nearly all cases to the same king, otherwise called Divodasa", nevertheless "a different Atithigva appears to be referred to in a Danastuti ('Praise of Gifts') where his son Indrota is mentioned".

3. Finally, there is the third Atithigva who is referred to in four hymns: I.53.10; II.14.7; VI.18.13; VIII.53.2.

This Atithigva is clearly not the hero of the references. All the four references relate to the defeat of Kutsa, Ayu and Atithigva at the hands of (according to I.53.10 and VI.18.13) Turvayana.

These references, if taken at face value, are absolutely incompatible with *all* other information in the Rigveda: all the other references to both Atithigva and Kutsa are favourable ones, while these references are clearly hostile ones in their exultation at their defeat. What is more, 1.53.8 exults in Atithigva's *victory* over Karanja and *Parnaya, while two verses later, I.53.10 exults in Atithigva's defeat* at the hands of Turvayana. Clearly, two different Atithigvas are being referred to. And this second Atithigva is compulsorily to be taken in combination with a Kutsa (obviously a different one from the Rishi Kutsa as well as the mythical Kutsa, the thunderbolt) and an Ayu (otherwise the name of an ancestral figure).

These references present an insoluble problem for all scholars engaged in a historical study of the Rigveda. Sayana, for example, tries to twist the meaning of the references in order to bring them in line with other references: Griffith notes, in his footnote to VI.18.13, that "Sayana represents the exploit as having been achieved for Kutsa, Ayu and Atithigva, but this is not the meaning of the words of the text".

Sayana's attempt to twist the meaning of the references is partly based on his knowledge of the identity of Turvayana: as Griffith notes, "according to Sayana, *Turvayana*, 'quickly going', is an epithet of Divodasa". But Atithigva is also an epithet of Divodasa. Hence Sayana finds what he probably considers to be an internal contradiction within the references; and the only way he can resolve this contradiction is by assuming, *against* the actual meaning of the words of the text, that Kutsa, Ayu and Atithigva must be the heroes of the references.

We have the following rational (if speculative) solution to offer towards the elucidation of these seemingly senseless references:

a. Atithigva, as we have seen, is the epithet of an ancestor of Sudas (*i.e.* Divodasa), as well as of a descendant. A natural inference is that Atithigva was a common epithet of Kings of the Bharata dynasty.

b. The word Kutsa (apart from its identity as a synonym of the thunderbolt) is found in the Rigveda in the names of two persons: the King Purukutsa and the Rishi Kutsa. Purukutsa is a King of the Trksi (Iksvaku) dynasty; and the Rishi Kutsa, as per tradition (outside the Rigveda), was also the son of an Iksvaku king. On the analogy of Atithigva, Kutsa may then have been a common epithet of Kings of the Trksi dynasty.

c. There are many references in the Rigveda where tribes are named in combinations purely in a figurative sense, often with special reference to their geographical locations, in order to indicate generality or universality.

Thus, VIII. 10.5: "Whether ye Lords of ample wealth (Asvins) now linger in the east or west, with Druhyu, or with Anu, Yadu, Turvasa, I call you hither, come to me."

Or I.108.8: "If with the Yadus, Turvasas ye sojourn, with Druhyus, Anus, Purus, Indra-Agni! Even from thence, ye mighty Lords, come hither, and drink libations of the flowing Soma."

However, the reference relevant to us is VI.46.7-8, which we have already seen earlier: "All strength and valour that is found, Indra, in tribes of Nahusas, and all the splendid fame that the Five tribes enjoy, bring all manly powers at once. Or, Maghavan, what vigorous strength in Trksi lay, in Druhyus or in Puru's folk, fully bestow on us, that, in the conquering fray, we may subdue our foes in fight."

The above is Griffith's translation. The meaning is: "Indra give us the strength and power of the tribes of Nahusas: the five tribes (Yadus, Turvasas, Druhyus, Anus, Purus). Give us the strength and power of all the tribes: the Trksis (in the east), the Druhyus (in the west) and the Purus (in the centre), that we may be invincible in battle."

Here, clearly the Trksis in the east, the Druhyus in the west, and the Purus in the centre, when named together, signify "all the tribes".

The same symbolism is probably expressed in the naming together of Kutsa, Ayu and Atithigva. The three names probably represent the common epithets of the Kings of the Trksis, the Druhyus and the Purus (*i.e.* Bharatas); and when taken in combination, they mean "all the tribes".

Therefore, what the four references mean is: "Indra is the Lord of all peoples and lands"; or, in two of them: "Indra made Turvayana (Divodasa) the sovereign of all the tribes."

In conclusion: we have conducted a full examination and analysis of the Rigveda from all the relevant angles, namely:

1. The inter-relationships among the composers.
2. The references to composers within the hymns.
3. The references to Kings and Rishis.
4. The family structure of the Mandalas.
5. The system of ascription of hymns in the Mandalas.

The chronological picture that we obtain, jointly and severally, in other words unanimously, from all these angles is that the chronological order of the Mandalas is: VI, III, VII, IV, II, V, VIII, IX, X (The upa-mandalas of Mandala I covering the periods of Mandalas IV, II, V, VIII).

The Geography of the Rigveda

The internal chronology of the Rigveda being firmly established, the next step in our historical analysis of the Rigveda is the establishment of the geography of the text.

The geography of the Rigveda has been the most misrepresented aspect of the text in the hands of the scholars: the geographical information in the Rigveda, to put it in a nutshell, more or less pertains to the area from Uttar Pradesh in the east to Afghanistan in the west, the eastern-most river mentioned in the text being the Ganga, and the western-most being the western tributaries of the Indus.

This geographical information is treated in a simplistic manner by the scholars, and the result is a completely distorted picture of Rigvedic geography:

1. Firstly, taking the, Rigveda as one monolithic unit, the information is interpreted to mean that the area of the Rigveda extended from western Uttar Pradesh to Afghanistan.

   It is further assumed that the habitat of the Vedic Aryans, during the period of composition of the Rigveda, was the central part of this area: the Saptasindhu or Punjab, the Land of the Five Rivers bounded on the east by the Saraswati and on the west by the Indus. Their eastern horizon was western Uttar Pradesh and their western horizon was Afghanistan.

   The consensus on this point is so general that even in our *own* earlier book dealing with the Aryan invasion theory, where we have *not* yet analysed the Rigveda in detail, we have automatically assumed the Punjab to be the habitat of the Vedic Aryans during the period of the Rigveda.

   However, as we shall see in the course of our analysis, the habitat of the Vedic Aryans during the period was considerably to the *east* of the Punjab.

2. Secondly, after taking the Punjab to be the habitat of the Rigvedic Aryans, the matter is not left at that. A further slant is introduced into the interpretation of the geographical data in the Rigveda: it is automatically assumed, on the basis of an extraneous theory based on a misinterpretation of linguistic data, and without any basis within the Rigvedic data itself, that a movement from west to east is to be discerned in the Rigveda.

   Thus, western places within the horizon of the Rigveda are treated as places old and familiar to the Vedic Aryans, being their "early habitats"; while eastern places within the horizon of the Rigveda are treated as new and unfamiliar places with which the Vedic Aryans are "becoming acquainted".

   The same goes for places *outside* the horizon of the Rigveda (*i.e.* places *not* named in the Rigveda): places to the west of Afghanistan, not named in the Rigveda, are treated as places which have been "forgotten" by the Vedic Aryans; while places to the east of western Uttar Pradesh, not named in the Rigveda, are treated as places "still unknown" to the Vedic Aryans.

3. Thirdly, and as a direct corollary to the above, it is automatically assumed that there was a movement of place-names as well from west to east.

   There are three rivers named in the Rigveda to which this applies: the Saraswati, Gomati and Sarayu. The Saraswati in the Rigveda is the river to the *east* of the Punjab (flowing through Haryana) and the Gomati and Sarayu in the Rigveda are rivers to the west of the Punjab (western tributaries of the Indus). This is the general consensus, and it is confirmed by an examination of the references in the Rigveda.

   But a Saraswati (Haraxvaiti) and a Sarayu (Haroiiu) are also found in Afghanistan; and a Gomati and a Sarayu are found in northeastern Uttar Pradesh. Clearly, there has been a transfer of name, in the case of these three river-names, from one river to another.

   The logical procedure would be to suspend judgement, till further evidence is forthcoming, as to the locations of the rivers which originally bore these three names. A second, and slightly less logical, procedure, would be to automatically assume that the Rigvedic rivers originally bore all the three names, since the oldest recorded occurrence of the three names is in the Rigveda.

However, a west-to-east movement is assumed in respect of all three names, and consequently, the western-most rivers bearing the three names are taken to be the original bearers of those names.

4. Thus far, the distortion in interpretation and presentation of the geographical data in the Rigveda is still relatively mild. It is in fact too mild for some extremist scholars who would like to present a more definitive picture of a west-to-east movement into India.

Some of these scholars attempt to connect stray words in the Rigveda, *often words not even having any geographical context*, with places far to the west of the horizon of the Rigveda: an extreme example of this is the attempt to suggest that a root word *rip*-in the Rigveda indicates a subdued memory of the Rhipaean mountains: the Urals.

Some scholars, not satisfied with the idea that the Vedic Aryans *came* from the west, attempt to show that they were *still* in the west even during the period of composition of the Rigveda: the Saptasindhu, it is suggested by some, refers to seven rivers in Central Asia, and the Saraswati in the Rigveda is *not* the river of Haryana, but the river of Afghanistan.

There is even an extreme lunatic fringe which would like to suggest that the Ganga and Yamuna of the Rigveda are rivers in Afghanistan. A political "scholar", Rajesh Kochhar, as part of a concerted campaign to show that the events in the Ramayana took place in Afghanistan, transfers the entire locale of the epic to Afghanistan: "Ravana's Lanka can be a small island in the midst of river Indus… by Vindhyas is meant Baluch hills, and by sea the Lower Indus." He does this under cover of examining the *geography of the Rigveda, in his book, The Vedic People: Their* History and Geography (Orient Longman, New Delhi, 1999), where he decides that in the Ramayana (which he examines for the geography of the Rigveda), Saraswati is identified with Helmand and Ganga and Yamuna as its tributaries in the hilly areas of

Afghanistan. He makes this revolutionary discovery on the basis of a verse in the Valmiki Ramayana (2.65.6) where "Yamuna is described as surrounded by mountains".

This is the level to which "scholarship" can stoop, stumble and fall.

In this book, we will examine the geography of the Rigveda, *not* on the basis of interpretations of verses from the Valmiki Ramayana or the Hanuman Calisa, but on the basis of the actual geographical data within the hymns and verses of the Rigveda itself, under the following heads:

I. The Rigvedic Rivers.
II. The Evidence of River-names.
III. The Evidence of Place-names.
IV. The Evidence of Animal-names.
Appendix: The So-called Negative Evidence.

The Rigvedic Rivers

The rivers named in the Rigveda can be classified into five geographical categories:

1. *The Northwestern Rivers (i.e. western tributaries of the Indus, flowing through Afghanistan and the north):*

   Trstama (Gilgit)
   Susartu
   Anitabha
   Rasa
   Sveti
   Kubha (Kabul)
   Krumu (Kurrum)
   Gomati (Gomal)
   Sarayu (Siritoi)
   Mehatnu
   Svetyavarai
   Prayiyu (Bara)
   Vayiyu
   Suvastu (Swat)

Gauri (Panjkora)
Kusava (Kunar)

2. *The Indus and its minor eastern tributaries:*
Sindhu (Indus)
Susoma (Sohan)
Arjikiya (Haro)

3. *The Central Rivers (i.e. rivers of the Punjab):*
Vitasta (Jhelum)
Asikni (Chenab)
Parusni (Ravi)
Vipas (Beas)
Suturi (Satlaj)
Marudvrdha (Maruvardhvan)

4. *The East-central Rivers (i.e. rivers of Haryana):*
Saraswati
DRS advati/Hariyupiya/Yavyavati
Apaya

5. *The Eastern Rivers:*
Asmanvati (Assan, a tributary of the Yamuna)
Yamuna/Amsumati
Ganga/Jahnnvi

A few words of clarification will be necessary in the case of the identities of some of these rivers:

1. *Hariyupiya/Yavyavati*: Hariyupiya is another name of the Drsadvati: the river is known as Raupya in the Mahabharata, and the name is clearly a derivative of Hariyupiya.

   The Yavyavati is named in the same hymn and context as the Hariyupiya, and almost all the scholars agree that both the names refers to the same river.

   It is also possible that Yavyavati may be another name of the Yamuna. M.L. Bhargava, in his study of Rigvedic Geography, incidentally (*i.e.* without making such an identification) makes the following remarks: "The old beds of the ancient Drsadvati and the Yamuna... ran very close to each other... the two rivers appear to have come close at a place about three miles southwest of Chacharauli town, but diverged again immediately after... the Yamuna... then again ran southwestwards almost parallel to the Drsadvati, the two again coming about two miles close to each other near old Srughna......"

The battle described on the Hariyupiya-Yavyavati may therefore have taken place in the area between these rivers.

However, pending further evidence (of this identity of Yavyavati with the Yamuna), we must assume, with the scholars, that the Yavyavati is the same as the Hariyupiya.

2. *Jahnnvi*: Jahnnvi, which is clearly another name of the Ganga, is named in two hymns; and in both of them, it is translated by the scholars as something other than the name of a river: Griffith translates it as "Jahnu's children" (I.116.19) and "the house of Jahnu" (III.58.6).

The evidence, however, admits of only one interpretation:

a. Jahnnvi is clearly the earlier Rigvedic form of the latler word Jahnavi: the former word is not found after the Rigveda, and the latter word is not found in the Rigveda.

   The word clearly belongs to a class of words in the Rigveda which underwent a particular phonetic change in the course of time: *Jahnavi* in the Rigveda becomes *Jahnavi after* the Rigveda; *Brahmana* becomes *Brahmana* in the Rigveda itself (both words are found in the Rigveda while only the latter is found after the Rigveda); and the word *Pavaka* has already become *Pavaka* in the course of compilation of the Rigveda (only the latter form is found in the Rigveda, but according to B.K. Ghosh, "the evidence of the metres... clearly proves that the actual pronunciation of the word *Pavaka* must have been *Pavaka* in the Rigvedic age").

b. The word Jahnavi (and therefore also the word Jahnavi which has no independent existence, and for which there is no alternative source of information since it is found only twice in the Rigveda and nowhere outside it) literally means "daughter of Jahnu", and not "Jahnu's children" or "the house of Jahnu".

And the word Jahnavi (and therefore also Jahnavi as well) has only one connotation in the entire length and breadth of Sanskrit literature: it is a name of the Ganga.

c. One of the two references to the Jahnavi in the Rigveda provides a strong clue to the identity of this word: *Jahndvi (I. 116.19) is associated with the Simsumara* (I.116.18) or the Gangetic dolphin. The dolphin is not referred to anywhere else in the Rigveda.

The Mandala-wise distribution of the names of the rivers in the Rigveda is as follows:

Early Mandala I

Saraswati: I.3.10-12.

Middle Mandala I

Saraswati: I.89.3.

Sindhu: I.83.1.

General and Late Mandala I

Gauri: I.164.4.

Rasa: I. 112.12.

Sindhu: I.44.12; 122.6; 126.1; 186.5

(plus the references to the Sindhu in the refrain of the Kutsas in the last verses of I.94-96, 98, 100-103, 105-115).

Saraswati: I.13.9; 142.9; 164.49, 52; 188.8

Jahnavi: I.116.19.

Mandala II

Saraswati: II.1.11; 3.8; 30.8; 32.8; 41.16-18.

Mandala III

Vipas: III.33.1.

Sutudri: III.33.1.

Saraswati: III.4.8; 23.4; 54.13.

Drsadvati: III.23.4,

Apaya: III.23.4.

Jahnavi: III.58.6.

Mandala IV

Sarayu: IV.30.18.

Kusava: IV.18.8.

Sindhu: IV.30.12; 54.6; 55.3.

Parusni: IV.22.2.

Vipas: IV.30.11.

Rasa: IV.43.6.

Mandala V

Sarayu: V.53.9.

Kubha: V.53.9.

Krumu: V.53.9.

Anitabha: V.53.9.

Rasa: V.41.15; 53.9.

Sindhu: V.53.9.

Parusni: V.52.9.

Saraswati: V.5.8; 42.12; 43.11; 46.2,

Yamuna: V.52.17.

Mandala VI

Saraswati: VI.49.7; 50.12. 52.6; 61.1-7, 10-11, 13-14

Hariyupiya: VI.27.5.

Yavyavati: VI.27.6.

Ganga: VI.45.31.

Mandala VII

Asikni: VII.5.3.

Parusni: VII.18.8, 9.

Saraswati: VII.2.8; 9.5; 35.11; 36.6; 39.5; 40.3; 95.1-2, 4-6; 96.1, 3-6.

Yamuna: VII.18.19.

Mandala VIII

Gomati: VIII.24.30.

Svetyavarai: VIII.26.18.

Suvastu: VIII.19.37.

Prayiyu: VIII.19.37.

Vayiyu: VIII.19.37.

Sindhu: VIII.12.3; 20.24, 25; 25.14; 26.18, 72.7.

Arjikiya: VIII.7.29; 64.11.

Susoma: VIII.7.29; 64.11.

Asikni: VIII.20.25.

Parusni: VIII.75.15.

Saraswati: VIII.21.17, 18; 38.10; 54.4

Amsumati: VIII.96.13.

Rasa: VIII.72.13.

Mandala IX

Sindhu: IX.97.58.

Arjikiya: IX.65.23.

Saraswati: IX.5.8; 67.32; 81.4.

Rasa: IX.41.6.

Mandala X

Sarayu: X.64.9.

Gomati: X.75.6.

Mehatnu: X.75.6.

Kubha: X.75.6.

Krumu: X.75.6.

Sveti: X.75.6.

Rasa: X.75.6; 108.1, 2; 121.4.

Susartu: X.75.6.

Trstama: X.75.6.

Sindhu: X.64.9; 65.13; 66.11; 75.1, 3-4, 6-9.

Arjikiya: X.75.5.

Susoma: X.75.5.

Vitasta: X.75.5.

Marudvrdha: X.75.5.

Asikni: X.75.5.

Parusni: X.75.5.

Sutudri: X.75.5.

Saraswati: X.17.7-9; 30.12; 64.9; 65.1,13; 66.5; 75.5; 110.8; 131.5; 141.5; 184.2

Asmanvati: X.53.8.

Yamuna: X.75.5.

Ganga: X.75.5.

The Proof of River Names

The names of the rivers in the Rigveda have always formed the basis for any analysis of Rigvedic geography.

Let us examine the geographical picture presented by these river-names when the Mandalas are arranged in their chronological order.

As the Chinese put it, one picture is worth a thousand words. The graph gives us the entire geographical picture in a nutshell:

1. In the pre-Rigvedic period and the early part of the Early Period (Mandala VI), the Vedic Aryans were inhabitants of an area to the east of the Saraswati.
2. In the course of the Early Period (Mandalas III and VII), and the early part of the Middle Period (Mandala IV and the middle upa-mandalas), there was a steady expansion westwards.
3. Though there was an expansion westwards, the basic area of the Vedic Aryans was still restricted to the east in the Middle Period (Mandala II), and even in the early parts of the Late Period: Mandala V knows the western rivers from the Kubha (Kabul) in the north to the Sarayu (Siritoi) in the south, but its base is still in the east. Saraswati is still the most important river in the Mandala: it is referred to by the eponymous Rishi Atri (V.42.12; 43.11) who also refers to the Rasa (V.41.15). All the other references to the western rivers (Sarayu, Kubha, Krumu, Anitabha, Rasa, Sindhu) occur in a single verse (V.53.9) by a single Rishi Syavasva, obviously a very mobile Rishi who also refers

elsewhere to the Parusni (V.52.9) and even the Yamuna (V.52.17).

4. In the later part of the Late Period (Mandalas VIII, IX, X, and the general and late upa-mandalas) the Vedic Aryans were spread out over the entire geographical horizon of the Rigveda.

Let us examine the evidence of the river-names in greater detail under the following heads:

A. The Westward Expansion in the Bharata Period.

B. The Evidence of Some Key Rivers.

The Westward Expansion in the Bharata Period: The graph of the rivers clearly shows that there was a *westward* expansion of the Vedic Aryans from the time of Sudas onwards.

In the Early period, right from pre-Rigvedic times to the time of Sudas, the Vedic Aryans were settled in the area to the *east* of the Punjab: Mandala VI knows of no river to the west of the Saraswati.

However, in the Mandalas and upa-mandalas following Mandala VI, we find a steady movement westwards:

a. *Mandala III refers to the first two* rivers of the Punjab *from* the east: the Sutudri and the Vipas.

b. Mandala VII refers to the next two rivers of the Punjab *from the east*: the Parusni and Asikni.

c. The middle upa-mandalas of Mandala I contain the first reference to the Indus, but none to the rivers *west* of the Indus.

d. Mandala IV contains the first references to rivers *west* of the Indus.

If the case for the westward expansion is strong enough even merely from the evidence of the *names* of the rivers, it becomes unimpeachable when we examine the *context* in which these names appear in the hymns:

1. The Sutudri and Vipas are not referred to in a casual vein. They are referred to in a special context: hymn III.33 is a special ode to these two rivers by Vishvamitra in commemoration of a historical movement of the warrior bands of the Bharatas led by Sudas and himself, across the billowing waters of these rivers.

What is important is that this hymn is characterized *by the* Western scholars themselves as a historical hymn commemorating the migratory movement of the Vedic Aryans across the Punjab.,

But the Western scholars depict it as a movement from the west to the east: Griffith calls the hymn "a relic of the traditions of the Aryans regarding their progress eastward in the land of the Five Rivers".

However, an examination of the facts leaves no doubt that *the direction of this historical movement was from the east* to the west: the very distribution of the river-names in the Rigveda, as apparent from our graph of the rivers, makes this clear.

But there is more specific evidence within the hymns to show that this movement was from the east to the west:

Sudas is a descendant of Divodasa (VII.18.25), Divodasa is a descendant of Srnjaya (VI.47.22 and Griffith's footnotes to it) and Srnjaya is a descendant of Devavata (IV.15.4): Sudas is therefore clearly a remote descendant of Devavata.

Devavata established the sacrificial fire on the banks of the Apaya between the Saraswati and the Drsadvati (III.23.3-4). The Saraswati is to the *east* of the Vipas and Sutudri, and the Apaya and Drsadvati are *even further east.* No ancestor of Sudas is associated with any river to the west of the Saraswati.

The historical movement of the Vedic Aryans across the Sutudri and the Vipas, at the time of Sudas, can only be a *westward* movement.

2. The Parusni and Asikni, also, are not referred to in a casual vein: they also are referred to in a special context. The context is a major battle fought on the Parusni by the Bharatas under Sudas and Vasishtha (who replaced Vishvamitra as the priest of Sudas).

   The direction of the movement is crystal clear in this case as well: Sudas with his *earlier* priest Vishvamitra is *associated with the Sutudri and Vipas, and with his later* priest Vasishtha is associated with the Parusni which is to the west of the two other rivers.

But there is more specific evidence in Mandala VII about the direction of movement in this battle, which is the subject of various references throughout the Mandala:

a. The battle is fought on the Parusni and the enemies of Sudas (who is referred to here as the Puru) are described in VII.5.3 as the people of the Asikni. The Asikni is to the west of the Parusni hence it is clear *that the enemies of Sudas are fighting from the west* of the Parusni while Sudas is fighting from the *east*.

   Curiously, Griffith mistranslates the name of the river Asikni as "dark-hued", thereby killing two birds with one stone: the people of the Asikni become "the dark-hued races", thereby wiping out the sense of direction inherent in the reference, while at the same time introducing the racial motif

b. In VII.83.1, two of the tribes fighting against Sudas, the Prthus and the Parsus, are described as marching *eastwards* (*praca*) towards him.

   Griffith again mistranslates the names of the tribes as "armed with broad axes" and the word praca as "forward".

c. VII.6.5 refers indirectly to this battle by talking of the defeat of the tribes of Nahus (*i.e.* the tribes of the Anus and Druhyus who fought against Sudas) as follows: "Far, far away hath Agni chased the Dasyus, and, in the east, *hath turned the godless westward*". Sudas is therefore clearly pressing forward from the east.

3. The first references to the Indus are in the middle upa-mandalas (I.83.1) and in Mandala IV (IV.30.12; 54.6; 55.3). There is, perhaps, a westward movement indicated even in the very identity of the composers of the hymns which contain these references: I.83 is composed by Gautama Rahugana *who does not refer to any river west of the Indus*, while the references in Mandala IV are by his *descendants*, the Vamadeva Gautamas, who also refer to two rivers to the west of the Indus (IV.18.8; 30.18).

Thus, we have a clear picture of the westward movement of the Vedic Aryans from their homeland in the east of the Saraswati to the area to the west of the Indus, towards the end of the Early Period of the Rigveda: IV.30.18 refers to what is clearly the western-most point in this movement, a battle fought in southern Afghanistan "on yonder side of Sarayu".

The Evidence of Some Key Rivers: The key rivers in the Rigveda are:

a. The Indus to the west of the Five Rivers of the Punjab.

b. The Saraswati to the east of the Five Rivers of the Punjab.

c. The Ganga and Yamuna, the eastern-most rivers named in the Rigveda.

The evidence of these key rivers is extremely significant:

1. *The Indus and the Saraswati:* The word Sindhu in the Rigveda primarily means "river" or even "sea"; it is only secondarily a name of the Indus river: thus Saptasindhava can mean "seven rivers" but not "seven Induses".

   The relative insignificance of the Indus in the Rigveda is *demonstrated by the fact that the Indus is not mentioned* even once in the three oldest Mandalas of the Rigveda.

   Since the word Sindhu, in its meaning of "river", occurs frequently throughout the Rigveda, scholars are able to juggle with the word, often mistranslating the word Sindhu as "the Indus" even when it means "river".

   However, even this sophistry is not possible in the case of the three oldest Mandalas (VI, III and VII): the word Sindhu, except in eight verses, occurs only in the plural, and can be translated only as "rivers".

   In seven of the eight references, in which the word occurs in the singular, it clearly refers to some other "river" which is specified within the context of the reference itself:

   a. III.33.3, 5; 53.9: Vipas.

   b. VII.18.5: Parusni.

   c. VII.33.3: Yamuna.

   d. VII.36.6; 95.1: Saraswati.

In the eighth reference (VII.87.6) the word means "sea": the verse talks of the sun setting in the sea.

In sharp contrast, the Saraswati is referred to many times in the three oldest Mandalas. In fact, there are three whole hymns dedicated to it in these Mandalas: VI.61; VII.95, 96.

All in all, the Saraswati is referred to in nine Mandalas out of ten in the Rigveda (*i.e.* in all except Mandala IV, which represents the western-most thrust in the westward movement of the Vedic Aryans). The Indus is referred to in only six Mandalas (I, IV, V, VIII, IX, X); and in three of these (V, IX, X), the references to the Saraswati far outnumber the references to the Indus.

It is only in the *latest* parts of the Rigveda that the Indus overshadows the Saraswati:

a. In Mandala VIII, the references to the Indus outnumber the references to the Saraswati (by six verses to four).
b. In the general and late upa-mandalas of Mandala I, the Indus, but not the Saraswati, is enumerated with other deities in the refrain of the Kutsas which forms the last verse of nineteen out of their twenty-one hymns.
c. In Mandala X, although there are more references to the Saraswati, it is the Indus, and not the Saraswati, which is the main river lauded in the *nadistuti* (X.75), the hynm in Praise of the Rivers.

The Saraswati is so important in the *whole* of the Rigveda that it is worshipped as one of the Three Great Goddesses in the Apri-suktas of all the ten families of composers (being named in nine of them and implied in the tenth). The Indus finds no place in these Apri-suktas.

The contrast between the overwhelming importance of the Saraswati and the relative unimportance of the Indus is so striking, and so incongruous with the theory of an Aryan invasion from the northwest, that many scholars resort to desperate explanations to account for it: Griffith, in his footnote to VI.61.2, suggests that perhaps "Saraswati is also another name of Sindhu or the Indus".

2. *The Eastern Rivers*: The Ganga and the Yamuna are the two easternmost rivers named in the Rigveda. One or the other of these two rivers (either by these names, or by their other names, Jahnavi and Amsumati respectively) is named *in seven of the ten Mandalas of the Rigveda, including the* three oldest Mandalas (VI, III and VII).

By contrast, the Indus and its western tributaries, as we saw, are named in only six Mandalas, which do *not* include the three oldest Mandalas of the Rigveda. But even more significant than these bare statistics is the particular nature of the four references to the Ganga, the easternmost river of them all:

a. The *nadistuti* begins its enumeration of the rivers with the Ganga and moves westwards.

   Whether this circumstance in itself is a significant one or not is debatable; but while many scholars, without necessarily having arrived at any specific ideas about Rigvedic chronology or geography, find it important, certain others seek to deflect its importance, and even to dismiss the importance of the Ganga itself in the Rigveda:

   Griffith, in his footnote to X.75.5, takes pains to suggest that "the poet addresses first the most distant rivers. *Ganga*: the Ganges is mentioned, indirectly, in only one other verse of the *Rigveda*, and even there, the word is said by some to be the name of a woman. See VI.45.31."

b. The reference in VI.45.31 is definitely significant: the composer compares the height of a patron's generosity to the height of the wide bushes on the banks of the Ganga.

   This makes it clear that even in the oldest Mandala in the Rigveda, the Ganga is a familiar geographical landmark, whose features conjure up images which are very much a part of traditional idiomatic expression.

c. The reference in III.58.6. is infinitely more significant. Griffith translates the verse as follows: "Ancient your home, auspicious is your friendship: Heroes, your wealth is with the house of Jahnu."

   Here, not only does Griffith mistranslate Jahnavi as "the house of Jahnu", he compounds it with a further misinterpretation of the grammatical form:

   Jahnavyam is clearly "on (the banks of) the Jahnavi" on the lines of similar translations by Griffith himself in respect of other rivers: *Parusnyam* (V.52.9: on the banks of the Parusni), *Yamunayam* (V.52.17: on the banks of the Yamuna), *Drsadvatyam... Apayayam Sarasvatyam* (III.23.4: on the banks of the Drsadvati, Apaya and Saraswati).

The correct translation of III.58.6, addressed to the Asvins, is: "Your ancient home, your auspicious friendship, O Heroes, your wealth is on (the banks of the Jahnavi."

What is noteworthy is that the phrase *Puranamokah* "ancient home" is used in the second oldest Mandala in the Rigveda, in reference to the banks of the Ganga.

d. The reference in I.116.19 associates the Jahnavi with Bharadvaja, Divodasa and the Gangetic dolphin (all of whom are referred to in the earlier verse I.116.18). It is clear, therefore, that the river is specially associated with the oldest period of the Rigveda, the period of Mandala VI (which is also the only place, outside the *nadistuti*, where the Ganga is referred to by that name).

The evidence of the rivers in the Rigveda is therefore unanimous in identifying the area to the east of the Saraswati as the original homeland of the Vedic Aryans.

The Proof of Place-names

The evidence of place-names in the Rigveda, usually ignored, is secondary to the evidence of river-names. Nevertheless, significant evidence in this respect does exist; and an examination of this evidence fully corroborates the geographical picture derived from our examination of the evidence of the river-names.

The places named directly or indirectly in the Rigveda can be classified into five basic geographical regions, from west to east, on the basis of present-day terminology:

A. Afghanistan.

B. Punjab.

C. Haryana.

D. Uttar Pradesh.

E. Bihar.

To go into further detail:

Afghanistan: The only place-name from Afghanistan that we find in the Rigveda is "Gandhari", and this name occurs only once *in the whole of the Rigveda: in the general and late upa-mandalas* of Mandala I (I.126.7).

But, the name is also found indirectly in the name of a divine class of beings associated with Gandhara, the gandharvas, who are referred to in the following verses: I.22.14; 163.2; III.38.6; VIII.1.11; 77.5; IX.83.4; 85.12; 86.36; 113.3; X.10.4; 11.2; 85.40, 41; 123.4, 7; 136.6; 139.4, 6; 177.2.

As we can see, the gandharvas are referred to in 20 verses in 16 hymns, and *all except one* of these references are in the very latest parts of the Rigveda: Mandalas VIII, IX and X, and the general and late upa-mandalas of Mandala I.

The one reference in an early Mandala (III.38.6) is not even *an exception which proves the general rule, it is in itself strong* corroboration of the late provenance of the gandharvas in the Rigveda: III.38 is one of the six hymns (III.21, 30, 34, 36, 38-39) which are specifically named in the Aitareya Brahmana (VI.18) as being late interpolations into Mandala III. As we saw in an earlier chapter, these hymns have been incorporated into Mandala III in the eight-Mandala stage of the Rigveda, and are contemporaneous with the hymns in Mandala VIII.

Punjab: The Punjab is known in the Rigveda as "Saptasindhu".

There are other phrases in the Rigveda which mean "seven rivers"; but these do not constitute references to the Punjab, as seven is a number commonly applied in the Rigveda to various entities to indicate "all" or "many": thus we have references to the seven horses and seven wheels of the Sun's chariot, seven mouths of Brhaspati, seven Rishis, seven priests at the sacrifice, seven holy places, seven castles of the aerial demon destroyed by Indra, seven holy singers, seven rays of the sun, seven flames of Agni, seven male children, seven elements, seven Adityas, seven foundations of the sea, seven races of men, seven heads, seven hands, seven tongues, seven threads, seven germs within the seed, seven metres, seven tones, and so on repeated throughout the Rigveda. The following verses are instructive in this regard:

> *I.164.3: "The seven who on the seven-wheeled car are mounted, have horses, seven in tale, who draw them onward. Seven sisters utter songs of praise together, in whom the names of the seven cows are treasured."*
>
> *VIII.28.1: "The seven carry seven spears; seven are the splendours they possess, and seven the glories they assume."*

However, the word "Saptasindhu" in the Rigveda (and, for that matter, Hapta-Handu in the Avesta) is clearly a name for a specific region, which is generally and correctly identified by the scholars with the Punjab (the Land of the Five Rivers ensconsed between two more: the Indus in the west and the Saraswati in the east).

The Saptasindhu is referred to in the following verses:

I.32.12; 35.8; II. 12.3, 12; IV.28.1; VIII.54.4; 69.12; 96.1; IX.66.6; X.43.3; 67.12.

If Afghanistan is directly or indirectly referred to only in the Late Mandalas, the Punjab is referred to only in the Middle and Late Mandalas.

Haryana: The region in Haryana known as Kuruksetra or Brahmavarta in ancient times was considered to be the holiest place on earth.

However, neither the word Kurukshetra, nor the word Brahmavarta, is found in the Rigveda.

But the Rigveda refers to this holy region by other names or epithets: it is known as *vara A prthivya* (the best place on earth) or *nabha prthivya* (the navel or centre of the earth); and two specific places in this region are named in the hymns: Ilayaspada or Ilaspada, and Manusa.

These two places are clearly named in III.23.4: "He (Devavata) set thee in the best place on earth (*vara A prthivya*) in Ilayaspada, on an auspicious day. Shine brightly, Agni, on the Drsadvati, on Manusa on the Apaya, and on the Saraswati."

The above is not Griffith's translation: he translates Ilayaspada literally as "ILA's place" and misinterprets it as a reference to a fire-altar (*any* fire-altar); likewise, he translates Manusa as "man".

However, the meaning of the verse is clear. And we find detailed confirmation of the identity and location of these two places in the Mahabharata:

The Mahabharata, in its Tirthayatra Parva section of the Vana Parva, devotes one part (III.81, containing 178 verses) to the Kurukshetra region, and gives details about the locations of the major pilgrim centres in this region.

Within a span of 21 verses (III.81.53-73) it gives details about the locations of the particular places with which we are concerned here:

Mbh. III.81.53-54: "Then from there one should go to the world-famous Manusa... By bathing (in the lake) there, a man who is chaste and master of his senses is cleansed of all evils, and (he) glories in the world of heaven."

Mbh. III.81.55-56: "The distance of a cry east of Manusa, there is a river called Apaga, visited by the Siddhas;... when one Brahmin is fed there, it is as though a crore of them have been fed."

Mbh. III.81.62-64: "Thereupon one should go to the world-famous Saraka... There is also there the Abode-of-IlA Ford (Ilaspada): by bathing there and worshipping the ancestors and Gods, one suffers no misfortune..."

Mbh. III.81.73: "By bathing in the Drsadvati and satisfying the deities, a man finds the reward of a Land-of-the-fire (Agnistoma) and an Overnight-Sacrifice (Atiratra)."

M.L. Bhargava, in his brilliant research on the subject points out that these places are still extant: Manusa is still known as Manas, still a pilgrim centre, a village 3½ miles northwest of Kaithal; the Apaya or Apaga *tirtha* is still recognised at Gadli between Manas and Kaithal; and Ilayaspada or Ilaspada at Saraka is the present-day Shergadh, 2 miles to the southeast of Kaithal: "Manusa and Ilaspada were thus situated on the right and left sides of the Apaya, about 5½ miles apart, and in the tract between the Drsadvati and the Saraswati."

What is more, ILA, the deity worshipped at Ilayaspada or Ilaspada, is one of the three Great Goddesses (one, as we saw, is Saraswati) who are worshipped in the Apri-suktas of all the ten families of composers in the Rigveda, and specifically named in all ten of them. The third Great Goddess is Bharati (named in seven of the Apri-suktas, called by another name Mahi, in two others, and implied in the tenth), and M.L. Bhargava points out that Bharati is the deity of the still extant "Bharati-tirtha of Kopar or Koer in the middle of Kurukshetra, 22 miles east of Kaithal and 12 miles south-southwest of Thanesar".

It is clear that the three Great Goddesses, who are worshipped in the Apri-suktas of all the ten families of composers in the Rigveda, are deities of places in Kurukshetra: this is specifically stated in II.3.7 which refers to the "three high places" (*adhi sanusu* trisu) in "the centre of the earth" (*nabha prthivya* = Kurukshetra). The next verse names the three Goddesses, Bharati, ILA and Saraswati; and this is the only reference, outside the ten Apri-suktas, where these Goddesses are named together.

Haryana therefore clearly occupies a central position in the Rigveda in more ways than one.

The following are the verses which refer to these places in Haryana:

a. *Vara A prthivya:* III. 23.4; 53.11.

b. *Nabha prthivya:* I.143.4; II.3.7; III.5.9; 29.4; IX.72.7; 79.4; 82.3; 86.8 X.1.6.

c. *Ilaspada/Ilayaspada:* I. 128.1; II. 10.1; III. 23.4; 29.4; VI. 1.2; X. 1.6; 70.1; 91.1, 4; 191.1.

d. *Manusa:* I. 128.7; III. 23.4.

(As the word Manusa can also mean "man", it is difficult to recognize the references to the holy spot of that name in other occurrences of the word in the Rigveda. Hence it will be safe to cite only the two above verses, in which the references are indisputable.)

The references to Haryana are fairly distributed throughout the Rigveda, right from the oldest Mandala VI: VI.1.2 refers to Agni being established at Ilaspada. Even more significantly, III.23.4 tells us that Devavata (an *ancestor* of Divodasa of the oldest Mandala VI) established Agni at that spot. (Incidentally this appears to reflect an ancient custom of maintaining a perpetual fire, a custom still preserved by the Zoroastrians).

The references to these places are particularly profuse in *Mandala III, the Mandala which represents the commencement of the* westward expansion of the Vedic Aryans.

Uttar Pradesh: The Uttar Pradesh of the present-day is more or less equivalent to the land known in ancient literature as Aryavarta or Madhyadesa. Neither the word Aryavarta, nor the word Madhyadesa, is found in the Rigveda. Nor is there any direct reference in the hymns to any place in Uttar Pradesh.

But, the Anukramanis provide us with a priceless clue: hymns IX.96 and X.179.2 are composed by a late Bharata Rishi who (like many other composers in Mandala X and the corresponding parts of Mandala IX) attributes his compositions to his remote ancestor, Pratardana. He, accordingly, uses the epithets of his ancestor: in IX.96, the epithet is Daivodasi (son or descendant of Divodasa); and in X.179.2, the epithet is Kasiraja (King of KASI).

Pratardana was a king of KASI, which is in eastern Uttar Pradesh. This can only mean that the Bharata Kings of the Early Period of the Rigveda were Kings of Kasi; and, in the light of the other information in the Rigveda, the land of the Bharatas extended from KASI in the east to Kurukshetra in the west. The above conclusion is inescapable: the information in the Anukramanis cannot be rejected on any logical ground (short of suggesting a conspiracy theory), and it fits in with *all* the other evidence:

a. The evidence of Indian tradition outside the Rigveda which knows the land from KASI to Kurukshetra as Aryavarta or Madhyadesa throughout not only the Puranic and Epic literature (which, moreover, clearly describes this land as the original homeland in its traditional accounts, as noted by Pargiter), but even the rest of the Vedic literature. The geography even of the Yajurveda is clearly an Uttar Pradesh-centred geography. That the geography of the Rigveda is also the same has escaped the recognition of the scholars purely and simply because these scholars are *so mesmerised by the Aryan invasion theory, and so obsessed with the vital need to locate the Rigveda in the northwest and* the Punjab for the sheer survival of the theory, that their ideas and conclusions about the geography of the Rigveda are based on the tenets of this theory rather than on the material within the hymns of the text.

   It may be noted that all the pilgrim-centres of Hinduism are located to the east of Haryana. There is no Hindu pilgrim centre worthy of particular note in the Punjab or the northwest. This also discounts the possibility that the oldest and hoariest text of Hinduism could have been composed in those parts.

b. The evidence of the rivers in the Rigveda, particularly the evidence of the references to the Ganga.

c. The evidence of the other place-names in the Rigveda, particularly the reference to Bihar.

Bihar: The most historically prominent part of ancient Bihar was Magadha, also known as Kikata.

While the word Magadha is not found in the Rigveda, the word Kikata is found in III.53.14. The reference is to Sudas's battle with the Kikatas and their king Pramaganda (whose name is connected by many scholars with the word Magadha = Pra-*maganda*).

This clinches the origin of the Bharatas in Uttar Pradesh: the expansion of the Bharatas under Sudas took place in two directions, eastwards into Bihar, and westwards across the Saraswati into the Punjab. Clearly, only a homeland in the area between KASI and Kurukshetra fits into this picture.

The evidence of the place-names in the Rigveda can be summarized as follows:

The Proof of Animal-names

The evidence of the river-names and the place-names is so clear that it does not really require further confirmation.

However, we may note the evidence of the animals named in the Rigveda, which tends to further confirm the eastern provenance of the Rigvedic Aryans.

There are many animals which are peculiar to India: that is, animals found only in India, or only in India and places cast (such as Southeast Asia), or, if they are found elsewhere, only in places (such as the interior of Africa) which cannot have any relevance to the history of the Vedic Aryans or the Indo-Europeans.

The following are examples of some such prominent animals named in the Rigveda:

1. *The Elephant (Elaphus Maximus: ibha, varana, hastin, srni):*

   I.64.7; 84.7; 140.2; IV.4.1; 16.14; VI.4.5; 20.8; VIII.33.8; IX.57.3; X.40.4; 106.6.

2. *The Buffalo (Bubalus Bibalus: mahisa):*

   I.64.7; 95.9; 121.2; 141.3; III.46.2; IV. 18.11; V.29.7, 8; VI.8.4; 17.11; VII.44.5; VIII.12.8; 35.7-9; 69.15; 77.10; IX.33.1; 69.3; 73.2; 86.40; 87.7; 92.6; 95.4; 96.6, 18, 19; 97.41; 113.3. X.8.1; 28.10; 45.3; 60.3; 65.8; 66.10; 106.2; 123.4; 128.8; 140.6; 189.2.

3. *The Indian Bison (Bibos Gaurus: gaura):*

   I.16.5; IV.21.8; 58.2; VII.69.6; 98.1; VIII.4.3; 45.24; X.51.6; 100.2.

4. *The Peacock (Pavo Cristatus: mayura):*

   I.191.14; III.45.1; VIII.1.25.

5. *The Chital or Spotted Deer (Axis Axis: prsati):*

   I.37.2; 39.6; 64.8; 85.4, 5; 87.4; 89.7; 162.21; 186.8; II.34.3, 4; 36.2; III.26.4, 6; V.42.15; 55.6.; 57.3; 58.6; 60.2; VII.40.3; VIII.7.28.

These animals are found mentioned in references throughout the different periods of the Rigveda.

Further, the names of all these animals are purely Aryan or Indo-European: the elephant, for example has four names, each of which has a purely "Aryan" etymology.

And the references to these animals are not casual ones. It is clear that the animals form an intimate part of the idiomatic lore and traditional imagery of the Rigveda: the spotted deer, for example, are the official steeds of the chariots of the Maruts; and the name of the buffalo (like that of the bull, boar and lion) serves as an epithet, applied to various Gods, signifying great strength and power. The Gods approaching the place of sacrifice to drink the libations evoke the image of thirsty bisons converging on a watering place in the forest. The outspread tails or manes of Indra's horses evoke the image of the outspread plumes of the peacock's tail.

The elephant is referred to not only in its wild form, with the image of a wild elephant crashing through the forest, uprooting the trees and bushes in its path, but in its fully domesticated form as well: one verse (X.40.4) refers to wild elephants being tracked by hunters; another (IV.4.1) refers to a mighty king with his (retinue of) elephants; another (IX.57.3) refers to an elephant (perhaps a temple elephant?) being decked up by the people; and yet another (VI.20.8) refers to Tugra with his (garrisons of) elephants in what is clearly a reference to a battle. (In IV.4.1 and VI.20.8, Griffith mistranslates *ibha* as "attendants" or "servants".)

In sharp contrast to these intimate references to typically Indian animals are the references to an animal which is restricted to the extreme northwest: the bactrian camel of Afghanistan and beyond.

This camel, *ustra*, is referred to only in the following verses:

I.138.2; VIII.4.7; 5.37; 46.22, 31.

The distribution of these references is restricted only to hymns belonging to the Late Period. It is clear that this distribution indicates an expanding horizon of the Vedic Aryans; and this is not the expanding horizon of a people from outside India expanding into India, but of a people from within India expanding out into the northwest.

The significance of the late "appearance" of the camel in the Rigveda may be expressed in the words of a modern Western scholar, a staunch and even fanatical supporter of the Aryan invasion theory: Michael Witzel, in referring to the geography of Mandala VIII tells us that "*Book 8* concentrates on the whole of the west of camels, *mathra* horses, wool sheep. It frequently mentions the Sindhu, but also the Seven Streams, mountains and snow." This book also "lists numerous tribes that were unknown to other books." Witzel further notes that "camels appear (8.5.37-39) together with the Iranian name *Kasu* 'small' (Hoffman 1975), or with the suspicious name Tirindra and the Parsu (8.6.46).

The combination of camels (8.46.21, 31), *mathra* horses (8.46.23) and wool, sheep and dogs (8.56.3) is also suggestive: the borderlands (including Gandhara) have been famous for wool and sheep, while dogs are treated well in Zoroastrian Iran but not in South Asia."

Although Witzel (whose writings we will be dealing with in an appendix to this book) tries generally to twist and distort the information in the Rigveda so as to demonstrate a movement into India from the northwest, his reaction to the information in Mandala VIII (a late Mandala, although Witzel does not admit it) unwittingly, but clearly, shows the expanding horizon of a people from "South Asia" coming into contact with "the borderlands (including Gandhara)".

The combined evidence of river-names, place-names and animal-names gives us a single unanimous verdict: the Vedic Aryans were inhabitants of the interior of India, and their direction of expansion was from the east to the west and northwest.

The So-called Negative Proof

The evidence of the Rigveda is so clear that it brooks no other conclusion except that the Vedic Aryans expanded from the interior of India to the west and northwest. However, there are certain points, raised by the scholars, which claim to negate such a conclusion and to establish that the Vedic Aryans were in fact newcomers into India who were still floundering around in the north-western outskirts of the land.

We will examine these points under the following heads:

A. Tigers and Rice.

B. Soma.

Tigers and Rice: According to the scholars, the Rigveda does not mention either the tiger or rice; and this is significant, since it shows that the Vedic Aryans at that time were still unacquainted with that common Indian animal and that common Indian cereal.

In delineating the parts of India which had become "known" to the incoming Aryans at the time of the Rigveda, Michael Witzel (whom we have already referred to earlier) declares: "It is also important to note that the tiger and rice are still unknown to the RV, which excludes the areas, roughly speaking, east of Delhi: the Ganga-Yamuna Doab and the tracts of land South of it."

Let us examine the logic:

The Tiger: It is "important to note" that the scholars claim that the Vedic Aryans were unacquainted with the tiger right from the time of composition of the earliest hymn of the Rigveda to the time of composition of the latest hymn (in whatever chronological order the hymns are arranged).

But what these scholars deliberately ignore, in their desperate attempt to grab at whatever straw they think is available, is that the tiger is not restricted to the area "east of Delhi": the tiger was a very common animal in the western Punjab (the seals of Harappa and Mohenjodaro contain many pictorial representations of the tiger, even when they do not have a single one of the lion) and *in fact, the tiger in ancient times was found as far to the northwest as northern Afghanistan, northern Iran and parts of Central Asia.*

Even if we follow the logic of the invasion-theorists and assume that the Vedic Aryans migrated into India from the northwest, these Vedic Aryans should have been very long familiar with the tiger well before they even glimpsed their very first elephant, spotted deer, peacock or Indian bison. It is clearly *impossible* that the tiger could have been "still unknown" to the Vedic Aryans who were so intimately familiar with all these animals, and whose area of acquaintance (even assuming that they came from outside) extended upto Bihar (Kikata) in the east.

Incidentally, when the tiger is mentioned in later texts (including the other Veda Samhitas), it has a purely "Aryan" name: *vyaghra,* which not only has a purely Indo-European etymology, but also has cognate forms in Iranian *babr* and Armenian *vagr.* And even in the Rigveda, while the word *vyaghra* does not occur even once in the text, it occurs in the name of one of the composers of IX.97: Vyaghrapada Vasishtha.

That the tiger is not mentioned even *once* in the whole of the Rigveda certainly does call for an explanation, but non-familiarity with the animal cannot be that explanation under any circumstance. Possible explanations are:

a. There was some kind of a ritual taboo on the mention of the tiger during the period of composition of the Rigvedic hymns, OR

b. The word *simha* (lion) which occurs in the Rigveda in the following references, stood for both the lion as well as the tiger (according to American archaeologist Mark Kenoyer, it probably stood for the tiger *rather* than for the lion):

   I.64.8; 95.5; 174.3; III.2.11; 9.4; 26.5; IV.16.4; V.15.3; 74.4; 83.3; VII.18.17; IX.89.3; 97.28; X.28.4, 10; 67.9.

Of these two possible explanations, the first is a more likely one.

***Rice*:** Rice is not mentioned in the Rigveda, *but nor is any other* specific grain: neither wheat, nor millet, *nor even barley* (the word *yava,* like the word *dhana/dhanya,* in the Rigveda is accepted by most of the scholars to be a reference to "grain" in general, and not to barley as it does in later times. The word is cognate to the Lithuanian word *javai* which also means "grain", the Lithuanian word for barley being *mieziai*). All these grains are known, to have been cultivated in the Indus sites, but not one of them is mentioned by name in the Rigveda which knows of lands as far east as Bihar (Kikata).

Yet not only do the scholars deduce that rice in particular was "unknown" to the Vedic Aryans, because it is not mentioned by name in the hymns; they even draw far-reaching and fundamental historical conclusions from this omission. And yet, is it true that *rice was unknown to the Vedic Aryans? And, more to the point, do these scholars themselves sincerely believe that this was the case?*

The Rigveda clearly refers to certain culinary preparations made from rice: *apupa and purolns* (varieties of rice-cakes) and *odana* (rice-gruel).

These are referred to in the following verses:

Apupa: III. 52.1, 7; VIII. 91.2; X. 45.9.

Purolas: I. 162.3; III. 28.1-6; 41.3; 52.2-6, 8; IV. 24.5; 32.16; VI. 23.7; VII. 18.6; VIII. 2.11; 31.2.

Odana: VIII. 69.14; 77.6, 10.

That these were rice preparations is something that cannot be easily denied outright. Even Witzel himself, elsewhere, somewhat qualifies, although negatively, his firm assertion that rice was "still unknown" to the Vedic Aryans: "Unless the Rgvedic words *(brahma)-udana and Purolas* mean a certain rice dish, as they do later on, cultivation and ritual use of rice first appear in the Atharvaveda..."

Griffith translates the words *apupa* and *Purolas* by neutral words like "cake", "sacrificial cake" and "me al-cake", and even suggests in one place (in his footnote to VIII.2.3, in reference to the word *yava*) that the sacrificial cake is "made of barley-meal".

But in his footnote to 1.40.3, he also admits that "the five-fold gift" offered to Agni consists of "an offering of grain, gruel, curdled milk, *rice-cake*, and curds".

And he clearly translates the word *odana* in VIII.77.6, 10 as "brew of rice" and "brew of rice and milk".

Soma: In the case of Soma, the argument is to the opposite effect: according to the scholars, the Soma plant was a species of Ephedra found in the extreme north-western parts of India extending to Central Asia and beyond. Species of Ephedra found further eastwards were not capable of yielding the kind of juice described in the Rigveda.

Hence, the fact that the ritual use of Soma formed such an integral part of the Rigvedic religion in every period of the text (and that this feature is shared with the Iranians) proves that the Vedic Aryans entered India from the northwest, bringing the Soma plant and cult with them. This is the argument. But is this argument either valid or logical, or in keeping with the facts of the case? One undeniable fact is that the Soma plant *was* a native of the extreme northwestern and northern regions: all the references to the sources of Soma, in the Rigveda, make it very clear that the plant grew in the mountains of Kashmir, Afghanistan, and the extreme northwest of the Punjab.

But, arguing, solely from this fact, that the Vedic Aryans, who used Soma prominently in their rituals, *also* came from the northwestern parts, bringing the plant with them, is like arguing that the Irish people, to whom potatoes constitute a staple food, came from America to Ireland, bringing the potato plant with them. Or, that the medieval Europeans, who used Indian spices in their culinary diet, went to Europe from India, taking the spices with them. Clearly, the use of a particular plant by a particular people cannot be the basis for historical conclusions about the *geographical origins of that people, unless this is demonstrated by their traditional understanding of their association with the plant in question.*

And the evidence in the Rigveda shows that:

1. The actual Soma-growing areas were distant and unknown to the Vedic Aryans in the early parts of the Rigveda, and became known to them only later after they expanded westwards.
2. The Soma plant and its ritual were not originally known to the Vedic Aryans and their priests, but were introduced to them in very early times by priests from the Soma-growing areas.
3. The expansion of the Vedic Aryans (and, by a chain of events, *the dispersion of the Indo-Europeans*, as we shall see in later chapters) into the west and northwest was a direct consequence of their quest for Soma.

The detailed evidence is as follows:

1. Soma is regarded as growing in distant areas: this area is so distant that it is constantly identified with the heavens (IV.26.6; 27.3, 4; VIII.100.8; IX.63.27; 66.30; 77.2;.86.24, etc.).

The only specific thing known about the place of origin of Soma is that it grows on mountains (I.93.6; III.48.2; V.43.4; 85.2;

IX.18.1; 62.4; 85.10; 95.4; 98.9, etc.). Nothing more specific is mentioned in the Family Mandalas or the early upa-mandalas of Mandala I.

The area of Soma is clearly not part of the Vedic area (nor is *there even the slightest hint anywhere in the Rigveda that it ever* was): it is constantly referred to as being far away (IV.26.6; IX.68.6; X.11.4; 144.4). This area is also known as the "dwelling of Tvastr" (IV.18.3); and this is what the scholars have to say about Tvastra: "Tvastra is one of the obscurest members of the Vedic pantheon. The obscurity of the concept is explained... (by) HILLEBRANDT (who) thinks Tvastra was derived from a mythical circle outside the range of the Vedic tribes."

Soma is mythically reported to be brought by an eagle to the Vedic people, and even to their Gods, from its place of origin:

> *I.80.2; 93.6; III.43.7; IV.18.13; 26.4-7; 27.3, 4; V.45.9; VI.20.6; VIII.82.9; 100.8; IX.68.6; 77.2; 86.24; 87.6; X.11.4; 99.8; 144.4, 5.*

That this place of origin is alien to the Vedic people is clear from the fact that this eagle is reported to have to hurry (IV.26.5) to escape the guardians of Soma, who are described as attacking the eagle (IV.27.3) to prevent it from taking the Soma away.

> *"Tvastra is especially the guardian on Soma, which is called 'the mead of Tvastra' (I.117.22)" and Indra is described as conquering Tvastra in order to obtain the Soma.*
>
> *In his footnote to 1.43.8, Griffith refers to "the people of the hills who interfere with the gathering of the Soma plant which is to be sought there".*

The Family Mandalas are generally ignorant about the exact details of the Soma-growing areas. Whatever specific information is there is in the later Mandalas:

> *The prime Soma-growing areas are identified in VIII.64.11 as the areas near the Susoma and Arjikiya rivers (the Sohan and Haro, northeastern tributaries of the Indus, in the extreme north of the Punjab and northwest of Kashmir) and Saryanavan (a lake in the vicinity of these two rivers). In VIII.7.29, the reference is to the Susoma and Arjika (in the masculine gender,*

> *signifying mountains; while the rivers of these names are in the feminine gender), clearly the mountains which gave rise to the Susoma and Arjikiya rivers, alongwith Saryanavan (which also appears in X.35.2 as a mountainous area, perhaps referring to the mountains surrounding the lake of the same name).*

In another place, the best Soma is said to be growing on the Mujavat mountains. The Mujavat tribes are identified (Atharvaveda V-XXII-5, 7, 8, 14) with the Gandharis. These mountains are therefore also in the extreme north of the Punjab and in adjacent parts of Afghanistan.

That Gandhari (Afghanistan) in the Rigveda is associated with Soma is clear from the specific role assigned in the Rigveda to the Gandharva or gandharvas (mythical beings associated in the Rigveda with that region). In the words of Macdonell: "Gandharva is, moreover, in the RV often associated (chiefly in the ninth book) with Soma.

He guards the place of Soma and protects the races of the gods (9.83.4; cp. 1.22.14). Observing all the forms of Soma, he stands on the vault of heaven (9.85.12). Together with Parjanya and the daughters of the sun, the Gandharvas cherish Soma (9.113.3). Through Gandharva's mouth the gods drink their drought (AV.7.73.3). The MS (3.8.10) states that the Gandharvas kept the Soma for the gods... It is probably as a jealous guardian of Soma that Gandharva in the RV appears as a hostile being, who is pierced by Indra in the regions of air (8.66.5) or whom Indra is invoked to overcome (8.1.11). ... Soma is further said to have dwelt among the Gandharvas..."

All these places are found mentioned only in the later Mandalas (*i.e.* after the westward expansion of the Vedic Aryans):

Arjika/Arjikiya:

VIII. 7.29; 64.11;

IX. 65.23; 113.2;

X. 75.5.

Susoma/Susoma:

VIII. 7.29; 64.11;

X. 75.5.

Saryanavan:

I. 84.14;

VIII. 6.39; 7.29; 64.11;

IX. 65.22: 113.1;

X. 35.2.

Mujavat:

X. 34.1.

Gandhari:

I. 126.6.

2. The special priests of the Vedic Aryans (*i.e.* of the Bharatas) were the Angirases, Vasishtha and Vishvamitra. These priests, however, are *not* specially associated with the Soma plant and ritual.

The nine priestly families are divided into two distinct categories: the Kasyapas and Bhrgus, who are very specially associated with Soma, and the other seven families which are not. The Bharatas separate the two groups.

Clearly, the Kasyapas and Bhrgus are the two families which are specially associated with Soma. And these are the two families which were originally alien to the Vedic Aryans: the Kasyapas are associated throughout Indian tradition with Kashmir (Kasyapa-mira); and the Bhrgus, except for one branch consisting of Jamadagni and his descendants, are associated with the enemies of the Vedic Aryans living to their north and northwest (as we shall see in greater detail in our chapter on the Indo-Iranian homeland). Both these families are thus directly associated with the Soma-growing areas to the north and northwest of the Vedic Aryan territory.

It is not only in the statistical analysis of the number of verses to Soma that the special relationship shared by these two families with the Soma plant and ritual becomes apparent; the joint testimony of the Avesta and the Rigveda also confirms this special relationship. As Macdonell puts it: "The RV and the Avesta even agree in the names of ancient preparers of Soma; Vivasvat and Trita Aptya on the one hand, and Vivanhvant, Athwya and Thrita on the other." According to the Avesta, the first preparer of Soma was Vivanhvant (Vivasvat), the second was Athwya (Aptya) and the third was Thrita (Trita). Vivasvat in the Rigveda is generally the Sun (note: in many references, the sky is referred to as "Vivasvan's dwelling", which may be compared with the reference to Ausija's dwelling or abode in our discussion on the word Ausija in our chapter on the chronology of the Rigveda); but Vivasvat is also the name of the father of two persons: Yama and Manu. In the Avesta also, Vivanhvant is the father of Yima.

Both Vivasvat and Yama Vaivasvata are identified in the Rigveda as Bhrgus and Manu Vaivasvata is identified in the Anukramanis of VIII.29 with Kasyapa.

Trita Aptya is not clearly identified with any family in the Rigveda, but it is significant that he is described by the Grtsamadas (Kevala *Bhrgus*) in II.11-19 as belonging to "our party" (Griffith's translation). The Kasyapas are indeed very closely associated with Soma: not only are 70.60% of the verses composed by them dedicated to Soma Pavamana, but the Apri-sukta of the Kasyapas is the only Apri-sukta dedicated to Soma (all the other nine Apri-suktas are dedicated to Agni).

But while the Kasyapas *are* exclusive Soma priests, the fact is that they entered the Rigveda at a late stage: they became exclusive Soma priests in the period *following* the expansion of the Vedic Aryans into the Soma-growing areas.

The identification of the Bhrgus with Soma is deeper, older and more significant: it is clear that the Soma plant originated among the Bhrgus of the northwest, and it is they who introduced the plant and its rituals to the Vedic Aryans and their priests:

a. The word Soma, which occurs thousands of times in the hymns of the Rigveda, is found in the name of only one composer Rishi: Somahuti Bhargava.
b. The word PavamAna, which occurs more than a hundred times in the Soma Pavamana Mandala, is found only once outside Mandala IX: in VIII.101.14 composed by Jamadagni Bhargava.
c. Both the Rigveda and the Avesta, as we have seen, are unanimous in identifying Bhrgus as the earliest preparers of Soma.
d. The overwhelming majority of the hymns to Soma in Mandala IX, as we have seen in our chapter on the

chronology of the Rigveda, are composed by Rishis belonging to the Middle and Late Periods of the Rigveda: the only two hymns (other than hymns by Bhrgus) which can be ascribed (and *only*, as we have pointed out, for the lack of clear contrary evidence) to. Rishis belonging to the period of the three Early Family Mandalas are IX.71 (ascribed to Rsabha Vaishvamitra of Mandala III) and IX.90 (ascribed to Vasishtha Maitravaruni of Mandala VII).

However, fourteen hymns are ascribed to Bhrgu Rishis. Of these, two which are ascribed to Jamadagni Bhargava (IX.62, 65) of the period of Mandala III, are clearly composed by his descendants; but the remaining twelve hymns are ascribed to remote ancestral Bhrgu Rishis of the pre-Rigvedic period, who are already ancient and mythical even in the oldest Mandalas: Vena Bhargava (IX.85), Usana Kavya (IX.87-89) and KavI Bhargava (IX.47-49, 75-79).

The oldest Soma hymns in the Rigveda therefore appear to be composed exclusively by Bhrgus.

e. The Rigveda clearly indicates that it was the Bhrgus who introduced Soma to the Vedic Aryans, and to their Gods and priests. According to at least three references (I.116.12; 117.22; 119.9), the location or abode of Soma was a secret; and this secret was revealed to the Asvins by Dadhyanc, an ancient Bhrgu Rishi, already mythical in the Rigveda, and older than even Kavi Bhargava and Usana Kavya. Dadhyanc is the son of Atharvana, and grandson of the eponymous Bhrgu.

Even the symbolism inherent in the eagle who brought Soma to the Vedic Aryans probably represents this role of the Bhrgus: according to Macdonell, "the term eagle is connected with Agni Vaidyuta or lightning (TB 3, 10, 5; cp. 12.1)"; and likewise, "BERGAIGNE thinks there can hardly be a doubt that *Bhrgu* was originally a name of fire, while KUHN and BARTH agree in the opinion that the form of fire it represents is lightning".

The evidence in the Rigveda thus clearly shows that the Vedic Aryans did not come from the Soma-growing areas bringing the Soma plant and rituals with them: the Soma plant and rituals were brought to the Vedic Aryans from the Soma-growing areas of the northwest by the Bhrgus, priests of those areas.

3. The expansion of the Vedic Aryans into the west and northwest was a direct consequence of their quest for Soma:

The westward movement commenced with the crossing of the Sutudri and Vipas by Vishvamitra and the Bharatas under Sudas, described in hymn III.33; and the fifth verse of the hymn clarifies both the direction and purpose of this crossing.

Griffith translates III.33.5 (in which Vishvamitra addresses the rivers) as: "Linger a little at my friendly bidding; rest, Holy Ones, *a moment in your journey..."; but he clarifies in his footnote: "At* my friendly bidding: according to the Scholiasts, Yaska and Sayana, the meaning of *me vacase somyaya* is 'to my speech importing the Soma'; that is, the object of my address is that I may cross over and gather the Soma-plant."

This crossing, and the successful foray into the northwest, appears to have whetted the appetite of Sudas and the Bharatas for conquest and expansion: shortly afterwards, the Vishvamitra perform an *Asvamedha* sacrifice for Sudas, described in III.53.11: "Come forward Kusikas, and be attentive; let loose Sudas's horses to win him riches. East, west, and north, let the king slay the foeman, then at earth's choicest place (*vara A prthivya* = Kurukshetra) perform his worship."

While some expansion took place towards the east as well (Kikata in III.53.14), the main thrust of the expansion is clearly towards the west and northwest: the first major battle in this long drawn out western war is on the Yamuna, the second (the Dasarajna) on the Parusni, and the final one in southern Afghanistan beyond the Sarayu.

While Sudas was still the leader of the Bharatas in the battles on the Yamuna and the Parusni, the battle beyond the Sarayu appears to have taken place under the leadership of his remote descendant Sahadeva in the Middle Period of the Rigveda.

Sahadeva's son (referred to by his priest Vamadeva in IV.15.7-10), who also appears to have been a participant. in the above battle beyond the Sarayu, may have been named Somaka in commemoration of earlier conquests of the Soma-growing areas of eastern Afghanistan by his father Sahadeva.

The Historical Legecy of the Vedic Aryans

We have examined the chronology and geography of the Rigveda, and seen the expansion of the Vedic Aryans from their original, homeland in the east to the west and northwest.

But a basic question that remains is: who exactly were these Vedic Aryans and what was their historical identity?

According to the scholars, the Vedic Aryans were a branch of the Indo-Iranians of Central Asia; and these Indo-Iranians were themselves a branch of the Indo-Europeans of South Russia.

That is, the Indo-Europeans were originally a people in South Russia; one branch of these Indo-Europeans, the Indo-Iranians, migrated towards the east and settled down in Central Asia; much later, one branch of these Indo-Iranians, the Indo-aryans, migrated southeastwards into the northwestern parts of India; and thus commenced the story of the Aryans in India.

These Indo-aryans are called Vedic Aryans since they composed the hymns of the Rigveda during the period of their earliest settlements in the northwest and the Punjab, before they came into contact with other parts of India.

These Vedic Aryans were faceless and anonymous groups of people, whose only historical identity is that they were the ultimate ancestors of the different tribes, peoples, priestly families and royal dynasties found throughout the Sanskrit texts.

But all this is the version of the scholars. As we have already seen, the scholars are wrong in their fundamental proposition that the Vedic Aryans moved into India from the northwest. They are also wrong in their conclusions about the historical identity of the Vedic Aryans.

The Vedic Aryans were not the ultimate ancestors of the different tribes and peoples found in the Sanskrit texts: they were in fact just one of these tribes and peoples. They have a definite historical identity: the Vedic Aryans were the Purus of the ancient texts.

And, in fact, the particular Vedic Aryans of the Rigveda were one section among these Purus, who called themselves Bharatas.

F.E. Pargiter, the eminent Western analyst of India's traditional history, came close to making this identification when he remarked that "the bulk of the Rigveda was composed in the great development of Brahmanism that arose under the successors of king Bharata who reigned in the upper Ganges-Jumna doab and plain".

And when he noted, in referring to the kings identified in the Puranas as the kings of North Pancala, that "they and their successors are the kings who play a prominent part in the Rigveda".? Unfortunately, Pargiter went off at a tangent, consciously trying to identify the presence of Aryans, Dravidians and Austrics among the tribes and dynasties in the Puranas; and thereby missed out on clinching the identification which is so crucial to an understanding. of Vedic, Indian and Indo-European history.

We will examine the evidence, identifying the Purus, and among them the Bharatas, as the Vedic Aryans of the Rigveda, under the following heads:

The Kings and Tribes in the Rigveda

We will examine the evidence under the following heads:

The Kings in the Rigveda: As we have seen in our chapter on the chronology of the Rigveda, the predominant dynasty in the Rigveda is the dynasty of Devavata, one of the descendants of the ancient king Bharata.

The kings in this dynasty, as we have already seen, are:

Devavata	Srnjaya
Vadhryasva	Divodasa
Pratardana	Pijavana
Devasravas	Sudas
Sahadeva	Somaka

These kings are Bharatas, but they are also Purus: according to the Puranas, *the Bharatas are a branch of the Purus*; and this is confirmed in the Rigveda, where both Divodasa (I.130.7) and Sudas (I.63.7) are called Purus, and where the Bhārata composer Parucchepa Daivodasi repeatedly speaks as a Puru (I.129.5; 131.4).

Some other names of kings in the Rigveda who appear in the Puranic lists as Puru kings (some belonging to the Bharata dynasty of Devavata, and some not) are:

AjamIlha (IV.44.6).

Dhvasra/Dhvasanti and Purusanti (I.112.23; IX.58.3). (Susanti and Purujati of the Puranic lists.)

Mudgala (X.102.2, 5, 6, 9).

Rksa (VIII.68.15, 16; 74.4, 13).

Srutarvan (VIII.74.4, 13; X.49.5).

Vidathin (IV.16.13; V.29.11).

Santanu (X.98.1, 3, 7).

Kusika (III.26.1).

Incidentally, the other Veda Samhitas also refer to the following prominent Puru kings:

Bhimasena of KASI (Yajurveda, Kathaka Samhita, VII.1.8)

Pariksita I (Atharvaveda, XX.127.7-10)

Pratipa (Atharvaveda, XX.129.2)

Vicitravirya (Yajurveda, Kathaka Samhita, X.6)

Dhrtarashtra (Yajurveda, Kathaka Samhita, X.6)

The only other prominent dynasty in the Rigveda is the Trksi dynasty of Mandhata, identifiable as a branch of the Iksvakus of the Puranas. The kings of this dynasty, as we have already seen, are:

Mandhata

Purukutsa

Trasadasyu

These kings are not Purus; but they are accorded a special position in the Rigveda only because of the special aid given by them to the Purus. According to the Puranas, Mandhata's father was an Iksvaku king, but his mother was a Puru, being the daughter of a Puru king Matinara. Moreover, the Puranas record that the Druhyus, who, in the earliest pre-Rigvedic period, were inhabitants of the Punjab, were pressing eastwards onto the Purus. In this context, Mandhata moved westwards, confronted the invading hordes of Druhyus, defeated them, and drove them out into Afghanistan and beyond.

The Rigveda itself records (I.63.7; VI.20.10) that Indra, through Purukutsa, rendered help to the Purus in a war against the Dasa tribes; and VII.19.3 refers to Indra aiding the Purus, through Trasadasyu, in "winning land and slaying foemen". IV.38.1, likewise, thanks Mitra and Varuna for the help which Trasadasyu, "the winner of our fields and ploughlands, and the strong smiter who subdued the Dasyus", rendered to the Purus.

It may be noted that most scholars, on the basis of these references, even go so far as to classify Purukutsa and Trasadasyu themselves as Purus. The only other kings of identifiable dynasty who are classifiable as heroes in the Rigveda (as distinct from kings who are merely praised in *danastutis* on account of liberal gifts given by them to the Rishis concerned: such liberal donors or patrons include Dasas and Panis, as in VIII.46.32 and VI.45.31) are Abhyavartin Cayamana and Vitahavya.

Abhyavartin Cayamana is an Anu king, and he clearly appears as a hero in VI.27. However, it is equally clear that this is only because he is an ally of the Bharata king Srnjaya: his descendant Kavi Cayamana who appears (though not in Griffith's translation) in VII.18.9 as an enemy of the Bharata king Sudas, is referred to in hostile terms.

Vitahavya is a Yadu, and he is referred to in VI.15.2, 3 and VII.19.2 (and also in the Atharvaveda VI.137.1). However, nothing more is known about him in the Rigveda; and it may be noted that he is associated in VI.15 with Bharadvaja, the priest of the Bharata king Divodasa, and again remembered in passing (though not in Griffith's translation) in the context of the Bharata king Sudas' battle with the ten kings.

Clearly, the only kings that really matter in the Rigveda are the kings of the Purus (and, in particular, of the Bharatas); and the only non-Puru kings who matter are those closely aligned with the Purus or those to whom the Purus as a race are deeply indebted.

The Tribes in the Rigveda: Traditional history knows of many different streams of tribes or peoples, but the two main streams are of those belonging to the Solar Race of the Iksvakus, and those belonging to the Lunar Race of the Ailas. The Ailas are further divided into five main branches: the Yadus, Turvasas, Druhyus, Anus and Purus.

The Rigveda is little concerned with the Iksvakus as a people, in spite of the fact that the second most important dynasty in the Rigveda (but *only*, as we have seen, because of the aid given by the kings of this dynasty to the Purus) is that of the Trksis, a branch of the Iksvakus. The word Iksvaku itself occurs only once in the Rigveda as a name of the Sun (X.60.4). The word Trksi occurs only twice, once in a list of enumeration of tribes or peoples (VI.46.8), and once as an epithet of Trasadasyu's son (VIII.22.7).

The five branches of the Ailas, however, are referred to much more frequently. Some of these references are those in which various tribes or peoples are merely enumerated (or in which the tribes serve as pointers of direction):

a. I.108.8: Yadus, Turvasas, Druhyus, Anus, Purus.
b. VIII.10.5: Yadus, Turvasas, Druhyus, Anus.
c. VI.46.8: Druhyus, Purus, (and Trksis).
d. VIII.4.1: Anus, Turvasas.
e. I.47.7: Turvasas.

But the other references to these five peoples, more concrete in nature, are quite conclusive in establishing the identity of the Vedic Aryans with the Purus:

Anus and Druhyus: The Anus and Druhyus (apart from the above-mentioned enumerations of tribes or peoples) are referred to only in a few verses:

Anus: V.31.4;
VI. 62.9;
VII. 18.13, 14;
VIII. 74.4.

Druhyus: VII. 18.6, 12, 14.

It is significant that most of these references are hostile references, in which Anus and Druhyus feature as enemies: VI.62.9: VII.18.6, 12-14.

Only two verses (both refering to the Anus) are more ambiguous:

a. In V.31.4, the Anus are described as manufacturing a chariot for Indra. The reference is clearly to the Bhrgus who were the priests of the people who lived to the northwest of the Vedic Aryans:, *i.e.* of the Anus, who lived to the northwest of the Purus. Griffith himself puts it as follows in his footnote: "*Anus:* probably meaning Bhrgus who belonged to that tribe."

This identity of the Anus and Bhrgus is clear in VII.18: verse 14 refers to the Anus and Druhyus, while verse 6 refers to the Bhrgus and Druhyus.

Likewise, while V.31.4 describes the Anus as manufacturing a chariot for Indra, IV.16.20 refers to the Bhrgus as manufacturing a chariot for Indra.

b. VIII.74.4 refers to Agni as Agni of the Anus: this again is probably a reference to the fact that the Bhrgus are credited with the introduction of fire.

The verse in question, in any case, does not refer to any Anu king or person, it refers to the Puru king Srutarvan, son of Rksa.

It is clear from these references that the Anus and Druhyus are not identifiable with the Vedic Aryans.

Yadus and Turvasas: The Yadus and Turvasas (apart from the verses which enumerate tribes or peoples) are referred to in many verses (often together):

Yadus and Turvasas:

I. 36.18; 54.6; 174.9;
IV. 30.17;
V. 31.8;
VI. 20.12; 45.1;
VII. 19.8;
VIII. 4.7; 7.18; 9.14; 45.27;
IX. 61.2;
X. 49.8; 62.10.

Yadus:

VIII. 1.31;6.46, 48.

Turvasas:

VI. 27.7;
VII. 18.6;
VIII. 4.19.

But these references make it very clear that the Yadus and Turvasas are not identifiable with the Vedic Aryans:

a. The two peoples appear to be located at a great distance from the land of the Vedic Aryans: they are described as coming "from afar" (I.36.18; VI.45.1), from "the further bank" (V.31.8) and "over the sea" (VI.20.12). Some of the verses refer to the Gods "bringing" them across flooded rivers (I.174.9; IV.30.17).

b. The very fact, that in spite of being two distinct tribes of the five, they are overwhelmingly more often referred to in tandem, is evidence of the fact that their individuality is blurred and they are thought of as a pair. This is definitely a measure of their distant location from the Vedic Aryans.

   Even among the six verses which refer to only one of the two, VI.27.7 refers to the Turvasas alongwith the Vrcivans, who are Yadus (cf. Vrjinivant of the traditional dynastic lists).

c. Four of the references to the Yadus and Turvasas are definitely hostile ones, in which they figure as enemies of the Vedic Aryans: VI.27.7; VII.18.6; 19.8; IX.61.2.

d. Although there are so many references to the Yadus and Turvasas, the majority of them refer to just two historical incidents in which (as in the case of Purukutsa and Trasadasyu) the Yadus and Turvasas appear to have come to the aid of the Vedic Aryans (thereby making it clear that they were not always enemies of the Vedic Aryans; unlike the Druhyus, and, to a slightly lesser extent, the Anus).

   The first incident is clearly a very old one, in which Indra is credited with bringing the Yadus and Turvasas safely over flooded rivers: I.174.9; IV.30.17; V.31.8; VI.20.12; 45.1.

   The second incident, in which the Yadus came to the aid of the Kanvas in fighting their enemies, in response to an appeal contained in I.36.18 (in which they are called "from afar" to come to the aid of Kanva), is referred to in I.36.18; 54.6; VIII.4.7; 7.18; 9.14; 45.27; X.49.8.

e. All the other references (apart from the hostile references and the references to the two historical incidents) are merely references in *danastutis* (and, as we have seen, even Dasas and Panis are praised in such circumstances) in VIII.1.31; 4.19; 6.46, 48; X.62.10.

Purus: The references to the Purus, on the other hand, make it very clear that the Purus, and in particular the Bharatas among them, are the Vedic Aryans, the People of the Book in the literal sense. The Bharatas are referred to in the following verses:

I. 96.3;
II. 7.1, 5; 36.2;
III. 23.2; 33.11, 12; 53.12, 24;
IV. 25.4;
V. 11.1; 54.14;
VI. 16.19, 45;
VII. 8.4; 33.6.

The references are very clear:

a. In many verses, even Gods are referred to as Bharataṣ: Agni in I.96.3; II.7.1, 5; IV.25.4, and VI.16.9; and the Maruts in II.36.2.
b. In other verses, Agni is described as belonging to the Bharatas: III.23.2; V.11.1; VI.16.45; VII.8.4.
c. In the other references to the Bharatas (III.33.11, 12; 53.12, 24; V.54.14; VII.33.6) it is clear that they are the unqualified heroes of the hymns.

There is not a single reference even faintly hostile to the Bharatas in the whole of the Rigveda.

The Purus (apart from the verses which enumerate tribes or peoples) are referred to in the following verses:

I. 59.6; 63.7; 129.5; 130.7; 131.4;
IV. 21.10; 38.1, 3; 39.2;
V. 17.1;
VI. 20.10;
VII. 5.3; 8.4; 18.13; 19.3; 96.2;
VIII. 64.10;
X. 4.1; 48.5.

The references make it very clear that the Purus are being referred to in a first-person sense:

a. The Vedic Gods are clearly identified as the Gods of the Purus:

Agni is described as a "fountain" to the Purus (X.4.1), a "priest" who drives away the sins of the Purus (I.129.5), the Hero who is worshipped by the Purus (1.59.6), the protector of the sacrifices of the Purus (V.17.1), and the destroyer of enemy castles for the Purus (VII.5.3).

Mitra and Varuna are described as affording special aid in battle and war to the Purus, in the form of powerful allies and mighty steeds (IV.38.1, 3; 39.2).

Indra is identified as the God to whom the Purus sacrifice in order to gain new favours (VI.20.10), and for whom the Purus shed Soma (VIII.64.10). Indra gives freedom to the Purus by slaying Vrtra (IV.21.10), helps the Purus in battle (VII.19.3), and breaks down enemy castles for the Purus (I.63.7; 130.7; 131.4).

Indra even speaks to the Purus and asks them to sacrifice to him alone, promising in return his friendship, protection and generosity (X.48.5.). In a Biblical context, this would have been a testimony of "God's covenant" with the People of the Book.

b. It is generally accepted by the scholars that the Saraswati represents the geographical heartland of the Vedic Aryan civilization. Saraswati is invoked (alongwith two other Goddesses who, as we have seen in our chapter on the Geography of the Rigveda, were deities of places close to the banks of the Saraswati) in the Apri-suktas of all the ten families of composers of hymns in the Rigveda.

   It becomes clear, in VII.96.2, that the Saraswati was a Puru river, and it flowed through Puru lands. The river is addressed with the words: "The Purus dwell, Beauteous One, on thy two grassy banks."

c. The identity of the Purus with the Vedic Aryans is so unmistakable, that the line between "Puru" and "Man" is distinctly blurred in the Rigveda:

   Griffith, for example, sees fit to translate the word Puru as "Man" in at least five verses: I.129.5; 131.4; IV.21.10; V.171.1; X.4.1.

   The Rigveda itself, in no uncertain terms, identifies the Purus in VIII.64.10 with "mankind": Purave... *manave jane.*

   In fact, the Rigveda goes so far as to coin a word Purusa/ Purusa (descendant of Puru) for "man", on the lines of the word *Manusa* (descendant of Manu).

While the word *Manusa* for "man" is representative of a general Indo-European word with counterparts in other Indo-European branches (Germanic, as in English "man"), the word *Purusa/Purusa* is purely Rigvedic in origin: the word is found in the Rigveda in 28 verses, of which 17 are found in the late Mandala X. Of the 11 verses in the other nine Mandalas, 9 are by the priests of Sudas and his descendant Somaka (*i.e.* by Vishvamitra, Vasishtha, Kutsa and Vamadeva). The word, therefore, was clearly coined during the period of Sudas, and gained increasing currency during the period of composition of the Rigvedic hymns.

d. There are two verses in which the Purus are referred to in hostile terms: VII.8.4; 18.3.

Far from disproving the general scenario, however, these references only further confirm the point that the Bharatas, themselves a branch of the Purus, were the particular Vedic Aryans of the Rigveda: both the verses refer to conflict between the Bharatas and the other Purus.

In VII.8.4. "Bharata's Agni" is described as conquering the Purus in battle.

In VII.18.3, Vasishtha, speaking on behalf of the Bharata king Sudas, addresses Indra with the plea: "May we, in sacrifice, conquer (the) scornful Puru(s)."

The Rishis and Priestly Families in the Rigveda

As we have seen, the Rigveda, by way of its ten Apri-suktas, recognizes ten families of Rishis or composers. The Apri-suktas are therefore a key to an understanding of some of the basic aspects of the system of priestly families in the Rigveda.

Two basic points which become apparent from the Apri-suktas are of great importance in identifying the Bharatas, among the Purus, as the particular Vedic Aryans of the Rigveda:

1. Nine of the ten families recognized in the Rigveda are identifiable with the seven primary and two secondary families of Rishis recognized in Indian tradition: the seven primary families are the Angirases, Bhrgus, Vishvamitra, Vasishtha, Agastyas, Kasyapas and Atris, and the two secondary families are the Kevala-Angirases (Kanvas in the Rigveda) and Kevala-Bhrgus (Grtsamadas in the Rigveda).

But the Rigveda also recognizes a tenth family, the Bharatas. This family does not figure as a separate family in later priestly traditions, which place kings who became Rishis among either the Angirases or the Bhrgus.

This special treatment shows that to the Vedic Aryans, there were nine families of priestly Rishis, but only one family of royal Rishis; and, by implication, the tribal identity of these royal Rishis is also the tribal identity of the Vedic Aryans.

2. There are three Great Goddesses invoked in the ten Apri-suktas. One of them is Bharati, who, as the very name suggests, was the tutelary deity of the Bharatas.

An examination of the references to this Goddess in the Apri-suktas brings out a significant state of affairs: the ten Apri-suktas fall into three distinct categories in line with our classification of the periods of the Rigveda into Early, Middle and Late.

As per our chronology, five families of Rishis originated in the Early Period of the Rigveda: the Angirases, Bhrgus, Vishvamitra, Vasishtha and Agastyas. All these five families refer to the Three Goddesses in a particular order of reference: Bharati, ILA, Saraswati (I.142.9; X.110.8; III.4.8; VII.2.8; I.188.9).

Two families originated in the Middle Period of the Rigveda, when the heyday of the Bharatas was waning, but the Rigveda was still a Bharata book: the Kasyapas and Grtsamadas. Both these families still refer to the same Three Goddesses, but in changed order of reference: The Kasyapas change the order to Bharati, Saraswati, ILA, (IX.5.8); and the Grtsamadas to Saraswati, ILA, Bharati (II.3.8). The Grtsamadas reverse the order and place Bharati last; but, in another hymn, they make amends for it by naming all the Three Goddesses in the original order: Bharati, ILA, Saraswati (II.1.11). This, incidentally, is the only hymn, apart from the Apri-suktas, to refer to the Three Goddesses by name.

Three families originated in the Late Period of the Rigveda, when the predominance of the Bharatas (of the particular branch whose ruling dynasty was descended from Devavata) was practically a thing of the past: the Atris, Kanvas, and the Bharatas themselves. Not one of the three refers to Bharati at all.

The Atris and Kanvas replace the suggestive name of the Goddess Bharati with the more general name Mahi (which is an epithet of the Goddesses in I.142.9 and IX.5.8) *and* change the order to ILA, Saraswati, Mahi (V.5.8; I.13.9).

The Bharatas, caught in a bind, since they can neither refer to the Goddess as Bharati, nor replace her name with another, follow a safe path: they *refer* to Three Goddesses, but *name* only one: ILA. (X.70.8).

All this proves one more thing contrary to general belief: according to the scholars, the Apri-suktas were late compositions. On the contrary, it becomes clear that each new family of Rishis, soon after it came into being and became a party to the performance of ritual sacrifices, composed its own Apri-sukta. The Apri-sukta, therefore, depicts the situation prevailing close to the time of the birth of the family (which, of course, does not apply to the two ancient pre-Rigvedic families, the Angirases and Bhrgus, whose antecedents go back deep into the pre-Rigvedic past).

It must be noted that any Rishi performing a particular sacrifice was required to chant verses appropriate to that particular sacrifice, regardless of the family identities of the composers of those verses. It is only at the point where an Apri-sukta was to be chanted, that he had to chant the particular Apri-sukta of his own family. Hence, the composition of an Apri-sukta, if no other hymn, was a must for any family, for a Rishi belonging to that family to be able to participate in certain sacrifices.

This, incidentally, also explains why the Apri-sukta of the Agastyas, whose other hymns were certainly composed in the Middle and Late periods of the Rigveda, clearly shows that it was composed in the Early period of the Rigveda. The Bharata-Puru factor is vital to an understanding of the very presence of the different families of Rishis in the corpus of the Rigveda:

1. The Angirases and Vasishtha are two families which are fully and militantly affiliated to the Bharatas throughout the Rigveda.
2. The Vishvamitra are a partially affiliated family: they were fully and militantly affiliated to the Bharatas in the period of Mandala III, and, moreover, the Vishvamitra were themselves descended from a branch of Purus (a different branch from that of Divodasa and Sudas, but possibly descended from Devavata) who also called themselves Bharatas.

However, their close affiliation with the Bharatas of the Rigveda ceased after the Vishvamitra were replaced by the Vasishtha as the priests of Sudas.

3. The Kasyapas and Grtsamadas are two families which are associated with the Bharatas, but not militancy affiliated to them.

   Their association is based on the fact that the provenance of these two families was in the Middle Period of the Rigveda, which was still the (albeit late) period of the Bharatas.

   The two families were more concerned with religious subjects (nature-myths and rituals), and hardly at all with politics or militancy; but the only kings referred to by the Kasyapas (as patrons) are the Puru or Bharata kings Dhvasra and Purusanti (IX.58.3), and the only prominent king remembered by the Grtsamadas is Divodasa (II.19.6).

4. The Bhrgus and Agastyas are relatively neutral families in the Rigveda, both being basically aloof from the Vedic mainstream:

   The Bhrgus were, in fact, the priests of the people (the Anus) who lived to the northwest of the Vedic Aryans, and therefore generally on hostile terms with the Vedic Aryans and their Rishis. However, one branch of the Bhrgus, consisting of Jamadagni and his descendants, became close to the Vedic Rishis; and these are the Bhrgus of the Rigveda.

   The Agastyas are traditionally a family of Rishis whose earliest and most prominent members migrated to the South, away from the area of the Vedic Aryans, at an early point of time in their history.

   Both these families owe their presence in the Rigveda to two factors:

   a. Agastya and Jamadagni, the founders of these two families, were closely related to, and associated with, two other prominent eponymous Rishis: Agastya was Vasishtha's brother, and Jamadagni was Vishvamitra's nephew.

   b. The two families were not affiliated to, or even associated with, the Bharatas, but nor were they affiliated to, or associated with, any other tribe or people.

Both the families, nevertheless, gained a late entry into the corpus of the Rigveda: even the oldest hymns of the Bhrgus are found in the late Mandalas; while the hymns of the Agastyas are, anyway, late hymns by Rishis belonging to a later branch of the family.

5. The Atris and Kanvas are also relatively neutral families, but in a different sense from the Bhrgus and Agastyas.

   These two families, in fact, are not only not affiliated to the Bharatas in particular or the Purus in general, but they are more often associated with non-Purus (Iksvakus, Yadus, Turvasas, Anus). This association is basically mercenary: the Atris and Kanvas appear to have officiated as priests for, and composed danastutis in praise of, any king (irrespective of his tribal identity) who showered them with gifts. This more catholic or cosmopolitan nature of these two families is also recognized (in the case of the *Atris) in I.117.3, where Atri is characterised as pancajanya* (belonging to all the five tribes).

   The Kanvas are even associated with the Yadus and Turvasas in the context of a battle, in which the Yadus and Turvasas came to their aid in response to an appeal by the Kanvas.

   All this raises a question: if the Purus alone, among the five tribes, are to be identified with the Vedic Aryans, and the Rigveda itself is a Puru book, what is the explanation for the presence of these two families in the Rigveda?.

   The answer is simple:

   a. These two families originated in the Late Period of the Rigveda, when the predominance of the Bharatas had ended, and the Purus in general had become more catholic and cosmopolitan in their attitudes.

   b. Tradition testifies that both these priestly families were themselves of Puru origin:

      According to the Vayu Purana (1.59), the earliest Atri Rishi was Prabhakara, who married the ten daughters of a Puru king Bhadrasva or Raudrasva, and had ten sons from whom all the Atri clans are descended.

As for the Kanvas, "all the authorities agree that they were an offshoot from the Paurava line".

c. While the Atris and Kanvas (though descended from Purus) were generally catholic or cosmopolitan in their associations, the most important Atri and Kanva Rishis in the Rigveda are closely associated with the Purus:

Among the Atris, Syavasva Atreya is closely associated with the Purus: according to Sayana's interpretation of V.54.14, Syavasva was himself a Bharata. He is also the only Atri to pay homage to the memory of Sudas (V.53.2).

Among the Kanvas, Pragatha Kanva and Sobhari Kanva are closely associated with the Purus: Pragatha identifies himself as a Puru directly in VIII.64.10, and also indirectly in VIII.10.5 (where he asks the Asvins to abandon the other four tribes, who are named, and come to the Purus, who are not directly named). Sobhari is the only Kanva Rishi to pay homage to the memory of Divodasa (VIII.103.2) and to call him an Arya. Sobhari Kanva and Syavasva Atreya are also two Rishis associated (VIII.19.32, 36; 36.7; 37.7) with Trasadasyu, whose importance in the Rigveda is due to the help given by him to the Purus.

It is significant that these three Rishis are perhaps the most important Atri and Kanva Rishis in the Rigveda: Syavasva Atreya has the largest number of hymns and verses (17 hymns, 186 verses) among the Atris in the Rigveda, more than those ascribed to the eponymous Atri Bhauma (13 hymns, 126 verses). Apart from these two Atris, all the other Atri Rishis have one, two, three, or at the most four hymns.

Pragatha Kanva does *not* have the largest number of hymns among the Kanvas in the Rigveda, but, Mandala VIII, associated with the Kanvas, is called the "Pragatha Mandala", and the dominant form of metre used in this Mandala is also named after Pragatha. These three Rishis are the only Rishis, belonging to the Atri and Kanva families, whose descendants have a place in the Rigveda: Andhigu Syavasvi (IX.101.1-3), Bharga Pragatha (VIII.60-61), Kali Pragatha (VIII.66), Haryata Pragatha (VIII.72) and Kusika Saubhara (X.127).

The presence of the Atris and Kanvas in the Rigveda is therefore fully in keeping with the Puru character of the Rigveda.

4

The Yajurveda

Humans are inspired to translate good thoughts into actions. Yajurveda inspires humans to walk on the path of Karma (deeds). That is why it is also referred to as Karma-Veda. The essence of the Yajurveda lies in those mantras (incantations) that inspire people to initiate action.

The first incantation of Yajurveda commands us to perform action

Devo Vaha Savita Praprayatu Shreshtamaya Karmane

Meaning: O Creator of the universe! inspire us to perform great deeds. Similarly the second mantra of the fortyth chapter of the Yajurveda commands us to perform deeds-

Kurvanneveha Karmani Jijivishechchat Samaha

Meaning: Desire to live for a 100 years performing ones deeds. Alike other Vedas there are many branches of Yajurveda. But 2 branches namely Krishna and Shukla Yajurveda have gained relatively more prominence. There is a beautiful story associated with this Veda.

Rishi Yagyavalkya acquired all knowledge related to Yajurveda from his uncle Vaishampayan. Because of some reason the Guru was angry on his student and told him to return to him the knowledge. The student vomited and returned to him all the knowledge acquired and on the orders of the Guru, the other disciples ate all the knowledge assuming the form of fowls. After this Yajurveda was named as Taitareya Samhita. After this Yagyavalkya worshipped Lord Sun ardently and in return he got the Yajurveda, named Shukla Yajurveda. Because of the impurity of the mind the Mantras (Yajus) became black and thereafter this Yajurveda was named as Krishna Yajurveda.

Alike Rigveda, Shukla Yajurveda is composed in a mantra and is poetic. The words like Yoju or Yajuhu have from:

"Yaja deva Puja Sangatikarna daneshu"

The Yajurveda includes mantras related to, worship of god, vedic rituals related to worship and religious sacrifices. The Yajurveda is classified into 40 parts/chapters consisting of 1975 mantras

The Brahmana textcome next to Vedas. The ultimate aim of these text was to throw light on the methods of conducting Yagya and its related ritual. The Brahmana texts are divided into 3 actions- (1)Brahmana (2) Aranyaka (3) Upanishads

The Shatpath Brahmana of the Shukla Yajurveda is very famous. It is divided into a 100 chapters and these depict the vedic religious scenario very authentically.

The Aranyaka texts comprise of many a part extracted from the Upanishads. The 14th "chapter of Shatpath Brahmana is referred to as Aranyaka. The 40th Chapter of the Shukla Yajurveda is referred to as 'Ishavasyopnishada'. The Brihadavanyaka upanished is the Upanishad of Shukla Yajurveda, while Kathopnishad, Taitariya, Shwetashweta Upanishad, Maitrayani. Upanishad and Kaivalyopnishad are th upanishads of Krishna Yajurveda.

(1) Devom Vaha Savita Prarpayatu Shreshtamaya Karmana
—(1/1 Yajurveda)

O Lord, the creator of all, inspire us to perform good deeds. Here we are inspired to indulge in good actions because then only is progress possible. Every person should strive to do such type of deeds so that they are respected and honoured for the same. By doing one can attain physical development, mental development, personal development and enhance communal development. One should eat wholesome food and should abstain from the wrong path.

(2) Ma Hvarma Te Yagyapatirhvarsheeta —(1/2,A, Yajurveda)

Do not become wicked,may your Yagya Pati (One who performed the religious sacrifice) also not become wicked.

It is important to be good and humble to tread on the path

of good action. A wicked person is unworthy of every thing he does. Here it is prayed at neither the person who performs the yagya and nor the means used should be wicked and evil respectively. Good work done with bad intentions is always a failure. That is why one should refrain from manipulative tendencies. In the same way the leader should abstain from such evil tendencies because this leads to harm more than good. One and all should therefore practice simple and good living. They should never seek recourse to manipulative tendencies.

(3) Sa Vishwayuhu Sa Viswakarma Sa Vishwa Dhayaha
—(1/4 Yajurveda)

The three Kamdhenus' (things that fulfil all wishes desired) are the life span, the energy to do action and the energy to sustain everything.

Every person who is blessed with long life performs all his duties meticulously and attains all the attainments (Purushastha). In this way he sustains throughout life.

Only by striving with perseverance and focus can one accomplish all his desired goals. With these three Kamdhenus humans can progress in all ways. One should not forget that without the energy to sustain, no one can perform action and without both these factors one cannot have a long life. One should, therefore utilise these energy's constantly and according to situations.

(4) Edamahamnrutat Satyamudaimi

I am renouncing untruth and embracing truth. One should accept truth, and should sacrifice their life to protect truth. This is known as the Satyapal vrata. O Lord! I take an oath that I shall always protect truth and may I be successful in observing and accomplishing this vow.

Unless we do not renounce our greed we cannot protect truth. Untruth inhibits self-development and physical, mental and spiritual growth. Therefore we should all adhere by truth.

(5) Ma Bherma Samviktha *—(1/23 Yajurveda)*

One should not deter, because of fear from the path of one's duties. One should perform all his duties without fear. The doors of progress are always closed for a person who fears. Only a fearless person can initiate self development and can also help in social and political progress. Therefore one should fearlessly perform all his duties.

(6) *Sam Jyotisha Jyotihi* —*(2/9, Yajurveda)*

May all knowledge come together and become radiant. A teacher gives knowledge to his student and enlightens him. Thereafter students give knowledge to someone else. In this way, one enlightens the other and knowledge increases. Increasing knowledge by knowledge is known as the Jnana Yagya. The ultimate aim of a Yagya is to increase the glory of knowledge.

(7) *Vedo Asi Yena Tvam Dev Veda Devebhyo Vedo Bhavastena Mahyam Vedoho Bhoyaha* —*(2/21, Yajurveda)*

The Vedas consists of all knowledge. Just in the way you became the giver of knowledge for the Gods in the same way you bless me with knowledge.

Vedas are an ocean of knowledge. The Gods acquired knowledge through the Vedas and even Human got knowledge from the same source. It is in the best interest of human to study the Vedas to acquire total knowledge.

(8) *Deva Gatuvido Gatum Vitva Gatumit* —*(2/21,8/21 Yajurveda)*

O Gods! know the path of truth and tread on the path of truth. Only by acquiring knowledge from the Vedas can one know the path of truth and righteousness, on acquiring knowledge human should tread on the path of truth, so that can do the good of one and all. Truth is unconcealable, that is why we should tread on the righteous path.

(9) *Asthuri Nao Garhapatyani Santu Shatam Himaha* —*(2/27 Yajurveda)*

May we both perform the duties of the family for a 100 years.

Family life can, only then be peaceful and happy if both the husband and wife performs their respective duties consistently for a 100 years without obstacles. A cart having only one buffalo is known as Sthuri and a cart pulled by 2 buffaloes is known as Asthuri, because two (husband-wife) pull them. It thus, becomes clear that one can perform their duties better when they are assisted by each other.

(10) *Tanupa Agne Asi Tanvam Me Pahyayyurda Agne Ayayu Me Dehi Varchoda Agne Asi Varcho Mem Dehi* —*(3/17, Yajurveda)*

O Agni! You are the protector of the body, so protect my body. You are the giver of long life, so give us long life. You are the giver of radiance, so bless us with radiance.

It is said that fire resides in the body, until the fire is there in the body it enkindles the life, when this fire ceases the body does not exist. When the health is sound one shall have a long life. It is because of fire that one grows with radiance. So one should maintain purity of the body, by regularly exercising and purify the mind by worship and self-study. As results of this one is blessed with long life and becomes radiant. Therefore we should do all those things that protect the body, life and radiance.

(11) Akran Karma Karma Kritaha Saha Vacha Mayobhuva
—(3/47, Yajurveda)

The person who is always working and active is always soft spoken all the time.

People who are striving for the attainments always speak softly and sweetly. When we speak in a good way it gives happiness to one and all and they are encouraged to do good to others. When we speak with hatred and anger it leads to unhappiness, pain and misery. So one should always be soft-spoken and all karma-yogis should tread on the path of righteousness so that one can do good to one and all.

(12) Na Aetu Manaha Punaha Kratve Dakshaya Jeevame Jyok Cha Suryadrishe *—(3,54 Yajurveda)*

May our mind, actions and strength be inspired all the time to seek the blessings of the sun for a long time.

Humans should always tread on the righteous path so that one can enhance one's strength, can remain healthy and can constantly for a longer duration. One should always seek blessings of the sun so that our vision remains unimpaired for long time. One should also do so that we may get inspired incessantly, just to do good work. One can after all attain perfection only after doing the same work repetitively. Therefore to enhance one's capabilities you should always seek the blessings of the sun god.

(13) Tryambakam Yajamahe Sugandhim Pushtivardhanam Urvarukamiva Bandhanan Mrityor Muksheeya Ma Mritat
—(3/60, Yajurveda)

We pray to lord Mahadev who is fragrant, has three eyes and

is the nourisher, may he liberate us from death. May our attachments cease alike that of Urvaaru (a species of cucumber) which ripens and falls of the tree i.e liberates itself from the material objects.

The person who recites this incantation regularly is freed from ailments, fear, and death. Tryimbak means the one with three eyes i.e Adhyatma, Adhiboot and Adhidaivik.

We should meticulously pray to lord Shiva so that all our attachments cease alike the fruit of urvaru and we are liberated from this vicious cycle of life and death.

(14) Parma Agne Dushcharita Dakshasva Bha Sucharite Bhaja
—(4/28, Yajurveda)

O Agni! Liberate us from the wrong doings and actions and inspire us to do good actions.

Please discourage us from doing wrong and encourage us to do good, O Agni! The result of good deeds are always good but the results of bad deeds are very bad. That is why help us to yearn and strive for the good of all so that it may yield good results.

(15) Prati Panthampadmahi Swastisamanehasam
—(4/29, Yajurveda)

One should always tread on that path which gives us happiness and where there is no fear of destruction and unhappiness.

We should always walk on that path, which is devoid of obstacles and hurdles. On which we can accomplish our duties properly and easily, and on which we progress.

We seldom go and do those things which we are not knowledge about and even if we have to do it, we take the opinion of experts in the respected fields, so that we may accomplish our duty perfectly, and punctually. Therefore, we should follow that path, that leads to happiness and where there is no fear of going astray.

(16) Bhavatam Naha Samnaso Sachet Savare Paso Ma Yagyam Himsishtam Ma Yagyapatim Jatvedaso Shivo Dhavatmadya Naha
—(5/3, Yajurveda)

O Agni! Make our mind stable, egalitarian an may you destroy the illusion. Do not destroy the Yagya and may you not destroy the Yagyapati.

We pray to Agni so that he may give us similarity in thought, there is no doubt and illusion. May he not destroy the religious sacrifice offered and also the performer of the religious sacrifice.

(17) *Yunjate Mana Uta Yunjate Dhiyo Vipra Viprasya Brihato Vidashchitaha* —*(5/14, Yajurveda)*

The scholars make their mind stable and engage in all religious activities with mind/intellect and Yoga by following the great soul who have contemplated acquired a lot of knowledge and have become important.

The commoners can only then become knowledge after they follow the sayings and teachings of the scholars. After doing so, then only they can engage in good actions and yoga (path) by applying intellect.

(18) *Mahirbhoorma Pridakurnamasta Ata Nanarva Prehi Ghritasya Kulyauparitasya Pathya Anu* —*(6/12, Yajurveda)*

O Scholar! The distributor or promoter of good, do not become short tempered as the snake, do not become proud alike the stupid, do not become aggressive as the tiger, come here, without obstacles and accept this water, and tread on the path of truth.

One should not become poisonous, aggressive and destructive. One should lead on the righteous path in the same way as a thirsty person who accepts water.

By doing so one shall grow and will be able to lead a simple life.

(19) *Ma Bherma Sam Viktha Urjaa Dhatsva Dhishane Veedvi Sati Veedyethamurja Dadhathaam Papma Hato Na Somaha*
—*(6/35, Yajurveda)*

O Woman! Your are blessed with physical and mental energy, so you do not fear your husband. Do not shiver but on the contrary become strong and courageous. Both(Husband-Wife) of you, become intelligent and courageous and engage in good deeds so that you shall be able to mitigate all the demerits present within and way alike the moon. In this way you shall mutually make each other happy.

Husband and wife are advised to destroy the fear and unstability in the mind and make the Aatma strong, full of enthusiasm and optimism. By this one shall engage in good actions which will result in domestic happiness and comforts. They shall become happy alike the waxing moon.

(20) *Upyamgrihito Ayantaryachcha Maghvan Pahi Somam Urushya Raya Aesho Yajasva* —*(7/4, Yajurveda)*

You are the followers of Yama and Niyama therefore take control of all your internal energies. Protect you energies which protect you and destroy all the miseries by your strength. As a result you shall be wealthy and happy.

One should regularly adhere to Yama(Non violence, truth, abstinence from stealing, celibacy and abstinence from amassing unnecessary wealth) and Niyama(cleanliness, Contention, penance, self study and devotion). This can protect all the internal energies, help you to vanquish all your miseries and become prosperous in all ways.

(21) *Swangkrito Asi Vishwebhya Indrebhyo Divebhyaha Parthivebhyo Manastvashtu Swaha* —*(7/6, Yajurveda)*

You should put your utmost efforts. I know that, you are the doer of good of all those scholars and great people who are blessed with good merits and senses.

The fate of that person often remains dormant who does not strive and on the contrary becomes lazy. Only by efforts can one become successful. Learn to strive for the good of others. May you be blessed with the power to think good and donate benevolently.

(22) *Sam Varchasa Payasa Sam Tanubhiraganmahi Mansa Samshivena*

Tvashta Sudatro Vi Dadhatu Rayo Anumarshtu Tanvo Yadvilishtama —*(8/14,16, Yajurveda)*

May we be blessed with radiance, good health, stable mind and energy. The giver of great donations, bless us with comforts and remove all the flaws and demerits from our body.

We should eat nutritious food so that we are healthy and should read good books that makes our mind pure and clean. Only by doing so we can do good to others. We should collectively work for the betterment of others. We should pray to god so that he makes us devoid of demerits and blesses us so that we become prosperous.

(23) *Upyamagrihito Asi Suryaya Tva Bhrajayaisha Te Yonihi Suryaya Tva Bhrajaya* —*(8/40, Yajurveda))*

Just as the sunrays can be seen by all similarly you are

committed to your rules. The sun rises and sets on time and is never unpunctual. Alike the sun, the activities of humans are subject to rules. Those who lead disciplined and orderly lifestyles they achieve all their goals and progress.

(24) *Vachaspatirvaja Na Swadatu Swaha* —*(9/1, Yajurveda)*

May the Lord of our voice make our voice sweet and soft. We should always be soft-spoken.

Sweet speech has the ability to attract one and all. Vitriolic speech keeps people away. That is why one should always be soft-spoken so that it enhances brotherhood and affection.

(25) *Graha Urjahutayo Vyanto Vipraya Matim*—*(9/4, Yajurveda)*

O men, the one who enhance their strength, please bless us with knowledge in different ways.

The scholars who incessantly contemplate and acquire strength and knowledge should engage in imparting knowledge to the ignorant also so that they can also develop their mental faculities which would result in self-development and spiritual progress. Ignorant naïve people should acquire maximum knowledge from the knowledgeable.

(26) *Apo Deva Madhumatir Gribhnannurjasi Vati Rajasuashchitanaha* —*(10/1, Yajurveda)*

The Gods took that food which was tasty, nutritious, wholesome, of that quality which could be given to kings, and which would bless people with knowledge and enlightenment.

One means to say that, the person who is soft-spoken, radiant with strength, has knowledge of politics and diplomacy peace and iron volition is fit to become a king.

Therefore one should imbibe all these good qualities in order to become a efficient ruler.

(27) *Devataya Prasutaha Pra Sarpami* —*(10/30, Yajurveda)*

O God, may we be inspired by good merits and thoughts and strive on the path of righteousness towards self-development. We should imbibe inspiring thoughts and should strive on the righteous path. In this way progress is sure. We should get inspired by thoughts and deeds of great scholars and great souls sager, etc. and become purusharthi (attainments)

(28) *Yuktena Manasa Vayam Devasya Savituhu Save Swargyaya Shaktya* —(11/2, Yajurveda))

In this world, created by the one and only sole creator, to become happy by living in solitude, one should work according to one's capabilities and limitations. We should condition our mind to be stable through study of Yoga and one should strive incessantly and selfessly to achieve the desired objective. Then only shall one become happy.

(29) *Sem Vastham Swavida Samichi Urasatmana Agnimantra Bharishyanti Jyotishamantam Jarasramit*—(11/31,Yajurveda)

You both realise the self, become calm and stable, and swallow that Agni which is always fiery, and keep that Agni within always enkindled. Realise yourself through self-analysis and introspection. By concentration, unkindle the flame of knowledge within the body and do not let it extinguish. This is a sure way to self-development and prosperity.

(30) *Punar Urja Ni Varttasva Pura Agna Isha Yusha Punarnaha Dahmam Hasaha* —(12/9, Yajurveda)

O Agni, I invoke you along with your energy. Give us good food, bless us with long life and protect us from sin.

The ultimate objective of human life is to be free from sin. Therefore, one should desire enhancement of strength, food and long life. One should always be free from any type of deficiency because this leads us to sin.

(31) *Avapatantirvadandiva Oshadhyaspari Vam Jeeva Ashnavam Ahai Na Sa Rishyati Purushaha.* —(12/91, Yajurveda)

The herbal medicines that incarnate from the heaven on earth say those who eat us, are never destroyed.

Medicine give us relief from all types of ailments. But one should take these medicines only on prescription of the doctor or *Vaid.* By taking these medicines one can also escape death why means, that they give us a long life.

(32) *Samyak Sravanti Sarito Na Dhena Antarhridda Manasa Pooyamanaha* —(13/38, Yajurveda)

Good thoughts, alike the water of a river, are purified by the mind and heart and flow from the mouth of the great scholars.

One should only speak those things, which are purified by the mind and heart and should avoid speaking things unpleasant to the heart and mind. One should therefore think twice and speak.

(33) *Ayurme Pahi Pranam Mem Pahma Panam Mem Pahi Vyanam Me Pahi Chakshur Me Pahi Shrotram Me Pahi Vacham Mem Pinva Mano Jinvatmanam Mem Pahi Jyotirmem Jachcham.*
—(14/17, Yajurveda)

O God! Protect our lives our lifespan, protect the Apan and Vyan Vayu, protect our eyes, both our ears and bless our minds and speech. Protect our souls and bless us with radiance.

If the heart, mind, body soul is protected or purified then only, shall the process of self-development be incepted. This shall unequivocally lead to success and prosperity.

(34) *Eshe Tvonje Tva Raiyayai Tva Poshaya Tva Lokam To Indram.*
—(14/22, Yajurveda))

I accept you for you are the giver of food grains and you nourish all. May you take care and protect this world. All people adore the great king Indra.

Agni or fire is the one that gives us food. Agni is imperative for growth and energy therefore one should use agni for the production of all things. Only by doing so will agni be used for the welfare of all and as a result we shall get all the comforts.

(35) *Rasmina Satyaya Satyam Jinda Pretina Dharmana Dharma Jinua.* *—(15/6, Yajurveda)*

Pacify truth, for truth with radiance and absorb the best form of divine knowledge and pacify Dharma.

One should always adhere by truth and accept it, then only can it be protected. One should absorb the divine knowledge and follow it then only can one protect Dharma. On the basis of these two one can hope for self-development. It is imperative that we love truth and Dharma for mutual protection.

(36) *Pratipadasi Pratipade Tva Anupadasyanupade Tva Sampadasi Sampade Tva Tejo Asi Tajase Tve.* *—(15/3, Yajurveda)*

You are the intellect, that is why I attain you, You are good, that is why I attain you. You are wealth that is why I attain you, you are radiance that is why I attain you.

With the increase in intellect one can grasp all knowledge and become a scholar. By eating good food the body gets energy and becomes nourished to perform the regular duties. By earning wealth, one prospers and becomes successful. By acquiring radiance the person becomes glorified. In this way human should adopt all those means that lead to mental and physical spiritual growth.

(37) *Pravrusdasi Pavrite Tva Vivrudasi Vivrute Tva Savridasi Savrute Tva.* *—(15/9, Yajurveda)*

You are the one to inspire all into work, that is why ? Why I accept you, Your are directly or indirectly related to each and every work. You possess a character and morality that is why I accept you.

We should imbibe qualities of good action from the sages and work. We should perform our deeds in such a way as to complete it easily. The scholar who has a good character is respected and honoured by all and his teachings are followed by all.

(38) *Yatha Naha Sarvamijjagada Yakshmam Sumana Asat.* *—(16/4, Yajurveda)*

O Rudra! may our entire universe be devoid of ailments and be engaged in good constructive thinking.

A healthy mind resides in a healthy body. Good thought can be imbibed by reading and studying good books and by contemplating on them. Therefore one should regularly exercise and take nutritious food

(39) *Niharena Pravrita Jalpya Chasutrip Ukatha Shashah Charanti.* *—(17/31, Yajurveda)*

Those humans who are ignorant, believe only in protecting the body and speak big things in reality do not follow divine knowledge at all. A person who is ignorant is a real atheist and does not know anything about divine knowledge. They seem to be satisfied wherever they are and whatever they are with. One cannot attain god unless ignorance is washed away. In reality god is within you and is in form of the conscience and in form of knowledge. One can attain god and experience divine happiness.

(40) *Udgrabham Cha Nigrabham Cha Bramma Deva Avivridhan I.* *—(17/64 Yajurveda)*

May the Gods bless us so that we become capable and apt to engage in good actions, so that we may defeat and punish our enemies and so that we may enhance our knowledge. May the Gods help us to become mighty and strong so that we may vanquish our enemies and punish them. May we be inspired to imbibe maximum knowledge so that we may become apt and adroit so that our enemies don't even come near us.

(41) *Eyakshmana Brububhihi Sajoshaha Swaryantu Yajamanaha Swasti.* —(17/69, Yajurveda)

Those who are interested in performing Yagya, destroy all their sins, love all humans alike, great souls and only these people attain Swarga Loke (heaven). These people incinerate all their sins in the religious sacrifice performed. They love all humans alike great souls. Such people definitely attain the state of bliss.

(42) *Vajashya Me Prasavashcha Me Prayatishcha Me*
Prasitishcha Me Dheetishcha Me Kratushcha Me
Swashcha Me Shlokashcha Me Shravashcha Me
Shrutishcha Me Jyotishcha Me Swashcha Me Yagyena Kalpantama. —(18/1, Yajurveda)

May I be blessed with food, comforts, perseverance, power of thinking, power of speech, energy to perform good deeds, energy to perform Yagya and to praise, power to listen, radiance and internal energy, by performing this Yagya.

By achieving the above-mentioned powers one shall undoubtedly become successful and prosperous.

(43) *Yadakutatsamsusroddhado Va Manaso Va Sambritam Chakshusho Va.* —(18/58, Yajurveda)

One should acquire all knowledge from the heart, mind and all the senses (external). The source of knowledge is undoubtedly within us. We have to just imbibe it by self-study, introspection, contemplation and action. We would strive to imbibe as much knowledge as we can.

(44) *Shamyuna Patnisanyajansamashti Yajusha Sanstham.* —(19/29, Yajurveda)

One should maintain restraint which can result in good relations with one's wife. Any plan made for the welfare of society becomes successful only without difference of opinion by the organisation or institution concerned.

Restraint is the enemy of passions. By controlling the senses the relations of a husband and wife can be cordial and healthy. When any organisation strives to bring changes, for welfare of society there is unity in society.

(45) *Vratena Dikshamapnoti Dikshaya Apnoti Dakshinam Dakshina Shradha-mapnot Shraddhya Satya Amapyate.*

—*(19/30, Yajurveda)*

Man can become intelligent only by accomplishing the vows and attains devotion on the basis of intelligence and attains truth on the basis of devotion.

When a person strives to accomplish a vow he becomes intelligent. By accomplishing the vow he attains devotion and consequently attains the ultimate truth. One should engage in vows, dikshas, and devotion for realization of higher ideals.

(46) *Riten Satya Indriyam Vipanam Shukramandhasa Indrasyendriyamidam Payo Amritam Madhu.*

—*(19/76, Yajurveda)*

On realisation of truth and on attainment of knowledge one can acquire comforts, food, radiance, glory, power of the army, milk and honey.

By following the righteous path one can get all the good results mentioned above. One should follow truth on attaining knowledge and by keeping undeterred faith on it.

(47) *Nishsada Dritvrato Varunaha Pastyaswa Samrajyaya Sukratuhu Marityoho Pahi Vidyotpahi.* —*(20/2, Yajurveda)*

May the person who is truthful and accomplishes all the vows be blessed with good intellect and earn honour and praise in society for his good deeds. May he protect the people from lightening and death.

The person who does all his deeds faithfully becomes the leader of the masses and thinks for their well-being and welfare. By doing so, he can earn name and fame and shall be honoured by the people.

(48) *Bahu Me Bala Indriya Masto Me Karma Viryam.*

—*(20/7, Yajurveda)*

May both my shoulders and every sense organ be strong. May both my hands be always engaged in deeds and may they be valiant.

When ones, sense organs and shoulders, hands and legs are active and engaged in deeds then only will the human become strong and radiant.

(49) *Maha Arnaha Saraswati Pra Chetayati Ketuna Dhiyo Vishwa Virajati.* —*(20/86, Yajurveda)*

Goddess Saraswati the goddess of knowledge enlightens the vast expanse of the sky and enlightens the mind with all kinds of knowledge.

It is explained that goddess enlightens all the minds with knowledge. That is why humans should always be conscious and enkindle the flame of knowledge in their hearts and minds.

(50) *Sham No Bhavantu Vajuno Haveshu Devatata Mitadravaha Swarkaha Jambhayanto Ahim Vrikam Rakshansi Sanemyasmadyu Yavananmivaha.* —*(21/10, Yajurveda)*

O Scholars! You are strong and intelligent, are disciplined and blessed with good knowledge and are alike the gods performing the Yagyas. Please destroy snakes, demons, wolves and bless us with eternal happiness, and good health. All the scholars who are blessed with divine knowledge and strength are requested that they should save the others from all evils and diseases and give all eternal happiness. By taking the right advice from the right people one can be successful in his or her endeavour and can attain happiness.

(51) *Tatsa Vitura Varenyam Bhargo Devasya Dhimahi Dhiyo Yonaha* ***Prachodayata.*** —*(22/9,30/2, Yajurveda)*

We contemplate on the God who is the protector and preserver of the Universe, the creator and is embellished with divine merits. He is the one who enlightens us and inspires us to engage in good, noble deeds.

This mantra of the Yajurveda is well known as Gayatri mantra and the above mantra is

> *Aum Bhur Bhuva Swhaha Tatsa Vitura Varenyam Bhargo Devasya Dhimahi Dhiyo Yonaha Prachodayaata.*

This mantra means-'AUM' the supreme cosmic soul is the creator of this universe, is the given comfort and luxury, who enlightens all the creature, who is pure and devoid of unchasteness is worth praying to.

We place this god in our heart and mind with inpeccable devotion and faith so that he may destroy all the bad thoughts that lead to bad deeds and encourages us to perform good deeds. One can certainly achieve peace and happiness by praying to god with mind and heart.

(52) *Ayuryagyen Kalpatama Prani Yagyen Kalpatama Chakihuryagyen Kalpatama Shrotram Yagyen Kalpatama Jagyagyen Kalpatama Mano Yagyen Kalpatama Atmayagyen Kalpatama Swaryagyen Kalpatama Prishtham Yagyen Kalpatama Yagyo Yagyen Kalpatama. —(22/23, Yajurveda).*

May we be blessed with long life because of Yagya may our prana be increased because of yagya, may our eyes become strong because of yagya; may our hearing improve because of yagya, may our sense of communication improve because of yayga, may our soul become strong and may our brahma become strong because of yagya, may a flame of self-knowledge be enkindled because of yagya, may we attain Brahmalok or swarga because of yagya and let the yagya be enhanced because of yagya.

(53) *Yaddevaso Lalamagu Pra Vishtiminmavishuhu*
Sakathna Dedishyate Nari Satyasyakshibhuvo Yatha.
—(23/29 Yajurveda)

When scholars become judges and start seeing the pros and con of each matter, then only can truth be seen by seeing things directly in the same way as the women can be known by seeing the thighs.

One should learn to see or experience truth face-to-face and understand the indepth meaning behind it. We should repose our faith in rumours. The jar of untruth shall break only when we realise the truth.

(54) *Rajata Harinihi Sisa Yujo Yujyante Karmabhihi ,*
Ashwasya Vajinastvachi Simaha Shamyantu Shamyanti.
—(23/27 Yajurveda)

Women who are loving, attractive, pious and engage in household work are married of-to strong and able men who give happiness to their husbands and themselves by leading disciplined lives. Women should therefore engage in good deeds and discipline so that they can lead a peaceful and cordial conjugal life.

(55) *Bahurupa Vaishwakarmanaha. —(24/17, Yajurveda)*

Different types or workers are under authorities who do different types of jobs.

A person who is all round and is blessed with talent to do all types of works he becomes famous because of his deeds and many people work under him and seek his valuable guidance that is why we should perform such deeds so that we become successful in all our endeavours.

It is the responsibility of the guide or leader to engage in activities that lead to welfare of society.

(56) Vache Krunchaha. *—(24/31 Yajurveda)*

The speech of a crane.

Every person should have the gift of speech so that they can express their thoughts accordingly. One should know to gauge a situation well and then speak, otherwise it could lead to animosity and embarrassing situations.

A person who learns to express maximum in minimum words is the person who shall definitely attain success on the basis of his eloquent speech.

(57) Ishtam Veetambhirguta Varshatkritam Tam Devasaha Prati Gribhnantyashwam. *—(25/37,Yajurveda)*

Those scholar call that person only, their leader who is radiant, loved by all, hard-working and progressive.

The person having the above qualities only can be accepted as the leader and people follow only such a person accordingly. That is why we should all strive to improve our skills.

(58) Sakamam Adhwanaskuru Sangyanamastu Me Amuna. *—(26/1 Yajurveda)*

You accept all these paths according to your desire may I attain knowledge by strength and object.

One should realise one's potentials and capabilities before treading on the path of either desired goal so that it may be easy to attain the eternal truth or knowledge of the self.

(59) Dhiya Vipro Ajayat. *—(26/15, Yajurveda)*

A thinker is gifted with a unique intellect.

A person who is contemplative and intelligent achieves all what he desires.

All people listen, but few of them contemplate. That is why we should all make an effort and contemplate.

(60) *Urdhva Asya Samidho Bhavantyurdhwa Shukra Shochinshyagnehe Diumattama Supratikasya Sunoho.*
—(27/11 Yajurveda)

The flames of fire in an altar rise up into the sky and the rays of light also move upwards. We learn that flames from the sacrificial altar and the rays of light emerging from it rise upwards. This means that the radiance of knowledge always helps the person to attain a high position and always be successful in all pursuits.

(61) *Emam Yagyamavatamdhwaram Na. —(27/17, Yajurveda)*

May our peaceful and non-violent religious sacrifice be protected in the righteous manner.

Just in the same way as a yagya needs fire and air, to be accomplished, in the same way every person should engage in constructive work so that he accomplishes the work properly.

(62) *Yutham Pata Swastibhihi Sada Naha. —(27/28 Yajurveda)*

O Sages! may your desire to do welfare of all, always protect us.

Scholars always desire the well-being of one and all in the same way as, fire and air add to the Yagya. The air protects fire by constantly airing it and keeping it alive. The scholars give guidance to the weak and people who have gone astray so that they fulfil all their desires by always treading on the path of righteousness.

(63) *Pahi Chatasribhirvaso. —(27/43, Yajurveda)*

O Agni! Protect us by the four types of knowledge, *i.e.* Rik, Yaju, Sama and Atharva.

The word "Vedas' means knowledge which is classified into four types. The characteristics of Rik are-welfare, attainment of the supreme soul, experiencing the beatitude of God, internal happiness, piousness, adhering to one's duties, love, penance, pity, altruism, benevolence and service, etc. The characteristics of Yaju are valiance, attainments, courageousness, protection, leadership, success, prestige and victory, etc. The characteristics of Sama are, performing arts, play, happiness, entertainment, literature, music art, sensual pleasure, progressiveness and contemplation. The characteristics of Atharva are, luxury and wealth, accumulation of things, aids of consumerism and accessories of household usage.

The four Vedas resemble Dharma, Artha, Kama and Moksha which help in our welfare. We can attain all these four states with knowledge.

(64) *Devistisrastitsro Devihi Patiminoram Vardhanayan. —(28/ 18, Yajurveda)*

The three goddesses help the protector Indra.

Bharati protects the Dyuloka. The companion of Rudragana Saraswati protects the Yagya and Ida protects the Bhuloka and help the performer of the Yagya in his work.

When the performer accomplishes the yagya he gets the desired results and benefits from it. The 3 goddesses definitely help that person who strive selflessly on the path of Karma (actions)

(65) *Ketum Krinavanna Ketave Deshomarya Apeshase*

Samushabh Dirajayatha Ha. —(29/37,Yajureda)

O Agni! Bless the ignorant with knowledge and bless the ugly or the not so beautiful with beauty. You are the one who rises alike the mornings and exhibit yourself in totality. Knowledge destroys ignorance and inspires us to do great and noble deeds. When a Karmayogi moves on the path of karma and attains the desired he experiences divine happiness and comes nearer to God. That is why one should start one's work early in the morning so that he progresses and moves on the path of success.

(66) *Rathe Tishthan Nayati Vajinaha Puro Yatra Yatra Kamayate Suparithana*

Abhishunam Mahimanam Panayata Manaha Pashchadanu Yachchanti Rashmayaha. —(29/43, Yajurveda)

The charioteer can direct the horses of the chariot to anywhere, he pleases, learn the importance of the 'reins' that control the mind which is alike uncontrollable horse.

To attain one's goal one can controls the mind which is fickle by the reins of purushartha(4 attainments). One should strive incessantly to control the mind.

(67) *Vishwani Deva Savitarduritani Parasuva*

Yudbhadram Tanna Asuna. —(30/3, Yajurveda)

O Lord! Destroy all that is evil and bring near us all that is good.

We should always be ready to accept good and abstain from all bad. We should strictly abhor bad thoughts, bad habits and bad deeds and should prefer good thoughts habits and deeds. This is the best path to purification, purification leads to self-development and consequently success.

(68) Brahmane Brahmanam,Kshatraya Rajanyam.

—(30/5,Yajurveda)

The person who is desirous of knowledge should go to a scholar and the person desirous of valiance should go to a Kshatriya.

Only by coming in the tutelage of the learned man can one acquire knowledge and the people desirous of becoming courageous should seek the tutelage of a Kshatriya. One should imbibe the best qualities by seeking the studentship of such great men.

(69) Tapase Kaulalam. *—(30/7, Yajurveda)*

The dignified should always practise penance.

Penana-basically includes following the set of rules, self-study, concentration, altruism, contemplation, worship giving sermons, inspiration to engage in good deeds and oneness in speech and action.

Those people who are born in the noble clan are incessantly engaging in wrong deeds. People born in noble clans should engage in good deeds and activities.

(70) Ritaye Stenahridayam. *—(30/3, Yajurveda)*

The best way to fight the enemy's army is to accompany such a person who keeps his thoughts concealed as a robber.

During war-time one should devoid acting independently. All the decisions should be taken in total secrecy. The person who conceals all his thoughts and does not exhibit it neither through speech nor actions, such a person is known as Sten-Hridya (One whose heart is alike a robber's heart)

(71) Yamaya Yamsoom. *—(30/15, Yajurveda)*

To know the rules and self-rules one ought to seek the guidance of the scholars.

One should properly adhere to the constitution of the country. The law-makers analyse the laws neutrally for the well-being of the country.

(72) *Pratishrutkaya Artanam.* —*(30/19, Yajurveda)*

Be sagacious to take the oath. He is known as an 'Atena' who criticizes the bad and praises the good and noble. An 'Atena' is straight forward and he is devoid of wickedness. One should therefore support the good should be away from bias and should always strive for the well-being of one and all. If you do so you shall fulfil all your desires and shall succeed in all endeavours.

(73) *Vedahametam Purusham Mahant Aditya Varna Tamasaha Parastata*

Tameva Viditvati Mrityumeti Nanyaha Pantha Vidyate Ayanaya. —*(31/18 Yajurveda)*

I am seeing this great soul alike the sun beyond the darkness. One who knows him is liberated from death. There is no other way to escape death.

It is only the light of knowledge that can conquer darkness. The person who knows the ultimate truth, does not fear darkness or death. Unconditional surrender at the feet of God is the easiest way to escape death.

(74) *Rucham Brahmam Janayanto Deva Agre Tadbuvan*

Yastvaiva Brahmano Vidyatrasya Deva Asan Vashe. —*(31/21,Yajurveda))*

The gods who have realised the Brahma Jnana have said in the beginning that the person who realises this truth can bring into his control all the gods and the senses.

Knowledge can facilitate the human to break bonds of the material world and to realise the eternal truth. That is why such a person has all his senses controlled. The gods reside in our body, and by controlling the senses, they too are into control. Then the senses work according to the human desire.

(75) *Hiranya Garbha Istyesh Ma Ma Hinsidityeshama Yasmanna Jata Istyeshaha.*

The God who is worshipped with the incantation *"HIRANYAGARBHAHA MA MA HINSIT VA YASMAMANNA* JATA" does not possess a form.

God does not possess a form and is omnipresent. The world moves and is preserved because of God's grace. The idol can just be a medium to experience divinity but is not god itself. One should therefore learn to experience the beatitude of God through meditation.

(76) *Paritya Bhutani Pariyta Lokan Paritya Sarvaha Pradisho Dishashcha.* *—(32/11,Yajurveda)*

Paridyava Prithivi Sadya Itya Parilokanaha Paridishaha Parishwaha. *—(32/12 Yajurveda)*

The first half of both these mantras mean the same. We should know everything about the worlds, the directions, etc.

The knowledge of the physical world is Avidya and the knowledge of the self is vidya. But we should know both. To understand nature, it is imperative to understand all the so-called elements or things that constitute nature. One gradually starts differentiating oneself from the entire nature. It is possible to attain this state by the knowledge of the self.

(77) *Yam Medham Deva Ganaha Pitarashchopasate*

Tatha Mamad Medhayagne Medhanivanam Kuru Swaha.
--(32/13 Yajurveda))

O Radiant Creator! Enlighten me with that divine knowledge which has always been praised by scholars and protectors, through self-surrender.

Here the human prays, surrendering himself to the will of god, saying O Lord, bless me with that divine knowledge praised by the scholars, who protect this knowledge and that is why are referred as noble souls. Please bless us with this knowledge which these noble souls are blessed.

(78) *Edam Mem Brahma Cha Kshatram Shriyashnutama.*
—(32/16 Yajurveda)

May I be embellished with the radiance of knowledge and the radiance of valiance. One should imbibe all the knowledge possible and tread on the path of truth and should also embrace courage. May the Brahmins and the Kshatriyas become radiant which is possible only if there is no animosity between them.

Both these type of people should spread that type of knowledge which increases, radiance, enthusiasm, zeal and strength.

The ascent of the individual is the ascent of society and the ascent of society shall doubtlessly lead to ascent of the nation.

(79) *Agne Shardha Mahate Saubhgaya Tava Dyumnanyutta-mani Santu*

Sam Jasqatyam Yuyamma Krinupva Shatruyatamabhi Tishtha Mahansi. —*(33/12, Yajurveda)*

O Agni! Bless us so that we may acquire all the comforts, may we be successful, discipline and assert the relation of the husband and wife, and destroy all the feelings of bitterness and enmity.

We should always engage in all activities that help us to acquire wealth and comfort and may we get success on the basis of our noble deeds. May there be always cordial relations between the husband and the wife and may all the obstacles and hurdles be crossed on basis of our pursuance and will-power.

(80) *Mahattadwidrishnaka Asurasya Nama Vishwarupi Amritanatassthao.* —*(33/22 Yajurveda)*

A brave and valiant person attains a lot of success and he becomes invincible. He conquers all the invincible comforts and consequently becomes famous.

The person who becomes famous on basis of his perseverance and griti he gradually assures control all the happiness and comforts. Therefore one should always strive so that there is growth and self-improvement.

(81) *Maham Indro Ya Ojasa Kadachana Stari Asi Kadachana Pra Yuchchasi.* —*(33/27 Yajurveda)*

You the great elegant Indra who does not indulge in violence and is never negligent of his duties, although being radiant and mighty.

Every person should therefore refrain from dereliction of duty and violence. Violence is the mother of all hurdles and obstructer and negligence is the doorway to misfortune.

(82) *Udutyam Jatavedasam Devam Vahanit Ketavaha Drishe Vishwaya Suryam.* —*(33/31 Yajurveda)*

In fact, all the scholars of the Vedas, to enlighten all the people, about the Divine cosmic energy or Parabrahma, and for his blessings distribute their knowledge to one and all, alike the emanation of effulgence.

Knowledgeable people distribute their knowledge so that they help all the people to emancipate and mitigate their miseries.

(83) *Shrayani Iva Surya Vishwendidrasya Bhakshat.*
Vasuni Jate Janmana Ojasaprati Bhagam Na Didhim.
—(33/41 Yajurveda)

O Humans! seek the refuge of the sun who inspires us to do everything and partake all the grains. We enjoy our hard-earned money, you also do so accordingly.

The sun helps in producing grains and other things on basis of his heat. In the same way we should also earn our living on basis of our courage and perseverance. Only by doing so can we attain success.

(84) *Vidadyadi Sarma Rugnamardrermahi Pathaha Parnya Saddyyankaha Agram Nayatsupadyaksharanamachcha Ravam Prathama Anati Gata.* *—(33/59 Yajurveda)*

The Vedas are unbiased and because of this merit they successfully enlighten the soul and destroy ignorance. We imbibe that knowledge which has discerned from the earlier generations. The Vedas speak of knowledge that is eternal and impeccable. It helps us in spiritual and mental development.

One can become knowledgeable only by imbibing the teachings of the Vedas, because the Vedas are the source of eternal and authentic divine knowledge.

(85) *Upa Naha Sunvo Giraha Shrunavanatvamritasya Ye*
Sumridika Bhavantu Naha. *—(33/77 Yajurveda))*

May our sons imbibe the knowledge of the Vedas which are given by the invincible gods and may it give us happiness.

It is obvious that the Vedas bless the person with happiness, who listens and imbibes that knowledge.

(86) *Praitu Brahmanaspatihi Pra Devyetu Sunrita*
Achcha Viramnarya Pankti Radhasam Deva Yagya Nayantu Na. *—(33/89,Yajurveda)*

May the scholars take part in the religious sacrifice. May we realise the eternal truth. May all the noble people, scholars and benefactors of the society help and assist us in accomplishing the Yagya.

Whenever one performs the Yagya, one should always invite noble-souls for the Yagya. Because, with their mere presence and blessing the Yagya gets accomplished. Therefore, all people should unite and work shoulder to shoulder for societal progress.

(87) *Yenedam Bhutam Bhuvanam Bhavishyat Parigruhita Mriten Sarvam Yena Yagyastayate Sapta Hota Tanme Manaha Shivjankalpamastu.* —*(34/4, Yajurveda)*

May that mind of mine be filled with good resolutions, which has absorbed everything from the past, present and future and can be performed properly with the help of the seven means.

Our life is alike a Yagya. This Yagya has seven means(body hands legs and mouth, mind, intellect) which fulfil the Yagya.

The speedy horse, *i.e.* the mind controls all of them if the mind is pure then all the deeds performed are also good deed; if the mind is impure then all the deeds performed are wasteful and futile. Therefore the mind should possess very good resolutions, then only can the Yagya be accomplished.

(88) *Pitum Nu Stosham Maho Dharmanam Tavishima Yasta Trito Vyojasa Vritram Viparvamardayata.* —*(34/7, Yajurveda)*

We praise the food grains that we behold on the basis of which lord Indra, the god of the three world destroyed Vritra.

We should eat only that type of food, which is nutritious, wholesome and gives energy. We should abstain from all types of junk food that vitiates our health, food that nourishes the mind and intellect and makes it efficient is the best food. Food should build up the resistance power of the body from bacteria and viruses.

(89) *Anvidanumate Tvam Manyasai Sham Cha Naskridhi Kratave Dakshaya No Hinu Pra Na Ayunshi Jarishaha.* —*(34/8, Yajurveda)*

O Scholars! Lead us to all that is noble and favourable so that our minds becomes sharp and sound. Please bless us with a long life.

We should always stay in the company of scholars so that they guide us constantly. The minds can be conditioned and strengthened by self study and good company of noble people. Consequently one is blessed with a long healthy life.

(90) *Tvada Kashchana Hi Praketaha.* —*(34/18, Yajurveda)*

We can attain all knowledge on being blessed by the god. The person can attain god or brahma jnana (knowledge of the divine cosmic soul) as a result of god's blessings.

(91) Tvam Jyotisha Vi Tamo Vavartha. —(34/22, Yajurveda)

You can destroy the darkness, by your radiance and light.

Ignorance(darkness) can be destroyed by light(knowledge) on acquiring knowledge human being can tread on the path of growth and progress.

(92) Trini Pada Vi Chakrame Vishnurgopa Adabhyaha Ato Dharmani Dharayana. —(34/43, Yajurveda)

The indestructable supreme god who is the protector and the controller, preserver of these three worlds is also the one who creates the rules and regulations of this world.

The supreme cosmic soul has all the energy to create, preserve and destroy the world. God himself is indestructible and is ommipresent. We should take inspiration from these merits of god and tread on the path of development and growth.

(93) Tadvi Praso Vipanyavo Jagrivansaha Samindhate Vishnoryotparam Padam. —(34/44, Yajurveda)

The scholars praise the Lord differently and are always alert, they always enlighten others with the effulgence of knowledge about the supreme God.

The scholars strive to enkindle the flame of knowledge in one and all. To realise divinity and the eternal truth we should seek the company of scholars.

(94) Ashmanvati Riyate Sam Ramadh Va Muttishtath Pra Tarta Sakhayaha Atra Jahimo Ashiva Ye Asanchivanvaya-muttaremabhi Vajan. —(35/10, Yajurveda)

Dear friends! A river filled with stones is flowing, try to cross it, stand up and strive to go beyond. Renounce all that which is painful and accept all, that which gives happiness.

This world is alike a river and the human being has to cross it to reach the paraloka(heaven) if the human being strives with preservance and grit he can easily cross the river of material life.

(95) Richam Vacham Pra Padye Mano Yajuhu Pra Padye Sama Pranam Pra Papadye Chakshuhu Shrotram Pra Papadye Vagojaha Sahojo Mayi Pranana Nao. —(36/1, Yajurveda)

My speech seeks the refuge of rigveda. My mind seeks the refuge of Yajurveda. My prana(life) seeks the refuge of samaveda. My ears seek the refuge of Atharvaveda. May the speech and strength and life (Prana) become stable and one.

May different senses seek the refuge of the vedas accordingly so that my speech becomes strong, so that the prana becomes stable and increases and so that I develop integrity of personality.

The knowledge of the Vedas can make a person capable and strong.

(96) *Drite Danha Mai Jyokte Sandrishi Jivyasam Jyokyte Sandrishi Jivyasam.* —*(36/19, Yajurveda)*

O the capable one! Make me strong and may all befriend me. May I develop a sense of brotherhood. May I develop a sense of brotherhood. May we all mutually develop a sense of brotherhood and affection.

May god bless us with the feeling of brotherhood so that we may live happily and peacefully, so that we can help and assist each other in our duties.

(97) *Tachcha Kshurdevhitam Purastachrukrammucharat*

Pashyem Sharadaha Shatam Jivema Shradaha Shatam Shrunuyama Sharadaha Shatam Pra Brayama Sharadaha Shatmadinaha Syam Sharadaha Shatam Bhuyashcha Sharadaha Shatam Bhuyashcha Sharadaha Shatataa.

—*(36/24, Yajurveda)*

He first arose who was the doer of good to the scholars and was blessed with pure eyes of knowledge. May he bless us with a long life of 100 years devoid of misery and pain so that we may live, may hear, give sermons, lead a comfortable life and dwell in happiness for more than a hundred years.

We should firstly acquire knowledge as much as possible. This shall lead to strengthening of the senses upto death. We will be blessed with a long healthy life, knowledge can facilitate in keeping the health and mind strong.

(98) *Vachamastame Ni Yachcha Deva Yuvam.*

—*(37/16, Yajurveda)*

Bless us with that type of speech so that we may be able to unite all the scholars together.

Speech should always be effectve and soft. Because of effective and good speech we can entice many a people. We should practise, patience and seriousness whilst we speak. Only because of this can we be successful in unity all the scholars together.

(99) *Mayi Tyandibriyam Brihanmayi Daksho Mayi Kratuhu.*
—(38/27, Yajurveda)

May I be blessed with divine energy, may I become intelligent and become responsible. We should bring into control all our senses and acquire the divine knowledge so that we become strong, intelligent. By doing so we can fulfil all our responsibilities properly. We should engage in that type of work that helps in honing our skills and increase our energy to perform work.

(100) *Manasaha Kama Akutim Vachaha Satya Ashiya.*
—(39/4, Yajurveda)

May I be blessed with a contemplative nature, an ability to grasp things well and speech which is truthful and righteous.

Those who acquire knowledge and contemplate on it they are blessed with all types of abilities. The strong conviction of a person helps him to focus on his desired objects and achieve it. By speaking the truth the desired object can be acquired easily. Only by doing so can one achieve the desired thing.

(101) *Kurvanneveha Karmani Jijivisheehadatam Samaha Aevam Khayi Nanya Yetho Asti Na Karma Lipyate Nare.*
—(40/2, Yajurveda)

While performing our deeds, we should desire to live for a 100 years. The essence of human life lies in deeds and nothing else. Accordingly a person who performs his deeds does not become attached to his deeds.

We should avoid lethargy. On the contrary we should perform noble deeds that eventually give good fruits. We should respect elders, honour and respect guests, have compassion towards one and all, respect all the divine forces that facilitate our work and consequently free it from flaws.

(102) *Asurya Nama Te Loka Andhena Tamasavritaha*
Tanste Pretyapi Gachchanti Ye Ke Chatmahano Janaha.
—(40/3, Yajurveda))

Those people who are self-destructive that live in ignorance(darkenss) and dwell in it even after death.

Physical energy is known as Asurya. Those who misuse their physical energy end in misery. We should abstain from, atheism,amassing wealth, greed, breaking unity, aimlessness, bad thoughts and thoughts that lead to failure and misery.

(103) *Yastu Sarvani Bhutanyatm Annevanu Pashyati.*
Sarvabhuteshu Chatmanam Tato Na Vi Chikitsati.
—(40/6, Yajurveda))

He does not have suspicion, who sees all the human beings with the experience of his soul through his soul.

The person who realises that there is one soul which dwells in one and all, and that there is no difference between the within and the body, does not hate anybody. He has no sort of suspicion because he experiences the real owners of divinity in multitudes. Such a person is egalitarian and has love and affection for one and all. He believes in reposing faith in all humans, equally which consequently results in peace and unity.

(104) *Sambhutim Cha Vinasham Cha Yastadweddbhaya Asaha*
Vinashena Mrityum Tirtva Sambhutyamrut Mashnute.
—(40/11, Yajurveda)

He who sees unity and diversity as one, he who conquers death by diversity, attains liberation with unity.

Unity is the energy being society. If there is no unity then the society shall undoubtedly disintegrate and consequently the unit of society (a human being) also shall cease to exist. When all the units of society come together then there is an increase in internal energy. This lead, to oneness of the world. Therefore a person should selflessly work by renouncing all forms of selfishness, for the growth of each and every one.

(105) *Vidyam Cha Avidyam Cha Yastadwedobhaya Asaha*
Avidyaya Mrityum Tirtava Vidyaya Amrutam Mashnute.
—(40/14, Yajurveda)

The person who acquires knowledge of the self and the science of nature he conquers death with the same and attains state of realisation with the help of the knowledge of the self.

The knowledge of the self helps in increasing one's moral strength, to acquire peace and to find a solution to all the problems. By acquiring the knowledge of nature one can fulfil all material needs. Both these types of knowledge is essential for spiritual and physical growth. One can be blessed with a long life if one practises yoga Sadhana and a balanced living. That is why human should acquire knowledge of nature and should lead the knowledge of the self and attain the higher goals of realisation.

(106) *Vayu Anil Amrit Athedam Bhasmant Ashariram*
Aum Krito Smada, Klibe Smari Krit Asmar.
—(40/15 Yajurveda))

This body is going to cease and the prana being celestial is immortal, O Purush/Soul! Meditate on the immortal soul, remember all the past karmas (deeds) and contemplate on them.

Human beings should become karma-yogis and incessantly meditate on the Supreme Soul. One should not forget that the body's mortal and is going to be destroyed eventually. He should therefore engage in good deeds that reap good fruits. One should introspect and contemplate on the past deeds so that one does not commit mistakes even inadvertently in the future.

(107) *Agne Naya Supatha Raye Asmanvishwani Devvayunani Vidwana.* *—(40/11, Yajurveda)*

O Lord! you are aware of all our deeds. Please enlighten us and lead us to the path of growth and spiritual development.

We should never forget that all our resolutions are God's resolutions, therefore they can never be concealed. We should therefore always engage in good deeds inspired by good thoughts. O Lord! therefore guide us, lead us on the path of righteousness so that we may grow spiritually and morally. In return of this, we can just prostrate before you.

(108) *Hiranmayena Patrena Satya Sthapihitam Sukham.*
—(40/17yajurveda)

The mouth of truth is covered with a gold vessel.

We should always be truthful and should be devoid of greed because greed is the root cause of all sins. Until the mouth of truth is closed, there shall be unhappiness and misery. But once the gold vessel is done away with, only peace and happiness shall dwell.

5

The Samveda

It is said in the Chandogya Upanishad that:

Ya Rik Tatsama. —*(1/3/4)*

A compilation of richas (shlokas) is known as Sama.

Richi Adhyoodha Sama. —*(1/6/1)*

Sama is dependent on the Richas.

Vachaha Rierasaha Richaha Samarasaha, Samna Udvitho Rasaha.

The beauty of speech lies in the Richas, The beauty of richas lie in the sama and the beauty of the sama lies in the style of pronunciation and singing.

Therefore, it is now clear that the knowledge of Sama itself is Samaveda. The singing of the sama can make the mind stable and can give peace to the vagrant mind. The singing of the Sama begins initially on the high pitch and gradually the pitch is lowered. These sound waves of the sama are capable of giving peace to the mind.

Yogeshwar Srikrishna has stated the importance of Samaveda in the following manner-*Vedanama Samavedo Asmi* meaning "I am samaveda myself, amongst the Vedas." (Geeta-10/22)

There are two parts of the Samaveda (1) Purvarchik (2) Uttararchik.

In between both of them is 'Mahanamnayarchik which comprises of 10 incantations

There are four parts of Purvarchika Aagneya, Aendra, Paavmaan and Aasanya.

The number of mantras in each skanda (Part) are as follows-

Name	*No. of Mantras*
Aagneya	114
Aendra	352
Paavmaan	119
Aaranya	55
Mahanamnyarchik	10
Total	650

There are 21 chapters in the Uttararchik which contain 1225 mantras. Cumulatively, there are 1875 mantras in the Samaveda.

On the basis of the style of singing and pronunciation there were once upon a time a thousand branches, but gradually became extinct. Now also we do not come across many that recite the Samagana. Many of them are found in Southern India, especially Mysore. The three branches now known as Ranayani, Kauthumi and Jaiminiya.

Many people believe that besides a few mantras, most of the Samaveda mantras are extracted from the Rigveda. It is important to know that the method of pronunciation of Samaveda and Rigveda is evidently different and in this language one alphabet can change the meaning and context of mantra altogether.

After the Vedas come the Brahmanas. Amongst the Samvedic Brahmana texts, Tandava and samavidhana are more famous. Because the Tandava Brahmana consists of 25 chapters; it is known as Panchvisha Brahmana. There are many a miraculous story in this Brahmana, therefore it is also referred to as Adhbhut Brahmana. The other Brahmanas of Samaveda are Arsheya, Vansha and Samhitopnishad Brahmana, etc.

The Aranyaka texts consist of extracts from upanishads. The Aranyaka of Samveda comes under the Samasamhita. The Samvedi Brahmans sing the metrical mantras, therefore the name of this Aranyaka text is Chandogya Upanishad. Amongst the Samvedic upanishads, the Chandogya and Kenopinshad are the most famous. The scholars state that Brahmana, Aranyaka and upanishads represent three states of life, Grihastha (householders), Vanprastha (going to the forest) and Sanyasa (Total renunciation).

All the mantras of the Samaveda are sung. Those mantras only are recited to invoke the Gods for whom the religious sacrifice is being offered to. The recitation of the Samaveda includes seven notes. One can therefore aptly find the roots of music embedded here. With respect to the evolution and development of Indian music, the samveda holds special significance. The sama-gana is capable of giving the listener, divine peace.

Part One: Purvarchik

Aagneya

(1) Agnirvritrani Janghanad —*(4, Samveda)*

Agni(fire) destroys the enemies (vritras). Agni destroys darkness by creating light. We have five fundamental enemies- pleasure instincts, anger, greed, attachment and ego. The fire of knowledge is capable of destroying these enemies. Ignorance (darkness) can be destroyed by knowledge of self.

(2) Agne! Naha Drishe Devaha Hi Asi —*(10, Samveda)*

Agni is the God, which leads and guides us. Agni destroys darkness and makes it easier for us to tread on the path towards knowledge. Therefore, Agni creates light and leads us towards our goal.

(3) Naha Rayim Vansate —*(22, Samveda)*

Agni blesses us with wealth. Agni gives us heat and energy so that we can fulfil all our duties. In return it yields good results, *i.e.* wealth. Therefore, it is a truth that Agni is the giver of wealth.

(4) Hey Agney! Mrid, Mahan Asi I —*(23, Samveda)*

O Agni, you are great and are giver of happiness. Agni is useful to us in many a way. As a result we get happiness. In this way Agni is giver of happiness and therefore is considered noble.

(5) Agney! Vishpatihi Rakshasaha Tapanaha —*(39, Samaveda)*

Agni is the protector of the people, is the destroyer of demons. Agni is useful in constructive activities. Agni is not only the protector but is also the destroyer.. The righteous usage of Agni can lead to good fruits but the abuse of Agni shall lead to sheer destruction and ruin.

(6) Hey Agney, Savita Devaha Na Urdhvaha Vajasya Sanita —*(57 Samaveda)*

O Agni! May you become alike the sun and bless us with food grains. O Agni! Nourish us and help us in all our constructive activities. Protect us and nourish us by creating the necessary food grains.

(7) Agnihi Suvirayasya Saubhagasya Ishe —*(60, Samveda)*

Agni is the master of noble valiance and fortune Agni is the one, which bestows all material happiness, destroys all darkness and is the ultimate source of energy. It is used in human welfare and allied constructive activities. It increases courage and bestows wealth, health and comfort.

(8) Havisha A Juhot, Marjayadhwam —*(63, Samveda)*

Perform the Religious sacrifice with the right means, may it purify everything. During the yagya, ghee, aromatic herbs, shrubs are offered to the fire. As a result the entire atmosphere becomes clean and pollution free. Fire can help in making the atmosphere devoid of pollution. Therefore, we should use the right things to purify the atmosphere, during the yagya.

Aendra Kanda

(9) Brahmadwishaha Avajahi —*(194 Samveda)*

Destroy hatred by knowledge. Light is the symbol of knowledge. When a person is filled with enmity and animosity he lacks judgement and fails to do good to others. With the emergence of knowledge, all the hatred ceases and the person engages incessantly in good deeds.

(10) Ugram Vachaha Apavadhihi —*(353, Samveda)*

Do not speak harsh words. We should always be soft spoken because people always like people who are soft-spoken. No body ever likes a person who speaks harsh words and hurts other. Our words should exhibit our good thoughts.

(11) Ahaha Ahaha Shundhyuhu Paripadam —*(396, Samveda)*

Cleanliness can keep one away from ailments and diseases. The people who keep themselves and their surroundings clean seldom fall sick. We should never forget cleanliness is next to Godliness. For proper growth and development, a clean mind and body are of utmost importance

(12) Avrataha Naha Hinoti —*(441,Samaveda)*

A person who does not fulfil the vows cannot accomplish anything. The person who does not have a firm conviction to accomplish the resolution is definitely a failure. A person who does not strive with mind, heart and body does not ever achieve anything. That is why one should become a karma-yogi and work constantly although he may or may not get the benefits. Eventually, hard work undoubtedly gets paid off.

Paavmana Kanda

(13) *Vicharshanihi Vishwaha Mrudaha Abhyakramit*

—(488,Samaveda)

The scholar is successful in vanquishing all his enemies. The scholar has a solution for every problem and crisis, may it be disease or an external enemy. Because he is endowed with wit and grit he surmounts all his problems successfully. He controls the fickleness of the mind by reciting mantras and eventually stabilizes the mind. He gives the right advice at the right time to the right people. In this way we should all strive to acquire as much knowledge possible because on attainment of total knowledge we shall be able to find a solution to all our problems.

(14) *Sukritya Mahana Abhyavardhayaha* *—(507, Samaveda)*

You become noble because of your good deeds.

By engaging in good deeds he or she becomes famous and gets honour and respect in society. If the good deeds result in the welfare of society then such a person is honoured and is respected, undoubtedly.

(15) *Vicharshanihi Hitaha Sa Chateti* *—(508, Samaveda)*

A scholar becomes a benefactor and gives knowledge. When a scholar is donating knowledge the ultimate aim of his knowledge is welfare of one and all. Because of knowledge, the darkness of ignorance ceases and we tread on the path of progress. We should imbibe all the knowledge and the merits from the scholars and should engage in activities that result in the welfare one and all.

(16) *Ratnadhaha Varyani Dayate* *—(528, Samaveda)*

A person who wears gems or precious stones becomes wealthy. People who wear precious stones and gems acquire a lot of wealth. During times of crisis, wealth is of utmost importance., Precious stones and gems are worn to improve ones health. We should, therefore always save for contingencies, otherwise we shall have to beg from others.

(17) Ma Te Rasasya Matsat Dwayawinaha —(561, Samaveda)

Those people do not dwell in happiness whose deeds and thoughts are not similar. A person who is a hypocrite never lives in happiness. Therefore, we should be beware of hypocrisy and try to bridge the gap between thoughts and action, *i.e.* we should perform deeds according to our thoughts.

(18) Ataptatturna Tadamo Ashnute —(565, Samaveda)

No one can overachieve anything without perseverance. When a human being engages in action and hard work until he does not achieve his goal, he undergoes metamorphosis and positive change. In this manner he makes himself all the more disciplined, patient and diligent. As a result of his diligence he gets good benefits such as total peace, happiness and contention.

Aranyaka Kanda

(19) Yaha Mam Dadati Sa Vata

The giver of food protects one and all. Donation of food leads to protection of others. That is why it is referred to as the noblest form of donation. By donating food one is blessed with limitless virtues. Similarly scholars who donate and impart knowledge, do so for the welfare of all. By knowledge, one become judicious and engages in earning a livelihood for him. Donation of knowledge enhances knowledge and this is a noble form of donation..

(20) Annam Adantam Aham Annam Admi —(594, Samaveda)

He who does not donate food, I (God) destroy his food. We should never store food more than what is required. If we do so the gods consider us selfish and destroy all the food. That is why we should always donate food whenever possible. Similarly if a scholar does not impart education and knowledge, the knowledge automatically stagnates and ceases. Therefore, the scholars should donate knowledge time to time. By doing so their ego ceases to exist.

(21) Mayavino Mamire Asya Mayaya —(596, Samaveda)

By imbibing knowledge the greatest of the ignorant can become noble and knowledgeable. By acquiring knowledge the darkness of ignorance is destroyed. As a result the wicked also become compassionate renounce their wickedness, their attachment and become noble. The flame of knowledge leads a person to the path of progress.

(22) *Amritaya Apyayamanaha Divi Uttamani Shravansi Dhishwa —(603, Samaveda)*

Attain success and tread on the path of progress to attain liberation. Humans are incessantly engaged in work so that they can liberate themselves from the bondages of material life. All the spiritual knowledge given by the great scholars help us in our endeavours to liberate ourselves. We tread on the path of progress by utilizing the means to attain liberation. This as a result gives us happiness and joy.

(23) *Tvam Jyotisha Vi Tamo Vavartha —(604, Samaveda)*

You destroy darkness by light. Light in form of knowledge is capable of destroying the darkness of ignorance. By doing so we can surmount all the difficulties and become successful in all our endeavours.

(24) *Abhubhdadra Niveshani Vishwasya Jagato Ratri —(608, Samaveda)*

The night is propitious because it gives all peace and relaxation. The night helps us to relax so that we become fresh and energetic to perform the next day's duties. In this way the night is beneficial to one and all.

(24) *Vaishvanaraya Matirnavyase Shuchihi —(609, Samaveda)*

The intellect of the Agni God is pure and auspicious for all. The person who strives selflessly for society automatically is respected and honoured. That is why we should engage in those deeds by which the entire society benefits. By doing so our mind and heart shall become pure and propitious. The ultimate aim of Agni is social welfare and the ultimate aim of every human being should be the same.

(25) *Ma Vo Vachanish Parichakshyani Vocham —(610, Samveda)*

O Gods! May I never speak anything harsh. We should always abstain from inauspicious and harsh words that inflict pain. Pain inflicted can not be taken back. Physical injury is sooner forgotten than insults and harsh words. The effect of good words is always good and in the long run it reaps good benefits.

(27) Yasho Ma Paratimuchyatama *—(611 Samaveda)*

May I be always blessed with success. Man can only be successful if he engages in work performed for the benefit of all. By doing he shall earn a lot of respect and honour. Success and fortune always bless such people.

Mahanamnyarchika

(28) Eshe Hi Shakraha *—(66, Samaveda)*

The lord is always capable. The person who controls all his senses is always capable. Every person should strive in order to have his skills and capabilities because the person who does so can only become the master.

We can make the body capable by exercising regularly and can make the mind capable by practising concentration and keeping the mind stable and calm. We can acquire maximum knowledge by self-study and by reading sublime literature. When we become capable in all ways we can become masters and as a result we shall be respected wherever we go.

Part Two: Uttararchika

(29) Yagyaha Chetanaha Jigati *—(670, Samaveda)*

The yagya enlightens the mind.

During the Yagya the samaveda is recited as a result of which the mind becomes stable and calm. Simultaneously the atmosphere also becomes pure and devoid of pollution. Consequently the atmosphere and the samagana enlighten the mind and facilitate spiritual progress.

(30) Soma Jatrasya Chetati *—(695, Samaveda)*

Soma infuses in us the enthusiasm to win.

The Vedas speak of the soma in some places. Some scholars believes it is synonymous to 'Bhang'. It is mentioned that Lord Indra's favourite drink is the Soma Rasa.

Soma infuses energy in each and every part of the body and improves blood circulation. As a result the body becomes energetic. It ushers enthusiasm and helps us to accomplish all our duties tirelessly.

Ritasya Jivha Pavate Madhu *—(701, Samaveda)*

A person who is truthful is always soft spoken. The truthful person is never indignant and harsh. He is devoid of fear, which is why he speaks sweetly to one and all.

(31) *Devaha Swapnaya Na Sprrihyanti* —(721, *Samaveda*)

The Gods do not favour the lazy and indolent.

The person who is lazy can never become a scholar. Laziness erodes a person's enthusiasm and energy. As a result the person loses all opportunities and finally becomes dejected and frustrated. Moreover he stops believing in the fact that he can ever succeed.

(32) *Devaha Sunvantam Echchanti* —(721, *Samaveda*)

The Gods favour the diligent and industrious.

One cannot achieve anything in life without engaging in action. A person who is diligent and consistently engaged in good actions shall attain all his goals and become successful in all his pursuits. So it is in the best interest to take part in the Karma Yoga and fulfil it to the best of ones abilities.

(33) *Ma Kim Brahmadwisham Vanaha* —(732, *Samaveda*)

Do not stay in the company of those who abhor knowledge. The people who abhor knowledge always dwell in ignorance. Good company can make a man and bad company can ruin a man. During the rains, the drop of water falls in and loses its existence and on the contrary the drop of water falls in conch and assumes the form of a pearl. That is why people who desire knowledge should refrain from people who believe that ignorance is bliss.

(34) *Martoho Na Vashta Taddhachaha* —(774 *Samaveda*)

One should not listen to anything bad. One should not listen and speak anything bad. By listening to bad things and contemplating on them, the person can engage in bad deeds. That is why one should refrain from listening to anything that is bad and negative.

(35) *Abhi Vishwani Kavya* —(775, *Samaveda*)

Always engage in all good deeds. One shall reap fruits on basic if the actions performed. Good deeds shall undoubtedly sooner or later fetch good fruits. People who engage in good deeds are always praised and respected. People who do so shall be blessed with all the desired things. Therefore, it is imperative that one should thoroughly abstain from bad actions.

(36) Dive Dive Vajam Sasnihi *—(981, Samaveda)*

You are always engaged in a war. Life is full of strife and turmoil. It is in therefore in the best interest of one and all to take part in the war without desiring anything. A life devoid of strife is a life devoid of happiness and realization. One realizes the significance of happiness only after pain. Therefore our aim should be to be take part in war and strive selflessly to be victorious.

(37) Mo Shu Brahmeva Tandrayurbhavo *—(826, Samaveda)*

After realizing the truth do not become indolent. The person who strives and attains the most divine form of knowledge should never while away his time. He should engage in performing great deeds. Knowledge leads to light and light leads us on the path of success and progress. We should therefore attain knowledge of the self and think of the welfare of others. Lethargy leads to failure therefore one should abhor it vehemently.

(38) Adha Hinvana Indriyam Jyayo Mahitvamanashe
Abhishti Kritdvicharshanihi. *—(839, Samaveda))*

The scholar achieves the ultimate goal on the basis of his abilities and its proper usage. Knowledge destroys ignorance. The scholar assimilates all the means required to fulfil a particular task on basis of his intellect and eventually becomes successful in achieving it. Because of this he becomes noble and great.

(39) Agninagnihi Samidhyate *—(844, Samaveda)*

Fire enkindles fire. It is fire that eliminates and destroys darkness. One karmayogi can be successful in creating another karmayogi. In this way one is successful in enlightening the other. That is the reason why the company of scholars is preferred and is considered very auspicious. Knowledge perpetrates knowledge and ignorance perpetrates ignorance.

That is why we should ourselves engage in good deeds and encourage others to engage in the same.

(41) Ritavridho Ritsprishao Brihantam Kratum Riten Ashathe
—(848, Samaveda)

The person who is truthful does all their deeds by treading on the righteous path. Truth is the instrument to engage in good deeds. The truthful is always ready to do good work. The greatness of truth is indecipherable, that is why it is mightier than anything in this world.

(42) Vacham Vardhaya —*(861 Samaveda)*

Improve your speech and speak only the truth. One should always speak softly and distinctly. Audience is always attracted towards those who are fluent and speak good things.

(43) Purandhim Janaya —*(861 Samaveda)*

Make us capable enough to engage in good actions. A person who is constantly engaged in good actions is never plagued by the dilemma of good and bad thoughts. By incessantly engaging in such actions he become capable and adroit in his work. Incessant practice makes a man perfect and his deeds reap rich dividends.

(44) Vacha Patirmakhasyata Vishwasyeshan Ojasaha
—*(873, Samaveda)*

If a scholar is radiant, *i.e.* an expert then he is respectable.

A distinguished person achieves name and fame only because of his adroitness and assiduity. People worship such noble souls because of their merits and qualities. That is why such scholars hold a respectable and honourable position in society.

(45) Pavitram Te Vitatam Brahmanaspate --*(967, Samaveda)*

Scholars, your deeds have disseminated all over the society.

The radiance of knowledge provides everything. Similarly the greatness of great deeds also is all-pervasive. The actions performed by great souls to spread knowledge, promote knowledge and disseminate to every stratum of society.

(46) Dhurvasya Kataha Ketavaha Pariyanti —*(997,Samaveda)*

The greatness of the heroic deeds performed by the valiant and courageous spread everywhere. One becomes successful by engaging in noble deeds. As a result, such a person also becomes prosperous and affluent. Such a person who attains knowledge does not need amenities of comforts, on the contrary he become mentally and physically strong. The courageous augments their success by their hard work performed selflessly and as a result reaps benefits.

(47) Dharmano Pavase —*(888, Samaveda)*

A person becomes pure by engaging in religious activities.

A person who is pious gradually becomes chaste and pure. Manu has said

Dashakam Dharma Lakshanam.

There are 10 merits of piousness:

(1) Stability of mind
(2) Forgiveness
(3) Benevolence
(4) Abstinence from larceny
(5) Internal and external cleanliness
(6) Control of senses
(7) Intellect
(8) Knowledge
(9) Truth
(10) Abstinence from indignancy.

(48) Vishwacharshana A Mahi Rodasi Prina —(896, Samaveda))

O Creator! Fill the heaven and the earth with your divine radiance. The sunrise brings light to the entire world. Similarly the humans are praying to soma so as to make them radiant as the sun and bless them with all the good qualities. Bless all the animate and inanimate objects with knowledge and effulgence.

(49) A Shurarsha Brihanmate Pari Priyena Dhamna
—(898 Samaveda)

O intelligent Vayu (Wind)! Come here embellished with all the merits. The wind is always active, agile, and that is why it is said that shun lethargy and become assiduous. Become swift and efficient. Inactivity is the root cause of failure. The ultimate aim of human life is incessant fulfilment of one's duties so that it accrues in the welfare of all.

(50) Suta Aeti Pavitra A Tvishim Dadhana Ojasa, Vichakshane Virochayan —(901, Samveda)

The person who engages in the good of other on the basis of his intellect, becomes successful and progresses rapidly on basis of his capabilities. This fact is self-proven that a person who engages in doing good to others, himself become successful. When such people do work they accomplish the Jnana Yagya and pave the way of knowledge for one and all.

(51) Rajanavanbhidruha Dhruve Sadasyuttame Sahasrastuna Ashate
—(911 Samaveda)

Those kings who do not conspire against each other sit amongst their courtiers in the court held by 1000 strong and firm pillars.

Noble people never engage in animosity. People who do so end up ruined and in misery. They are always devoid of stability, peace and success. If all people work shoulder to shoulder by renouncing the credit altogether, such a society is bound to prosper and grow. People who rise above and abhor rebellion pave the way for national welfare.

(52) *Dharmana Vayumiruha* —*(921 Samaveda)*

Attain the wind on the basis of independent merit.

The person who is pious always treads on the path of growth on basis of internal energy. By doing so he attains moral strength and gives our mind stability and orientation.

(53) *Ayam Yatha Na Abhuvattvashta Rupeva Takshya*
Asya Kratva Yashaswataha —*(947, Samaveda))*

Just as the carpenter gives shape to wood, in the same way Agni (Fire) purifies us and makes us successful in our concerted actions to achieve our goal. We learn from this shloka that, anyone who is assiduous and with a firm conviction can accomplish the desired task and become successful. A person who lacks conviction and perseverance is always unfortunate.

(54) *Jyeshtam Namasyata Saha* —*(951, Samaveda)*

Let us prostrate before the capable. The person who is blessed with innumerable capabilities is respected and honoured. We should become diligent so that we achieve all our desired goals. We can become successful only on the basis of our capabilities and oriented efforts.

(55) *Yatihi Na Valam Vibheda* —*(954, Samaveda)*

The person who practises restraint killed a demon named Vala. It is said that Indra kills an enemy in the same way, the restrained killed the demon Vala.

The one who controls his senses suppresses the five evils—sexual pleasure, anger, greed, attachment and ego and practices restraint; he conquers all his enemies easily.

(56) *Vayam Syama Bhuvaneshu Jeevase* —*(956, Samaveda)*

May we lead a prosperous life in this world.

Every person should lead a prosperous life and should attain whatever is essential to do so. Here we seek the blessings of God so that he may bless us with a good, prosperous life.

(57) *Tava Vrate Soma Tishthantu Krishtayaha—(957, Samaveda)*

O Soma! May all humans adhere by your rules.

All people should lead a disciplined life. By doing so all our endeavours can be achieved very easily.

(58) *Sahvanvishwa Abhi Sprithaha —(968, Samaveda)*

The knowledgeable defeats all in the race to attain godship.

If one has to become successful it is imperative that we remove all the hurdles and obstacles that are in forms of impediments or hindrances. We should conquer fear of struggle and turmoil. By doing so only can the hindrances be cleared.

(59) *Meghakaram Vidathasya Prasadhan Agni Aun Hotaram Paribhutaram Matim —(984, Samaveda)*

We praise Agni, who is the one who bestows intellects upon us, who invokes the gods, who is the primary requirement of a sacrifice and is the destroyer of all the enemies. The scholar who consistently engages in action vanquishes all his enemies is honoured and respected. We should therefore acquire maximum knowledge so that we can suppress the enemies and be victorious in all our pursuits.

(60) *Indragni Sham Bhuva —(991, Samaveda)*

Indra and Agni are the givers of happiness. The importance of water and fire is known to all of us. Life itself is impossible without these elements. We should therefore imbibe the qualities of water and fire and become successful..

(61) *Asi Dabharasya Chit Vridhaha —(1003, Samaveda)*

The knowledgeable mould the ignorant. He attains knowledge of the self who controls all his senses.. Therefore one should engage in controlling and orienting the senses properly so that one become intelligent.

(62) *Abhi Vratani Pavate Punanandho —(1021, Samaveda)*

The person who is in the process of purifying himself practises Yama and Niyama regularly. The person who desires knowledge should practise restraint and discipline because by doing so only, he can surmount all the hindrances

(63) *Vishwakarma Vishwa Deva Maham Asi—(1026, Samaveda)*

They are noble alike the gods who engage in all types of work. He who is multi talented does not hesitate to do any type of work.

Consequently, because of his diligence he is showered with praises and honour. Therefore, we should constantly engage in deriving our talents and constructively utilizing them.

(64) *Jyotiryayasya Pavate Madhu Priyam —(1031, Samaveda)*

The flames of the yagya are pleasing and lovable. When a karmayogi incessantly strives to achieve the goal there is ardent of divine and celestial feelings in the mind which are pleasant and lovable. When we attain our desired goal, we experience real happiness.

(65) *Agre Vajasya Bhajase Mahadwanam Swayudha Ha*
—(1033, Samaveda)

The valiant who possesses maximum number of good weapons, during the war, only is successful in amassing wealth. Accordingly, the person who possesses noble actions and firm conviction only becomes successful and prosperous. He experiences the real happiness.

(66) *Sana Jyotihi Sana Swarvishwa Cha Soma Saubhaga*
Atha No Vasyasaskridhi —(1048 Samaveda))

Bless us with radiance, happiness and fortune and welfare. Those who imbibe the qualities of gods and bring it in use, they automatically become radiant and fortunate. In this way they attain the energy, which they can utilize to do good to the multitudes.

(67) *Sana Dakshamuta Kratumap Soma Mridho Jahi*
Atha No Vasyasaskridhi —(1049 Samaveda))

Give us energy and make us capable. Destroy all our enemies and bless us. If a person realizes his capabilities and tries to augment his abilities through incessant practice he can destroy all the enemies on the path of success and prosperity.

(68) *Tvam Surye Na A Bhaja Tave Kratava Tavotibhihi*
—(1051, Samaveda)

Assist us on the basis of your capabilities and by constantly protecting us. Here we realize that if a person performs his duties corresponding to his capabilities and abilities, he can attain everything desired.

(69) *Usra Deva Vasunam Martasya Devyavasaha*
—(1058, Samaveda)

The early morning (dawn) knows how to protect us. The person who gets up early in the morning is blessed with good health, beauty and intellect. Because of this the person remains energetic and active throughout the day. The mind is refreshed and remains alert throughout the day. Therefore, we should make it a habit to get up early in the morning.

(70) Te Chitayantaha Pauvana Parvana Vayam—(1065, Samveda)

May we contemplate upon you before every chapter. We should meditate upon the lord everyday, in the morning as well as in the evening. Meditation improves faith, devotion and confidence in all our endeavours.

(71) Jeevatave Prataram Sadhaya Dhiya Agne—(1064, Samaveda)

Accomplish our Yagya of Karma (actions) and bless us with a long life. We can then only attain our goal if there is assiduity and perseverance. Good knowledge inspires us to engage in good actions. Therefore, we should always work hard and try to imbibe maximum knowledge so that we are successful in our pursuits.

(72) Samaso Raye Akramu Hu —(1119, Samaveda)

The devotees work assiduously to earn wealth.

Devotees are always desirous of salvation. If one is determined and is ready to tirelessly work then attaining liberation is possible.

(73) Dharman Ritasya Patha Asrigram —(1128, Samaveda)

People, who are pious, tread on the path of truth and righteousness.

Truth is always victorious. Those who owe their allegiance towards truth undoubtedly achieve their goals, sooner or later. People who are religious-minded and god-fearing do not dare to tread on the wrong path. They always prefer the right path of truth and honesty.

(74) Sakha Sakhyurna Pra Minati Sangiram—(1152, Samaveda)

Friends do not hurt or inflict pain on each other.

The person who is favoured alike a friend can not, at any cost, cause harm to anyone. We should always prove to be true, reliable friends.

(75) Raksha Toka Mutatmana —(1246, Samaveda)

Protect your children through your own efforts.

Every person should take care of all those people who are in his refuge, in the same way as Agni who does well to people on the basis of his independent efforts.

(76) Satrajit Agohyaha Vishwataha Prithu —(1247, Samaveda)

You are the mightiest, who vanquishes all his enemies and is unoppressable. Here we praise Lord Indra who controlled all his senses and became mighty. Similarly if we control all our senses and free ourselves from the five evils then we shall definitely be successful in surmounting the insurmountable.

(77) Aeva Surya Mro Chayatpavamano Adhi Dyavi I
—(1284, Samaveda)

The sadhaka makes his life pure and divine by enkindling the flame of knowledge in the mind. When the flame of knowledge is enkindled in the mind the sadhaka does not go astray. He realizes the path ahead and treads on the path of success. One can become knowledgeable by self-study or by studying under the tutelage of an experienced teacher (Guru).

(78) Pavmaniryo Adhyetryushibhihi Sambhritam Rasam
Tasmai Saraswati Duhe Ksheeram Sapirmadhydakam
—(1299, Samaveda))

Those who accompany the sages and imbibe knowledge, Goddess Saraswati blesses by milk, ghee, honey and water. Knowledge can bestow us with proper intellect, which helps us to earn our livelihood. Milk, ghee, honey and water are useful to nourish the mind.

(79) Papamanihi Swastyayanistabhirgachchanti Na Anandami
Punyama Shva Bhakshanbhakshayatyam Rutatvam Cha Gachchati —(1303, Samaveda)

May humans be blessed with happiness because of the incantations (shlokas) which purify and facilitate the welfare of people. He eats pure food and attains immortality. Those who imbibe the knowledge of the Vedas and utilize it in practical life attain happiness. We need to conduct a detailed study of the Samaveda if we desire to be blessed by pure food and plentiful of food grains.

(80) Hey Kavey, Tanu Na Pata —(1348, Samaveda)

O Agni, you do not allow the body to get decayed.

Until fire is present within our body we do not cease to exist. The fire present within maintains and protects our body from decay. To be blessed with sound health it is important that we nourish our body and mind with nutritious and wholesome food.

(81) Kariney Na, Dhanam Pra Yansat —*(1358, Samaveda)*

May we be blessed with wealth alike the ones that are blessed to perform yagya. The fruits of good actions are good and the fruits of bad deeds are bad. Students imbibe knowledge on basis of their conviction and efforts. Similarly we also should work assiduously to be blessed with all good things.

(82) Vyakhyanmahisho Divam —*(1377, Samaveda)*

This great sun illuminates the heaven.

The energy and light emanated from the sun is of a lot of use to earth. Similarly, the scholars impart knowledge to all and enlighten the minds of the ignorant. Therefore, we should take inspiration from the sun and should work constantly so that we become prosperous and successful.

(83) Raja Riten Vivvridhe —*(1396 Samaveda)*

The king benefits by speaking truth.

The kind who adheres to righteousness and truth becomes famous and immortal. By doing so the kind is favoured by all and is honoured. As a result the king becomes all the more prosperous.

(84) Uru Bavyuthihi Abhayani Krinvam —*(1410,Samaveda)*

May he, whose path is wide and broad, protect us.

Every person becomes successful corresponding to his or her limits and capabilities. Capabilities should be honed or sharpened so that they are successful in removing all the obstacles and impediments on the path towards our goal.

(85) Asman Avantu Te Dhiyana —*(1421, Samaveda)*

May your intellect protect us.

One can imbibe only that amount of knowledge that can be absorbed by the intellect. On being blessed by knowledge we are naturally protected because we become immune to purity, ignorance and frivolity. Therefore we should always engage in activities that help us to enhance our intellect.

(86) Bhuyasa Te Sumatao Vajino Vayam —*(1422, Samaveda)*

May we become equally intelligent, alike you and become strong.

We pray to Indra so that we become equally intellectual and prosperous as him. As a result of this we can become equally radiant successful and prosperous as the Gods.

(87) *Ma Na Starabhimataya* —*(1422 Samaveda)*

May pride and ego never plague us.

We should guard ourselves from pride because pride of wealth, energy and knowledge shall only lead to misery. Pride takes the person to the isles of nothing.

(88) *Tvamam Hi Shooraha Sanita Chodaya Manusho Ratham* —*(1434 Samaveda)*

You are brave and benevolent. Incite the desires of human beings.

Here we pray to Lord Indra to incite the desires so that we can fulfil them and become prosperous. The person who lacks inertia should practise self-study and introspection and try to enkindle the flame of knowledge within us. This flame of knowledge shall help us to inspire ourselves and help us to tread towards our goal.

(89) *Sahavandasyumavratamoshaha Patram Na Shochita* —*(1434,Samveda)*

Alike Agni, who incinerates everything according to its capability, you destroy the wicked and the ignorant.

Those who are not assiduous, who are engaged in wrong deeds and do not adhere by the vows definitely end up in misery.

Therefore we should avoid bad deeds and fulfil all our vows.

(90) *Manashchinmanasanspatihi* —*(1448, Samaveda)*

Realise the potential of the mind and reign over it.

That person, who introspects and contemplates, enhances the potentiality of the mind. He gains controls over the reins of the mind and command it. Therefore one should practise concentration and take control of the mind.

(91) *Saraswati Stomya Bhut* —*(1461, Samaveda)*

The Goddess of knowledge Saraswati is worth praising.

Worship of Goddess Saraswati helps us to enhance our memory and intellect. Therefore we should all take guidance and imbibe knowledge from the Guru. In this way we shall become enlightened.

(92) *Tatsa Vitura Varenyam Bhargo Devasya Dhimahi*
Dhiyo Yo Naha Prachodayata —*(1462, Samaveda))*

May we meditate upon that radiance by which Savita inspires

and enlightens our minds. One should always concentrate on the energy that inspires us because by doing so the flow of inspiration within us is maintained.

(93) *Ketum Krunvannaketave Desho Marya Apeshase*
Samush Abhdirjayathaha —(1470, Samaveda))

O Humans! The sun rises after dawn. Similarly bless the ignorant with knowledge and the ugly with beauty.

The Sunrays bless us with knowledge, good health and radiance, Therefore we should respect the greatness of the Sun and we should imbibe qualities of knowledge and radiance from him.

(94) *Hota Devo Amrtyaha Purastadeti Mayaya*
Vidathani Prachodayan —(1477, Samaveda))

Agni, which is used in the Yagya, always inspires the Gods to perform their duties and very swiftly keeps moving.

Similarly we should take inspiration from Agni and imbibe it. We should, therefore, always work towards our goal, selflessly.

(95) *Sa E Namada Mahi Karma Kartave Mahamuram Sainam*
—(1486, Samaveda)

They inspire us to do great, heroic and noble deeds.

It is our duty to get inspired by the knowledge given to us by the noble souls. By acquiring all the knowledge one should engage in good actions, constantly.

(96) *Sadyo Dashushe Ksharasi* —(1498, Samaveda)

The donor immediately begets the fruits of his actions.

The donor is always blessed with happiness and prosperity. Donation, is the greatest form of virtue, Which is why we should be always willing to donate. By donation, the means of earning wealth relatively increase. The Lord also blesses them who do charity.

(97) *Dadhati Ratnam Vidhate Suviryamannirjanaya Dashushe*
—(1514, Samaveda)

Agni blesses that person with success and wealth who performs the Yagya and donates benevolently. Those who are inspired by Agni tirelessly and selflessly work and donate accordingly. They are blessed with the fruit of liberation and enjoy the real happiness of life.

(98) Dadgajjyotirjanebhyaha —*(1530, Samaveda)*

Give light to the people.

Agni and the Sun are eternal sources of energy. We should imbibe the qualities of the Sun and Agni and work selflessly. As a result we shall become famous and successful.

(99) Dahi Vishwasmadrakshaso Aravnaha —*(1545, Samaveda)*

O Agni! Protect us from the ominous, demonic forces and the diabolic tendencies.

The person who is plagued by diabolic tendencies cannot do charity. He is always engaged in bad karma. So we pray to Agni, so that he protects us from all these evils present within us. We should therefore imbibe good qualities and thoughts.

(100) Chikidvi Bhati Bhasa Brihata —*(1546, Samaveda)*

A scholar is always radiant by the light of knowledge he possesses. Scholars enhance their knowledge by donating as much knowledge as possible. Therefore we should acquire this knowledge and use it in day-to-day life. By doing so the flame of knowledge burns all the more brightly.

(101) Saha Tigmajambha Rakshaso Daha Prati—*(1563, Samaveda)*

O Agni! Destroy one by one all these diabolic forces. Here we pray to Agni so that he may vanquish all the ominous, the devilish forces tendencies present within us and inspire us on the path of righteousness and truth.

(102) Ma Bhem Ma Shramishmograsya Sakhye Tav
—*(1605, Samaveda)*.

May we neither fear, nor become tired by your friendship.

He, who has undeterred devotion and faith towards the Lord, is blessed with perseverance and moral strength. Such a person does not fear and nor does he get tired. On the contrary he fearlessly treads on the path of truth and righteousness.

(103) Uto Kridant Dhityo Devanam Nama Vigratihi
—*(1633, Samaveda)*

The fingers of the scholars are always engaged in constructive activities. He who is always assiduous and diligent is always a scholarly figure. Such a person seldom likes to waste his time. He engages in work and strives for perfection. We all should imbibe these qualities and become alike the scholars.

(104) *Ma No Agne Mahadhane Para Vararbhara Bhrudyatha Samvarga Sam Rayim Jay* —*(1650, Samaveda))*

O Agni! Don't keep us away from strife and turmoil. May we be blessed with wealth and be prosperous.

We should imbibe qualities of fire and should take active part in the struggle or maelstrom of life. In return we shall definitely earn wealth, become prosperous and successful. We should suppress all our weakness and tread on the path of growth.

(105) *Vishnoho Karmani Pashyat Yato Vratani Paspashe*

O Human! Think of those heroic deeds of Vishnu and follow them after contemplation. We should imbibe good thoughts and actions and perform our duties accordingly. By doing so we can become successful in all our pursuits.

(106) *Ritasya Pathya Anu* —*(1694, Samaveda)*

The knowledgeable always tread on the path of truth and righteousness.

The scholar who incessantly performs his duties is always successful. He who treads on the righteous path is always enlightened. Therefore we should also engage in good actions and deeds.

(107) *So Agniryo Vasuhu* —*(1739, Samaveda)*

Agni helps all to settle well.

He, who knows the art of treading on the path of knowledge, knows the art of living. He who does not struggle does not gain anything. We should imbibe the qualities of Agni and should bring them in practical usage.

(108) *Preta Jayata Nara* —*(1862, Samaveda)*

We should dare each and everything and should not hesitate to sacrifice ourselves in the maelstrom of life. Without orienting ourselves, we cannot expect to be victorious. Therefore, the struggle for attainment of truth shall unequivocally yield good benefits,

6

The Atharvaveda

The *fourth veda* is the *Atharvaveda*. The meaning of the word Atharveda (A+tharva) is devoid of *movement* or *concentration*. The word Tharva means *fickleness* or *movement* and accordingly the word *"Atharva"* means that which is unwavering, concentrated or unchanging. That is why it is said

Tharva Gati Karma Na Tharva Eti Atharva

The philosophy of Yoga speaks that-

Yogash Chitta Vritti Nirodhaha

which means controlling the different impulses of the mind and senses in yoga. The Gita re-iterates that when the mind is free from impulses and flaws, the mind becomes stable and the person becomes neutral when the impulses of the mind and the other senses are in control, then only the mind is freed from instability and purterbances.

The word *"Atharva"* therefore refers to *neutrality of personality. The Atharvaveda speaks more about Yoga, the human physiology, different ailments, social structure, spirituality, appreciation of natural* beauty, national religion, etc. This knowledge is practical and is worth bringing in use.

The Atharvaveda is a fusion of prose and poetry together. A number of facts related to Ayurveda are seen here, that is why *Ayurveda* is considered to be the *Upaveda (Sub-Veda)* of this Veda.

The Brahmanas come next after Vedas. There are three categories of Brahmanas texts, *i.e. Brahmana, Aranyaka* and *Upanishads*. The one and only Brahmana text of Atharvaveda is Gopinath, which is famous.

There are two parts

(1) Purvardha (first half)

(2) Uttarardha (second half).

The Purvardha comprises of a number of lectures while the Uttarardha comprises of critical appreciation of rituals, etc. We come across no Aranyaka text of the Atharvaveda but there are a number of Upanishads.

The prominent ones are *Mundak, Mandukya, Prashna* and *Mrusinghapini.* The Muktikopanishad speak and mentions 93 Upanishads of Atharvaveda.

Chapter 1:

(1) Vachaspatirni Yachchutai —(1/3, Atharvaveda)

May the scholar become disciplined.

The people who live disciplined lives accomplish all their duties, without obstacles and easily. By doing so one can achieve a lot of success scholars should guide all to lead disciplined lives.

(2) Sam Shrutena Gamemahima Shrutena Vi Radhishi
—(1/4, Atharvaveda)

May all become knowledgeable and may never detest from knowledge.

One can attain all the knowledge from a Guru. That Guru who teaches and imparts knowledge properly to his disciple is a good guru. He who acquires theoretical and practical knowledge and utilizes it in day to day life, in the real sense becomes knowledgeable.

Knowledge helps us materially and spiritually. Therefore we should try to acquire as much knowledge as possible and should abstain from wrong or false knowledge. By doing so we can break away from the chains of ignorance and misery.

(3) Apsvantarmritmapsu Bheshajam —(4/4 Atharvaveda)

Water is,the elixir of life, water has medicinal value.

Water is the primary necessity of the human body. Water is alike the elixir of life because of which the body is purified and we become energetic. Water also possesses medicinal value. It frees the body from different doshas (ailments) and is known as *Bheshagya.* It gives us good health, happiness and contentment.

(4) *Sham Mem Chaturbhya Angebhyaha Shamastu Tanve Mam*
—(12/4 Atharvaveda)

May my four organs be free from ailments. May my entire body be healthy and strong. The body should be sound and healthy. A healthy body houses a healthy mind.

If the body is unhealthy then it cannot enjoy any happiness. Therefore one should strive to maintain good health by taking balanced diet, exercise and by reading good literature.

(5) *Adarasrid Bhavatu* *—(20/1, Atharvaveda)*

May there be no one to create a rift between us.

The cause of war is mental or satisfaction of one's ego. Because of the effort to dominate over each other, it leads to rifts and animosity. Where there is discordance, that place shall always be devoid of stability and peace. But where there is concordance even the enemy will fear attacking such a place. Unity and oneness leads to success and prosperity, concordance does not entertain bad actions, hostility and failure at any cost.

(6) *Brahmanaspate Abhi Rashtraya Vardhya*
—(29/1, Atharvaveda)

O Scholar! Work for the benefit of the nation

To keep the nation to grow and succeed it is imperative that we become strong, healthy capable and mentally, morally strong. When social and other forces shall be enhanced, they shall unequivocally result in national prosperity. People should engage only in those actions, which are in the nation's favour and facilitate development and progress. Every person should dedicate himself for the betterment and advancement of the country.

(7) *Ya Ashanamashapalashchatvara Sthan Devah*
Te No Nirrityaha Pashebhyo Muchatanhaso Anhasaha.
—(31/3, Atharvaveda)

O God! You are the protector of the four directions. Free us from sin, failure and misery.

Alike the four directions North, South, East and West the body *also possess four openings or entrances. The East entrance (Mouth),* West entrance (Rectum), North entrance (Head), South entrance (Penis).

It is important that the body performs all its functions properly and perfectly.

The *"Life"* enters the body via the north entrance and also is liberated from the bonds of the body because of concerted effort. The southern entrance is the penis, which consists of semen. One who keeps this balanced and restrained becomes noble but he who is devoid of restraint ends up in misery. The Eastern and the Western entrances are related to intake of food and excretion of waste matter respectively. Human body should try to abstain from the demerits of the personality.

(8) *Vacha Vadmi Madhumada Bhuyasam Madhu Sandrishama*
—(34/3, Atharvaveda)

I speak sweetly and softly so that I emerge as an epitome of sweetness.

This sukta of Atharvaveda speak of MadhuVidya or the knowledge of sweetness. According to this we should perceive the world a like nectar which is sweet and pleasant.

In this way everyone should be devoid of hatred, harshness and filth. We should strain our feelings incessantly by constantly contemplating upon oneself.

Every person should become amicable so that he befriends one and all. The sweetness and pleasantness of personality should be evident in all our actions and thoughts. In this way we shall be successful in establishing global peace and happiness and help in ushering the feeling of brotherhood.

Chapter 2:

(9) *Kshtrenagne Swena Sam Rabhasva Mitrenagne Mitradha Yatasva*

Sajatanam Madhyameshtha Rajamagne Vihavyo Didiheeha
—(2/4,Atharvaveda)

O Agni! May you become enthusiastic on basis of your own capabilities, may I act like a friend with the friends, may I hold a respectable position in my community, may I be honoured by scholars and become enlightened.

We derive inspiration from here to become successful on the basis of assuidity and capabilities. We should always be ready to work diligently. By maintaining friendship with friends, it helps us to improve upon our capabilities. We should assume that aptitude and ability so that we are respected in our community and honoured in the company of scholars. The person who does so is blessed with success and prosperity.

(10) Vishwa Hyagne Durita Tar —(6/5, Atharvaveda)

O! Agni! Surmount all the evils and sins. We should *abstain from violence, debauchary, evil deeds, sensual attachment, hatred, anger* and *ego*. We should strive to become pure and chaste. By renouncing these evils and sins, one becomes prosperous and successful.

(11) Shaptarametu Shadatho Yaha Suharta Tena Naha Saha —(7/5, Atharvaveda)

May the curse go back to the person who curses.

May we befriend them who are kind and polite.

If the person, who is cursed, is mentally strong then the curse shall backfire and recoil and go back to the person who has given the curse. The person who curses shall definitely suffer if the curse backfires.

Those whose minds are stable, pure and chaste are mentally and morally strong. Therefore one should only befriend those people who are kind-hearted, polite and engaged in good actions.

(12) Yashchakar Sa Nishkarat —(9/5,Atharvaveda)

He who constantly engages in action attains perfection.

Those people who work assiduously with interest, become conversant and expert in their respective fields.

He who engages in practice and actions becomes noble and utilizes this discipline in all spheres of life.

(13) Pashe Sa Baddho Durite Ni Yujyatama Yo Asmakam Mana Idam Hinasti —(12/2, Atharvaveda).

All that, which pollutes the mind, falls prey to evil and sin. All this should be kept in total control.

Bad thought pollute our minds that's why need to discipline our mind. The sinner should be punished severely, considering the gravity of the crime committed.

(14) Aya Yamasya Sadadamagniduto Arankrutaha —(12/7,Atharvaveda)

Become messenger of Agni, become powerful and then embrace death. The person who is fearless and embraces death fearlessly is great and noble. People fear death because of ignorance. When the flame of knowledge is enkindled in the mind the fear of death ceases to exist. He, who controls his senses gains control all over the vital forces of life. He who sacrifices himself in the fire of knowledge does not have the slightest of trepidation and fear. Those who desire material and sensual pleasure and approach death with fear they fall prey to the wrath of death.

Therefore one sees that there is a differences in the death of the ignorant and the knowledgeable.

(15) *Paridamvaso Adhithaha Swastaye Abhurg Rishtinamabhi Shastipa U*

Shatam Cha Jeeva Sharadaha Puruchi Kayascha Roshmupasamvyayasva —*(13/3, Atharvaveda)*

Wear this attire for your welfare, you are the one who protects human from destruction. In this way live for a hundred years and become healthy (nourished) and wealthy.

Weave the cloth of life with the help of good health and wealth. By wearing such attire you shall be blessed with a long life and save all from destruction. The people who wear the cloth that is intricately woven with threads of comfort, health and wealth are devoid of destruction, illness and misery. Such people are always blessed with a long life and a healthy body.

(16) *Yathabhutam Cha Bhavyam Cha Na Vibhito Na Rishyataha Aeva Mem Prana Ma Vibhehe* —*(15/6, Atharvaveda)*

The past and present are fearless that is why they are indestructible. Alike them O Life! Don't fear anything.

All human fear the present not the past and the future. The past exhibits everything, which is truthful. People seldom fear the past and the things probable and improbable, *i.e.* the future. He, who takes lessons from his past and improves on himself, does not fear the future. Truth is eternally vicious, that is why humans should fearlessly, accomplish all the duties properly. Fearlessness leads to immorality.

(17) *Yatha Jeeva Aditerupasthe Prana Apanabhyam Gupitaha Shatam Himaha* —*(28/4,Atharvaveda)*

So that your life and energy increases and you are blessed with a life of hundred years in the lap of your motherland.

The upper half of the body till the navel is known as Prana and the lower half below the navel is known as *Apana*. When prana is enhanced, it exerts a good effect even on the *Apana* and as a result all the function of Apana are performed perfectly. One, who enhances the strength of Prana and Apana through Yoga Sadhana, is blessed with long healthy life.

Chapter 3:

(18) *Te Adharanchaha Pra Palvatama Chinna Naoriva Bandhanata*
Na Vaibadhpranuttanama Punarasti Nivartanam.
—(6/7, Atharvaveda)

Those who create new obstacles can never be rehabilitated. A like a boat without an anchor, they end up in failure and misery.

People, who inflict pain upon others, end up in misery and in deplorable condition. Those who harass others and ostracize others can never ever think of reaching higher ideals. That is why we should think in the welfare of others and by doing so we shall become successful and prosperous.

(19) *Sam Vo Manansi Sam Vrato Samakutirnasamasi*
Ami Ye Vivrata Sthan Tantaha Sam Nabhayamasi
—(10/5,Atharvaveda)

May your mind be infused with one type of thought, may every action of yours be embellished by one-one thought, may your resolution be one. If you are isolated and work incessantly, your action shall result in another form of thought.

May your thoughts, resolution and actions culminate into one form of strength, republican strength. Human beings are social animals and cannot be isolated from society because the society possesses strength. Growth is possible only by working shoulder to shoulder. That is why we are encouraged to bring unison in words, deeds and thoughts. This only shall accrue in social development and national growth.

(20) *Emamagne Sharanim Mimrusho No Yamdhwanamagam Aha Duram*
No Astu Prapano Vikrayashcho Pratipanah Falinam Ma Krinotu
Edam Havyam Samvidani Jushethama Shunam No Astu Charit Uttithama Cha *—(15/4,Atharvaveda)*

O Agni! Forgive us for the commissions and omissions. To the extent, which we have come let the dealing be profitable. Let every action be profitable to me. Please partake this Yagya.May our actions and our rise be fruitful.

Here we pray to Agni so that he may forgive all the bad we do and help us in making all the dealings profitable. We should abstain from miserliness, cruelty, larceny, gambling and misconduct of any type. Therefore, we should do all our work by putting our minds in it, without negligence. Secondly there should be stability and consistency of work. We should regularly pray to god. By doing so our mind shall become stable and calm and engage in faithful actions.

(21) Kshinami Brahmanamitrayannayami Swana Ham
—(19/3,Atharvaveda)

I destroy the enemies by acquiring knowledge and consequently enlighten myself.

Human beings should vanquish their enemies by acquiring maximum knowledge and should tread on the path of growth and success. In this way he makes his own people proud and also enlightens them.

(22) Shatahasta Samahar Sahasrahasta Sam Kir
Kritasya Karyasya Chahe Sfatim Samavaha
—(24/5,Atharvaveda)

O Human! You amass wealth with a hundred hands and donate with thousand hands. In this way escalate in the fulfilment of your duty.

One cannot progress without being benevolent. Community prosperity shall only then result if we all accomplish our duties properly. Human should try and enhance all their skills. The doorway to peace and prosperity is that we should engage in amassing wealth and should accordingly engage in donation.

(23) Sahridayam Sammanasyamavidvesham Krinomihi Vaha
Anyo Atyamabhi Haryat Vatsam Vatmi Vandhya
—(30/1,Atharvaveda)

I become understanding, kind-hearted and mutually amicable for you. May all love you mutually in the same way the cow loves her new-born calf.

Our heart should be devoid of hatred and indignance, hostility and jealous, on the contrary it should be embellished by auspicious thoughts and affection towards one and all. We should love each other mutually in the same way the cow loves her newborn calf. Good resolution and mutual affection shall definitely accrue in peace and happiness.

(24) *Vyartya Pavmano Vi Shakraha Papa Krityaya*

A person who is pure doesn't inflict pain on others even inadvertently and the person who is assiduous shall always abhor sinful deeds.

One who refrains from sinful deeds becomes healthy and is blessed with long life. One can engage in good actions and become pure and chaste. By doing so he can attain all the anticipated attainments. One should avoid all sins performed by the mind, action and thought. By doing so we pave our way to success and peace. Those who are mentally strong and chaste liberate themselves from suffering and pain.

Chapter 4:

(25) *Yatsanyamo Na Vi Yamo Yanna Sanyamaha*
—(3/7,Atharvaveda)

What is already controlled and restrained should not be suppressed, but what is not controlled and is vagrant needs to be brought under control.

One should control all the senses but if they are unnaturally controlled or rather suppressed they start reacting contradictorily. After controlling the senses, one should keep a strict vigil on them rather than suppressing them. A virtuous diet helps to control sensual desires and anger.

A mind, and the senses, which are vagrant and instable, should be strictly brought under control.

(26) *Otsuryamanyantsvapavyusham Jagritadaha Indra Ivarishto Akshitaha* *—(5/7,Atharvaveda)*

Put others to sleep until sunrise but I, the brave the indestructible and devoid of decay, wake up.

The person who is the protector should allow others to have sound sleep and he himself should be awake and should protect others.

(27) *Bhuto Bhuteshu Payaa Dadhati Sa Bhutanamadhi Patirbabhuva*
—(8/1,Atharvaveda)

He who himself becomes radiant, effectual and donates milk, etc. to all his subjects, becomes the king of all.

The person who strives for the good of others, engages in action for people's welfare and impresses all his subjects is fit to become the king or leader of the masses.

(28) *Anadvanindraha Sa Pashubhyo Vi Chashte Trayam Chakro Vi Mimeete Adhvanaha Bhutam Bhavishyadbhavana Duhanasarva Devanam Charati Vratani*

Indra in form of a bullock protects all the animals. Indra is the creator of the three elements and creates matter coveted to the past, present and future.

Indra in form of a bullock takes care of all, knows all the three paths, transverses beyond the 3 tenses and observes all the vows to be observed by gods. The three directions are Sat, Raj and Tamas. Indra knows which way he should go. He gives everyone, whatever he has to give, by milking the past, present and future.

The vow of the sun is to give light, the vow of the water is to flow, and the vow of the air is to "dry up" These are the vows of the external gods. The internal gods stay in the body. The vow of the eyes is to see, of the ear is to hear, of the prana is to juvenate, and of the nose is to smell. All these vows can be accomplished on the basis of internal energy and divine inspiration.

(29) *Ahamuttrareshu* —*(22/1, Atharvaveda)*

May I rise to the highest level.

Every person should desire to acquire maximum knowledge, to engage in the noblest of deeds, earn maximum social status, success, fame and prosperity, authority.

Only when a person aspires for higher, he becomes successful and prosperous.

(30) *Sansrushtam Dhanmunnaye Sama Kritbhasmabhyai Varunashcha Manyuhu*

Bhiyo Dadhana Hridayeshu Shasravaha Parajitaso Apa Nilayantama —*(31/7,Atharvaveda)*

Bless us with wealth along with enthusiasm and nobleness. May the enemy fear us and run away.

Enthusiasm and seniority come hand in hand. And these both fetch us wealth, wealth which is self-created and accumulated.

Enemies of the enthusiastic person are easily defeated. That is why we should aspire to become great and noble. When we are enthusiastic and jealous we take a lot of interest in accomplishing our work. People who are cynical do not see that the wealth accumulated is caused by assiduity, hard work and enthusiasm. They become jealous and do bad to themselves.

Chapter 5

(31) *A Yo Dharmani Prathamaha Sasada Tato Vapunshi Krinuve Puruni*

Dhasyuryoni Prathama A Vivesha Yo Vachamanudham Chiketa
—*(1/5,Atharvaveda)*

He who becomes religious and pious acquires all the physical powers. He understands and deciphers the secret speech and attains the highest state.

The person who treads on the righteous path attains all powers and becomes noble by realizing the meaning of the divine and secretive speech.

(32) *Sapta Maryadaha Kavastata Kshustasamidekabhyam Huro Gata*

Aryoraha Skambha Upamasya Neede Datham Visarge Dharuneshu Tasthao —*(1/6,Atharvaveda)*

The scholars have determined seven types of conduct and one who isolates them is a sinner. He who takes the support of all seven pillars is the noble one. The person who takes support of all these pillars, *i.e.* adheres to all these rules or conditions attain the highest state, where many a path converges or ends. In such state there is stability

The rules determined are-

(1) Abstinence from stealing
(2) Abstinence from sensual pleasure
(3) Abstinence from violence or slaughter
(4) Abstinence from abortion
(5) Abstinence from alcohol
(6) Abstinence from misconduct
(7) Abstinence from lies

(33) *Mumuktamasmanduri Tadavadyajjushethama*

Yaeya Amrutamasmasmasu Dhattam —*(6/8,Atharvaveda)*

Liberate us from this repugnable sin.

Please accept this yagya, this oblation and infuse within us Amrit or the Elixir of life. Stay away from evil, engage in noble deed, surrender yourself and eventually become immortal.

(34) Uta Nagna Bobhuvati Swapnya Sachase Janam
Arate Chittam Virtsantyakurti Purushesya Cha
—(7/8,Atharvaveda)

Miserliness becomes shameless and makes a person indolent, it vitiates the mind and the resolutions taken.

Those who are miserly do not utilize their wealth properly and become lethargic. Lethargy mars one's assiduity and impedes the person of fulfilling the duties.

The one who is benevolent and liberal is always happy and his wealth grows by leaps and bounds.

(35) Trayaha Suparnastrivrita Yadayatre Kaksharmabhi-sambhuya Shakaha Shakra
Pratyohanmrityu Mriten Sakamantardadhana Duritani Vishwa
—(7/8, Atharvaveda)

They're three energies, which unite together and are exhibited in one alphabet. They destroy all that is inauspicious, destroy death and bless us with immortality. There are three energies that unite together to for *"AUM"*, they destroy all that is inauspicious, death, misery. These three alphabets of A,U and M are like 3 fibers of the Yagyopaveeta (thread). These 3 alphabets unite to create the resonance of Omkar.

These three alphabets resemble three states of the human *mind, i.e. consciousness, subconscious's* and *dream state.*

One should definitely experience the divinity of the Omkar, which improves concentration. All work done with a stable mind saves us from all that is inauspicious and also the fear of death.

Chapter 6:

(36) Pavmanaha Punata Ma Kratve Dakshya Jeevase
Atho Arishta Tatye —(10/2,Atharvaveda))

May the god who bless us with actions, fruits and welfare and a long life make me pure and chaste. We should become mentally and physically strong, should keep our thoughts pure and chaste so that we are blessed with a long life and prosperity and so that we attain all what is concerted and pre-determined according to our wishes.

(37) *Sanjanidhwam Sam Pricchayadhwam Sam Vo Manansi Janatama*
Deva Bhaeam Yatha Purve Sanjanana Upasete
—(64/1, Atharvaveda)

May your mind be cultured. Acquire equal amount of knowledge and with this equality build bond within yourself. Perform all your duties alike the earlier ancestors and ideals established by them.

Oneness is the characteristic of a group. Oneness should lead to unity of thought and action. People who are embellished with good cultural traits, sense of unity, equality, fraternity and brotherhood can never be vanquished by their enemies. On the contrary life shall be full of peace and happiness.

(38) *Apamityam Pratitam Yadasmi Yamasya Yena Balilana Charami Edam Tad Agne Anuruno Bhavami Tvam Pashana Vichritam Vettha Sarvan* *—(117/1, Atharvaveda)*

I have become a creditor although I could have paid up my credit and have not done so that is why O Agni! Now I intend to pay up the credit and free myself from it. You are the one who knows all the bonds that engulf the credit. We should without fail return the things we have taken or borrowed. If this does not happen the creditor is considered responsible. We should free ourselves from all credits before death, this is a sure way to peace and happiness.

Chapter 7:

(39) *Bhadradhi Shreyaha Premi Brihaspatihi Puraeta Te Astu — (8/1, Atharvaveda)*

May you be benefited more than merely attaining happiness, and may the scholar be your guide and leader. It is preferable that humans rather than indulging in material happiness, should follow the path of spiritual growth. To attain this we should stay under the tutelage of a learned teacher or Guru. In this way we can liberate ourselves by realizing the true self.

(40) *Tam Savitaha Satyamsava Suchitrabha Ham Vrine Sumati Vishwaram*

Yamasya Kanvo Aduhatprapinam Sahasra Dharama Mahisho Bhagaya —*(15/1,Atharvaveda)*

O Lord! I accept the greatness, the truth of the mightiest, the most knowledgeable, who believes in the welfare of all. I accept that knowledge that is acquired by scholars.

It is imperative that one engages in self-study to acquire maximum knowledge. The mind becomes enkindled because of knowledge and all the good qualities and powers emanate from the mind.

(41) Akshyao Nao Madhu Sankashe Anikam Nao Samanjanam

Antaha Krinushva Mam Hridi Man Innao Sahasati

—*(36/1, Atharvaveda))*

May our eyes (of husband/wife) be full of love and affection. May our eyes be embellished with collyrium. May there be a sense of caring and may our relations be cordial and peaceful.

May the relation of the husband and wife always be cordial and loving. May there be no discord or hatred, anger in the relation. The eyes should be pure, impeccable and chaste.

Collyrium (Anjan) keeps the eyes healthy while knowledge makes vision all the more pure and clear. May they dwell eternally in each other's heart. May there be unison of thoughts and feeling towards each other.

Chapter 8:

(42) Bodhashcha Tva Pratibodhashcha Rakshatama Swapnashcha Tvanavadranashch Rakshtam

Gopayanshcha Tva Jagrivishshcha Rakshatama

—*(1/3, Atharvaveda))*

May knowledge and science protect you. May he who is always awake and fearless, protect you, may the protector and he who is enlightened, protect you.

Knowledge, alertness, fearlessness and enlightenment help to us to be awake and protect ourselves. He who acquires knowledge should bring it into use so that he attains the desired fruit. Knowledge that creates mere illusion is not anything but deception. By realizing the real truth we can become healthier and can be blessed by a long life. Therefore we should adhere to the abovementioned rules and work incessantly to accomplish our desires.

(43) *A Rabhasvemam Amritasya Shnushtimi Chchidyamana Jaradashtirastu Tei Ansuta Ayuhu Punara Bhadami Rajastamom Mopa Ga Ma Pra Meshthaha.* —*(2/1, Atharvaveda))*

May you start drinking the elixir of life so that you are blessed with a long life. I fill your life and prana with you again. May you go towards knowledge and enlightenment and may you never cease to exist.

Here the diseased is telling us that we should drink the elixir of life so that we become healthy and long lived. They, who go towards ignorance and superficial pleasure, die early. To be blessed with a long life it is imperative that we become mentally and physically strong. We should do all that makes our mind and body healthy and energetic.

(44) *A Jihvaya Muradevantabhasava Kravyado Vrishtvapi Dhatsvasan* —*(3/2, Atharvaveda)*

Emancipate the stupid through the tongue in form of a flame and eat up all those violent people who eat flesh.

Here we see that the scholar is told to sermon the stupid and enlighten them and to dissuade the violent from cruelty. By doing so our society shall become noble and peaceful.

(45) *Suvijnanam Chikiteshu Janaya Sacchasaccha Vachasi Paraspridhate*

Tyoryatsatyam Yatarahajiyastadit Somoauati Hantyasat —*(4/2, Atharvaveda)*

For the person who acquires knowledge this is considered as special knowledge that there is incessant tug-of-war or competition between truth and untruth. The Soma God protects all that is truthful and straightforward and destroys all that is untruth.

God only protects all that which is pure and truthful, what is not righteous shall always cease. It should never be forgotten that truth is always victorious.

(46) *Ulukayatum Shushulakayatum Jahi Shwayatumut Kokayatum*

Suparnayatumut Gridhrayatum Vrishdeva Pre Mrina Raksha Indra —*(4/22, Atharvaveda)*

O Indra, destroy all those people and demons the way people kill birds, who are lustful as birds, angry like the wolves, greedy a like the vultures, enticed or attached like the owls, proud alike the eagle, and the jealous like the dogs. We should destroy all those who are lustful, angry, greedy, enticed, proud and jealous.

We should strictly abhor such people otherwise it would be detrimental.

Chapter 9:

(47) Indra Mitram Varunambnimahuratho Divyaha Sa Suparno Gurutman! Aekam Sad Vipra Bahuda Vadantyagni Yamam Mitarishwanamahuhu —(10/28, Atharveda))

Scholars describe one eternal truth in different ways. That truth is known by so many names, *i.e.* Indra, Mitra, Varuna, Agni, divya, suvarna, Garutbhana, Yame, Matarishwa.

There is only truth in this world but scholars describe that truth differently according to their respective experiences and revelations. He who treads on that path of truth is always victorious.

Chapter 10:

(48) Brahmabhyavatem

Tanme Dravinam Yachchatu Tanmebrahman Varchasam —(5/40, Atharvaveda)

I am led by my knowledge, may it bless me with wealth and radiance of knowledge.

That person who is engaged in good actions on the basis of knowledge acquired knowledge is the stepping stone to achieve success an enlightenment.

(49) Tiryagbilash Chamasa Urdhvabudhnastasmin Yasho Nihitam Vishwarupam

Tadasat Rishayaha Sapta Sakam Ye Asya Gopaa Mahto Babhuvuhu —(8/9, Atharvaveda)

A human being is like a pot or vessel, which has a horizontal opening or an opening which, is on the top. This vessel contains success in different forms. Along with that are, seven sages who are seated and who protect this body, *i.e.* vessel they are in.

All the abilities of a human being are in the brain. If the brain is imbalanced then the humaneness of the human body is destroyed.In this vessel of the mind the seven sagas, *i.e.* two eyes, two ears, one nose, one mouth are seated who protect this vessel of the mind. People should realize the importance of this and should take utmost care to protect it because the balanced mind is the epitome of humanity.

(50) *Anantam Vitatam Purutrananta Bhantavacha Samante*
Te Nakpalashcharati Vichinvan Vidwanbhutamuta Bhavyamasta
—(8/12, Atharvaveda)

The endless, limitless, is omnipresent and the one who is limitful is united with limitless, The scholar, thinks about the past present and future and such a person dwells in happiness.

The one and only eternal truth is omnipresent. The limitful and limitless are fused and absorbed in each other. Scholar think and contemplate on the past, present, and future and tread on path of growth and self- development this should be an ideal for all human beings.

Chapter 11:

(51) *Aema Aguryoshitaha Shumbhamana Uttishtha Nari Tavasam Ramasva*
Supatni Patya Prajaya Prajavatya Tva Agna Yagyaha Prati Kumbham Gribhaya *—(1/14 Atharvaveda)*

These women have decorated themselves and have come here. You get up and acquire strength. May you become a good wife with a good husband, may you be blessed by good children. The yagya has reached you, fill the pot.

It is important for a woman to wear good ornaments and should acquire a good husband on basis of work, give birth to noble children, take care of the house and keep it happy and peaceful. The women are apprised of their duties, which they should adhere and accomplish.

(52) *Vrishabho Si Swarga Rishinarveyana Gachcha*
Sukritam Loke Seeda Tatra Nad Sanskritam
—(1/35 Atharvaveda))

You are strong and are the giver of happiness. You shall become cultured and enlightened only if you stay in the company of sages, sons of sages and other noble souls.

Humans here are advised to become mighty and dwell in happiness they should follow the ideals of the scholars and make themselves cultured.

(53) *Samachinushvanusam Prayahmagne Pathaha Kalpaya Devyanan* —(1/36,Atharvaveda))

O Agni! unite all and create a path, which is favourable for all the Gods.

Unity will only accrue if humans have mutual intellectual equity. Therefore we should follow the ideals established by the scholars. In this way we shall be successful in accomplishing our desired work.

(54) *Ma No Hinsiradhi No Bru Hi Parino Vringdhi Ma Kradha Mam Tavya Samaramahim* —(2/20, Atharvaveda))

Do not kill us, advise us, protect us, do not become angry on us. May we not oppose you at any cost.

We should never be indignant and resentful. We should acquire knowledge by refraining from violence. We should work with unity and co-operation because opposition leads to obstacles and hurdles.

(55) *Pranaya Namo Yasta Sarvamidam Vashe*—(4/1,Atharvaveda)

I prostrate before that Prana (breath) which controls the entire universe.

It is the Prana that helps us to maintain our existence. Our life sustains on Prana. Our body is dependent upon prana (breath) for all its functions. We should bring this mighty force into our control, by practising pranayama.

(56) *Brahmacharishn Anshcharati Rodasi Ubhe Tasmin Devaha Sammanaso Bhavanti* —(5/1, Atharvaveda)

A brahmachari (a person who practises celibacy) makes the heaven and the earth favourable to tread, that is why all the Gods always reside with him. He controls the earth and heaven and fulfills his life on the basis of his penance.

A brahmachari is he who is incessantly trying to realize the eternal truth about life and works assiduously to attain immortality. He acquires intellect, sublimeness, knowledge, essence of immortality and treads on the path towards truth. All gods favour such a person and reside within him. Because of this all the elements of nature rather than creating hurdles assist him in his pursuit. Without knowledge no one can be inspired to engage in the righteous action.

Chapter 12:

(57) *Sa No Bhumirvi Srujatam Mata Putraya Me Pachaha*
—(1/10,Atharvaveda)

May earth provide us with all the things we require alike a mother who breast-feeds her child.

The earth gives us all what we need. Food grains to eat and water to drink. Alike the mother who breast feeds her child, the mother earth provides minerals, etc. to humans who are like her children. Therefore, we should protect our mother earth by realizing her nobleness.

(58) *Ta Naha Prajaha Sam Duhatama Samagra Vacho Madhu Prithivi Dhehi Mahya* *—(1/16,Atharvaveda)*

O Motherland! May we, your subjects come together and speak softly. Bless all of us to maintain cordial relations by talking politely to one and all. Soft speech results in unity and co-operation. On the contrary harsh speech leads to hostility and obstacles.

Therefore, we should all practise speaking softly and politely.

(59) *Udirana Udaseenastishthantaha Prakamantaha*
Padbhyam Dakshinasavyabhyam Vyathishmahi
—(1/28,Atharvaveda))

May we not inflict pain on anyone while walking, sitting, moving from left to right or vice-versa. The world is more in misery than in happiness, that is why one should not hurt anyone. We should not engage in any action that results in giving pain to others.

(60) *Bhume Matarni Dhehi Bha Bhadraya Supratishthitam*
Samvi Dana Diva Kave Shriyaam Ma Dhehi Bhutyaam
—(1/63,Atharvaveda))

O Motherland! Bless us with a benevolent mind, make us realize each and everything day by day, and may I acquire wealth from the earth.

Here one prays to mother earth so that she blesses one with the knowledge of the earth, consisting of invaluable wealth so that we may become happy and acquire a good position in our community and on earth. One can even be blessed by diligence and assiduity, on being inspired by earth. We should therefore always engage in good actions.

(61) *Nirito Mrityum Niraratimajamasi*

Yo No Dveshti Tamadadhagne Sakravyada Dvishmastamu Te Pra Suvamasi —*(2/3 Atharvaveda)*

Liberate us from pain, death and enemies. O Agni! Destroy all of them who oppose us. We hand over them to you who oppose us. Here we pray to Agni so that he may emanciapate us from death, pain and enemies. We should work hard so that we are freed from the bondage of the suffering and poverty. We should become mighty and destroy all our enemies so that we have a long life and don't fear death.

(62) *Yat Tva Krudhaha Pradhakrurmanyuna Purushe Mritee Sukalpamägne*

Tat Tvaya Punastvoddipayamassi —*(2/5 Atharvaveda)*

O Agni! you are right when you incinerate the body of a person after death with flames of your anger. So we again enkindle you.

After incinerating the body of a dead person there is no fear on the contrary peace dwells. This body created with five elements and after death Agni fuses the body with the five elements.

(63) *Ye Shraddha Dhankamya Karvyada Samasate*

Te Va Anyesha Kumbhim Paryadadhi Sanrvada

—*(2/51 Atharvaveda)*

All those who are devoid of devotion, and are greedy those who eat flesh together definitely have an eye on others' wealth.

Such people who are greedy and avaricious end up in misery because of their evil deeds and are short lived.

(64) *Piteva Putranabhi Samsuajasva Naha* —*(3/12 Atharvaveda)*

Alike a father who loves his children you come and meet all of us.

Let us all love each other the same way a father loves his children

Mutual affection only leads to co-operation and peace this helps us to dwell in happiness.

(65) *Yadyajjaya Pachati Tvat Paraha Paraha Patirva Jaye Tvat Tiraha Ist Tat Sujeta Saha Vam Tadastu Sampadayantao Saha Lokam Aekam* —*(3/39 Atharvaveda)*

May you bring all those things together that your wife cooks separately and the husband does separately may it all constrive into one act and may both of you attain the same state.

If there is difference of opinion between husband and wife then the household shall collapse. To avoid this, relation ship between husband and wife should be cordial and loving. Concealing anything would lead to serious consequences. Therefore, it is in the best interest of both to share whatever they have so that it embellishes their household.

(66) Priyam Priyanam Krinvam Namaste Yantu Yatem Divshanti
—(3/49 Atharvaveda)

May we be affectionate towards our friends. May those who hate us end up in ignorance and darkness.

We should never have any malevolent feelings towards our friends. Hostility pollutes the mind and actions and results in our bad. Therefore, we should always be loving towards our friends.

Chapter 13:

(67) Paritva Dhata Savita Devo Agnirvarchasa Mitravaruna Vabi Tva

Sarva Arantirvakramannehidam Rashtra Akar Sanrita Vat
—(1/20, Atharvaveda)

O Savita, may all the gods be around and besides you. May Mitra, Varuna, and Agni with his radiance protect you. Attack all the enemies and move ahead. May the nation be full of happiness and joy. May all the gods assist us and destroy all the enemies. This shall definitely result in national prosperity and happiness. We should engage in such action that naturally lead to national development growth and progress.

(68) Yo Yagyasya Prasadmanastanturdeveshvatataha

Tamahutamshimahi —(1/60 Atharvaveda))

May we imbibe those qualities or elements, which are present in the gods. May we posses all those qualities and sublime merits which the gods posses. Human should try to inibibe all qualities from gods by doing so we shall prosper and be successful. Our good resolution to good deeds shall definitely yield rich benefits.

(69) Ayukta Sapta Shundhyuvaha Suro Stharasya Naptyaha

Ta Abhiryati Swayuktibhihi —(2/24 Atharvaveda))

The chariot of the sun god (epitome of eternal knowledge) comprises of seven horses, which are well concerted and disciplined. The sun corresponding to his pre-concerted plans does good to the world. Similarly humans should also engage in doing work so as to benefit one and all. We should imbibe good qualities from the sun and enhance one's internal energies. The person who engages in doing good to the others naturally become prosperous and successful

(70) *Atandro Thasyan Harito Yadasthada Dve Rupe Krinate Rochamanaha*

Ketumanudyantusahamano Rajansi Aditya Mavato Vibhasi —(2/28Atharvareda)

He, who is not indolent, assumes two forms when he decides to go and sit on the horses. O Sun! You are radiant and you capture the entire world. The greatness of the sun is indispensable. When the sun rises the entire world is illuminated. He who sheds indolence and seated on the high seat of performing duties self-lessly, is honoured and respected.

(71) *Kirtischa Yashashchambhashcha Brahman Varchasam Cha Annam Cha Annadya Cha*

Aetam Dev Eka Vritam Veda —(5/14 Atharvaveda))

He who realizes the supreme god achieves, fame, success, rest, radiance, food and knowledge

The person who selflessly and assiduously works towards his goals is never devoid of mental and physical energy. Such a person is blessed with all merits, and all his desires are satisfied. Faith in the Supreme Force facilitates this and he becomes all the more prosperous.

Chapter 14:

(72) *Archamanam Yaja Mahe Subandhum Pativedanam*

Urvaru Kamiva Bandhanatpreto Munchami Namutaha —(1/17, Atharvaveda))

May we honour those minds that help us, to select a good husband with a good family. I free you from the paternal clan but not from your husband's clan alike a Urvaru (a specie of Cucumber) which detaches itself from the tree after it ripens. One should seek the help of the noble souls while finding a good husband. Just alike Urvaru, which detaches itself from the tree after it ripens, the girl after marriage leaves the father's house and builds a new relation with her husband's family. The detachment from the father's clan is favourable, but the detachment from the husband's clan is not at all favourable.

(73) *Yuvam Bhaeam Sam Bharatam Samriddha Mritam Va Dantivrddyeshu Brahmannaspate Patimaniyai Rochaya Charu Sambhalo Vadatu Vachametama*
—(1/31, Atharvaveda)

May you both (husband/wife) act righteously and be blessed by luck and fortune. O Scholar! Create interest in the mind of the wife towards her husband. May the husband be soft-spoken and polite.

For good, congenial martial life, the husband and wife should be truthful and faithful. One should not forget that the wife should always respect her husband. The husbands also should be soft-spoken, polite and loving so that he attracts his wife and there is constant growth in their love and affection.

(74) *Ashayana Saumanasam Prajam Saubhagyam Rayim Patyurnyvrata Bhuvva Sam Nahmaswamritaya Kam*
—(1/42,Atharvaveda)

You desire a good mind, children fortune and wealth. Act according to your husband's wishes and work towards immortality.

A woman should always think good of her family and should work according to her husband's wishes so that she creates peace and happiness in her family, and paves her way towards immortality effortless and peaceful. If one adheres to the principal and leads a proper life then family life can be peaceful and full of happiness.

(75) *Aemam Panthamaru Ksham Sugam Swastivahanam*
Yasmin Viro Na Rishyatyanyesham Vindate Vasu
—(2/8,Atharvaveda))

Tread on this path, which is not arduous and is accessible easily. On the path when the brave are not vanquished and on which relatively one acquires more wealth than others.

We should tread one that path which is easy and devoid of obstacles so that there is no fear whatsoever. Consequently we can achieve the desired goal without any problem.

(76) *Aghor Chakshur Patindhi Syona Shagma Susheva Suyama Grihebhyaha*

Vir Ardevrikama Sam. Tvaidhishimahi Sumanaysa Maha
—(2/17,Atharvaveda))

May we become wealthy because of her, who is not indignant, who does not owe malevolence towards her husband, treads on the righteous path, gives happiness to all, serves all, gives birth to good sons, satisfies her brother-in-laws demands and gives good food.

A woman should be full of good qualities and a house in which such a woman dwells is always prosperous and full of comforts and luxuries.

(77) *Sharma Varmetada Harasyai Narya Upastare*
—(2/21,Atharvaveda)

A woman should be showered with happiness and should be protected.

It is the duty of the husband to earn for the wife and give her all types of happiness. He should protect her and satisfy all her demands. The husband should realize his duties towards his wife and children. That household is the happiest where all are satisfied and content.

Chapter 15:

(78) *Parishkanda Asantsankalpaha Prahayya Vishwani Bhutanyu Pasadaha* *—(3/10, Atharvaveda)*

The God becomes his protectors. His resolution, his messengers and all people believed and followed him.

The person who takes a resolution and becomes ready to work diligently to attain a goal is helped and blessed by gods. He gets easy access to all the means possible. Therefore, efforts put to acquire a good resolution never go in vain.

(79) *Saha Visho Anu Vyachalat* *—(9/1, Atharvaveda)*

He became favourable to his subjects and walked along.

The person who engages in people's welfare realizes one thing that the meetings, committees, treasury and the army become the centre of cynosure for him. Such a person does well to the nation and also to his subjects.

Chapter 16:

(80) *Sushrutao Karno Bhadrashrutao Karnao Bhadram Shlokam Shruyasam* —*(2/4, Atharvaveda))*

May both my ears listen to good knowledge, good speech, and good praises. Every person should listen too only good and should abhor bad altogether.

By listening to good thoughts we get inspired to engage in good actions. When we listen to praises that do well to one and all we feel positive and optimistic. On the contrary when we listen to bad thoughts we become cynical and skeptical about each and everything.

(81) *Brihaspatrima Atma Nrimana Nama Hridyaha* —*(3/5,Atharvaveda)*

My soul is embellished with knowledge and whoever contemplates, he resides in the heart. When humans indulge in self-analysis the mind becomes enlightened and enkindled. This type of person engages in good actions. The "reflective" by nature are not plagued by indignance.

(82) *Nabhiraham Rayinam Nabhihi Samananam Bhooyasam* —*(4/1, Atharvaveda)*

May I be wealthy and be in the company of the alike. Human should work assiduously and earn wealth so that he can come in the company of the elite. The person who is wealthy will be centre of cynosure for one and all. Therefore, one should achieve his goal by working assertively on the basis of the knowledge acquired.

(83) *Usho Yasmad Dushvapnyad Bhaishmapa Taduchatu* —*(6/2, Atharvaveda)*

O Morning. May we be freed from the nightmare that frightened us. It is said that dreams seen at day or dawn or daybreak often come true. Therefore humans should avoid seeing nightmares.

The person who engages in people's welfare and good actions is never plagued by bad dreams. If we see dreams regularly then we should try to get rid of them.

(84) *Jitamasma Kamudbhinnamasmak Amritamasmkam*
Tejo Asmakam Brahamasamakam Swa Rasmakam

Yasyo Asmakam Pashvo Asmakam Pragya Asmakam Vira Asmakam *—(8/1, Atharvaveda))*

May we be victorious, may we rise, may we realize the truth, may we become all the more radiant, may we enhance our knowledge, may our light increase, may our yagya be successful, may we be blessed with animals, good subjects and may we become valiant.

When a human being shall take the above resolution and shall strive to attain all this, that day he shall be blessed with all these things.

(85) Vasyobhuyaya Vasumana Yaeyo Vasu Vashishiya Vasumana Bhuyasam Vasu Mayi Dhehi *—(9/4, Atharvaveda)*

May I become all the more wealthy and get all the luxuries and comforts. Comforts are like a yagya, may I attain it.

Every person should strive to become wealthy so that he can lead a good life. The attainment of yagya depends on ones diligence. Therefore, we should become industrious so that wealth runs behind us rather than we becoming poor and running behind wealth.

Chapter 17:

(86) Devanam Prajanam Samananam Pashunanam Priyaha Bhuyasam Ayushyaman Bhuyasam *—(1/1-5, Atharvaveda)*

May I be, favoured by all the gods, subjects, equally mighty people, animals and may I be blessed with along life.

When a person remains healthy then he shall acquire all abilities. He shall religiously work towards his goal and shall be blessed with a long life.

We should engage in such actions so that God's people and animals favour us similarly. If you want attention and affection of people, it is initially important that we take the onus of others on our shoulder and shower on them love and affection.

(87) Adabdhena Brahmana Vavri Dhanaha—(1/12, Atharvaveda)

May I rise with knowledge that is sublime and divine. Knowledge inspires us to engage in good deeds that accrue in the welfare of others. Knowledge arms us in such a way as to make us valiant and brave. It also helps us in constructive activities.

(88) *Shukro Asi Bhrajo Asi Sa Yatham Tvam Bhrajata Bhrajo Asyevaham Bhrajatama Bhrajata Bhrajasyam*

You are radiant, dazzling and may I become radiant and enlightened as you are. Human should imbibe the best of qualities and become alike them. By doing so all the obstacles in the path are mitigated easily. Therefore we should become radiant and enlightened.

(89) *Udyate Nam Udyate Nam Uditaya Namah*

Viraje Namaha Swaraje Namaha Samraje Namaha

—(2/22, Atharvaveda))

I greet him, who rises, who is radiant with his own light, who is radiant and embellished with the most sublime form of light. One and all who tread on the path of growth respect him. Therefore, one should strive tirelessly to rise up in society. He who does so shall get honours and fame.

(90) *Aditya Nava Arukshaha Sharitram Swastaye*

Arurmatyapiparo Ratrim Satrati Parya

O Sun god! Climb on a hundred oared boat to do good of us. Help me to cross this during the daytime and night-time by staying with me. The sun engages in good actions so as to benefit all on the basis of his rays. Humans also alike the sun should attain the desired goals by perseverance and assiduity. The night and day pass smoothly and one eventually reaps good dividends.

(91) *Riten Gupta Ritubhishcha Sarvaibhuten Gupto Bhavyen Chaham*

Mama Prapat Pamma Mota Mrityunantardadhe Aham Salilena Vachaha *—(2/9, Atharvaveda)*

May I dwell here protected by truth, all the seasons, past and present. May I be liberated from sin and death. I engross or submerge myself in the water of the divine knowledge of Vedas. Human should tread on the righteous path of religion so that he is protected by the past, present and future.

Everyone should try to take a holy dip in the waters of the knowledge of Vedas and become immortal. We should strive to bring changes in the present because the present breeds the past and the future.

Chapter 18:

(92) *Shpad Eandharviranya Cha Yoshna Nadasya Nade Paripatu No Manaha*

Ishtasya Madhye Aditirni No Bhrata Nojyeshtha Prathamo Vi Vochati *—(1/19,Atharvaveda)*

The knowledge of the Vedas, which praise the greatness of great souls and is consistently engaged in the benediction of others, praises the Agni. May Agni protect the people who praise us make us prepared to achieve the anticipated and like a elder brother advice us.

The Vedas praise Agni who is the supreme God. God protects all those who ought to be honoured and blesses them with all that is desired. He advises and guides us like an elder brother. The person who engages in good deeds is considered noble and god fulfills all the desires of such a noble soul.

(93) *Yaste Agne Sumatim Marto Akhyat Sahasaha Suno Ati Sapra Shrunave*

Isham Dadhano Vahamano Ashvaira Sa Dyumam Abhvan Bhushati Dyuta *—(1/24, Atharvaveda)*

O Agni! Those people who praise you, they become famous, are never devoid of wealth and food grains, beget vehicles such as horses, etc., become mighty and assume a special position in the hearts of all.

He who imbibes all these divine qualities and praises the God gets in return food, wealth, vehicles and all the comforts he desires. Such a person is also blessed with a long life.

(94) *Sakhaya A Shishamahe Brahmendraya Vajrine*

Stusha U Shunritmaya Dhrishnave *—(1/37, Atharvaveda))*

Let us become friends and desire for Indra, Divine knowledge so that he becomes a good leader, destroyer of all enemies and the Vajra Dhara.(The one who holds the Vajra in his hand)

We should become friends and desire for the prosperity and growth of each other. By doing so only can become capable of praising Indra. Until we do not become capable of praising the Indra we cannot seek his blessing.

(95) *Saraswati Devayanto Havante Sa Swatimadhware Tayamane Saraswatim Sukrito Havante Saraswate Dashushe Varyadata*
—(1/41, Atharvaveda)

Those who want to become gods invoke the Goddess Saraswati and invoke her in a non-violent yagya. Saraswati blesses the benevolent with the desired things. The person, who acquires maximum knowledge and donates it, is blessed by Goddess Saraswati. If a person wants to become noble then he has to invoke Goddess Saraswati, *i.e.* become knowledgeable.

(96) *Mainamagne Vi Daho Mabhi Shushucho Masya Tvacham Chikshipo Ma Shariram*

Shritam Yada Karasi Jatavedo Athemena Pra Hinutat Pitru Rupam *—(2/4, Atharvaveda)*

O Agni! Incinerate this dead body (corpse) in such a way as to avoid giving it pain. Do not make it sorrowful. Do not throw the skin. Burn the entire body so that nothing remains. You, the knower of Vedas, totally incinerate the corpses so that the soul goes to the Pitru Loka (The abode of the deceased ancestors)

(97) *Pra Chayavasva Tanua Sam Bharasua Ma Te Gatra Vi Hayi Bho Shariram*

Mano Ni Vishthmanusan Vishasva Yatra Bhumerjushase Tatra Gachcha

More ahead! Nourish and nurture the body properly. May your hand, legs and body not be destroyed by death. Go wherever your mind desires and go to that place which you have attraction and love.

Humans should take care of the body. They should stay wherever they adjust and love. They should do whatever they want without troubling others.

Chapter 19:

(98) *Ta Apaha Shiva Apo Ayakshmankaraniyaha*
Yathaiva Tripyate Mayastasta A Datta Bheshajihi
—(2/5,Atharvaveda))

This water is beneficial to one and all, it cures all the ailments. Like the happiness, which increases, that water is like a panacea for all the diseases, please accept it.

The medicinal value and nobleness of water is omniscient. Water itself is alike a panacea to cure many a disease.

(99) Yato Bhaya Abhayam Tanno Astvav Devanam Yaja Hedo Agne
—(3/4, Atharvaveda))

May we become fearless, where there is fear. O Agni! Pacify the gods, so that they shed their anger.

One should never invite the wrath of the Gods. But we should learn to be fearless and praise the Gods. Similarly we should imbibe the sublime qualities of Gods and work selflessly and tenaciously.

(100) Akutya No Brihaspat Akutya Na Upa Gahi
Atho Bhagasya No Dhehmatho Naha Suhano Bhav
—(4/3, Atharvaveda))

O Jupiter! Come here with a strong will-power. Bless us with a good fortune, easily and swiftly. Human should strive to acquire maximum knowledge, knowledge facilitates influx of income, wealth and teaches us to protect ourselves, despite adversities.

(101) Abhayam Mitrad Abhayammitradbhayam Gyatada Bhayam Puro Yaha
Abhayam Nakta Abhayam Diva Naha Sarva Asha Mam Hitram Bhavantu *—(15/6, Atharvaveda)*

May be we devoid of fear from friends, enemies, death, future, day, night and all the directions.

Human should engage in such actions so that they become audacious, assertive and fearless. The minds of the malevolent people can never be devoid of fear. One should refrain from bad actions and engage in good deeds.

(102) Varcha A Dhehi Me Tanvam Saha D Jo Vayo Balam
—(37/2,Atharvaveda)

May you bless me with radiance, courage, energy and strength.

Humans should engage in such actions that help in aggrandizing radiance, courage, energy, strength and divinity.

(103) *Pashmeya Shradaha Shatam, Jivem Shradaha Shatam*
Budhyem Shradaha Shatam, Rohem Shradaha Shatam
Pushum Shradaha Shatam, Bhavem Shradaha Shatam
Bhuyem Shradaha Shatam, Bhuyasi Shradaha Shatam

May we witness a 100 years, live for a hundred years, imbibe knowledge for a 100 years, grow for a 100 years, become strong and nourished for a 100 years, become embellished for a 100 years. Live for more than 100 years. Here we see the greatness of 100 years. To live a hundred years it is important that the body is healthy, devoid of weakness and ailments.

Chapter 20:

(104) *Indra Prehi Purastvam Vishwasyeshana Ojasa*
Vrittani Vritraham Jahi *—(5/3, Atharvaveda))*

O Indra, move ahead, you are the saviour of this universe by your capabilities, destroy all the Vrittras.

Human being should become mighty and strong. By doing so all the obstacles should be destroyed and we shall move ahead. Moreover we should lead and guide the multitudes.

(105) *Vayam Rajabhihi Prathama Dhan Anyasmakena Vrijanena Jayem*
—(17/10, Atharvaveda))

May we become leader like the kings and amass wealth by our own strength.

Humans should strive to acquire knowledge and to eschew poverty. In this way we should learn to amass maximum wealth.

(106) *Yaha Shardhate Nanudadati Shudhyam Yo Dasyorhanta Sa Janasa Indraha* *—(34/10, Atharvaveda))*

He is Indra who does not need to pride of the proud and is the vanquisher of all dasyus.

Pride is like a demon and Indra is the one who destroys ego and pride. Ego, pride corrodes a person's ability to acquire knowledge.

To seek the blessing of Indra it is imperative that we renounce pride. Pride makes a man end up in misery and in a deplorable condition.

(107) Yo Jamya Amethayastadyatsakhayam Dughurshati
Jyeshtho Yadprachetastdahu Radharagiti
—(128/2,Atharvaveda))

The person who mistreats a noble woman does bad towards a friend, he who is senior but is ignorant is known as a degraded person.

A person should refrain from all those thing that take him towards, fallacy, misery and degradation.

(108) Yudbhadrasya Purushasya Putro Bhavati Dadhrishihi
—(128/3, Atharvaveda)

The son of the noble man is always victorious.

Like the noble man the son of such a person is equally noble. He becomes victorious on his own capabilities and assiduity. The noble people should therefore engage in making people in their refuge noble and great.

Bibliography

Adikaram, E. W.: *Early History of Buddhism in Ceylon,* D. S. Puswella, Migoda, 1946.

Agrawala, V. S.: *Shiva Mahadeva: The Great God,* Veda Academy, Varanasi, 1966.

Ahmad, Imtiaz: *State and Foreign Policy: India's Role in South Asia,* Vikas, New Delhi, 1993.

Ahmad, Jamil-ud-din: Some Recent Speeches and Writings of Mr. Jinnah, Lahore, Ashraf, 1952.

Aiyar, R. Krishnaswami: *Outlines of Vedaanta,* Chetana, Bombay, 1978.

Archer, W. G.: *The Kama Sutra,* Unwin Hyman, London, 1990.

Ashton, S.R. : *British Policy Towards the Indian States, 1905-1939,* London, Curzon, 1982.

Aurobindo, Sri: *Vyasa and Valmiki,* Acharya Press, Pondicherry, 1956.

Avalon, Arthur and Ellen: *Hymns to the Goddess,* Ganesh and Co., Madras, 1964.

Aziz, Ashraf: *Light of the Universe: Essays on Hindustani Film Music,* Three Essays Collective, New Delhi, 2003.

Bagchi, P. C.: *Studies in Dharmashastra,* University of Calcutta Press, Calcutta, 1939.

Bahadur, K.P.: *The Wisdom of Vedaanta,* Sterling Publishers Private Limited, New Delhi, 1996.

Banerjea, J. N.: *Pauranic and Vedanta Religion,* University of Calcutta, Calcutta, 1996.

Bankimchandra, C.: *Essentials of Dharma,* Sanskrit Book Depot, Calcutta 1979.

Basu, Manoranjan: *Dharmashastra: A General Study,* Shrimati Mira Basu, Calcutta, 1976.

Beaumont, Roger : *Sword of the Raj: The British Army in India, 1747-1947*, Indianapolis, Bobbs-Merrill, 1977.

Benjamin, Joseph : *Scheduled Castes in Indian Politics and Society*, New Delhi, Ess Ess Publications, 1989.

Bhattacharyya, B.: *Nispannayogavali of Mahapandita Abhyakara Gupta*, Oriental Institute, Baroda, 1949.

Borchert, Bruno: *Mysticism: Its History and Challenge*, Samuel Wiser, York Beach, 1994.

Bose, D. N.: *Dharmashastra: Their Philosophy and Occult Secrets*, Kali Press, Calcutta, 1965.

Bowle, John: The Imperial Achievement: The Rise and Transformation of the British Empire, Little, Brown, 1974.

Brockington, J. L.: *Righteous Rama: The Evolution of an Epic*, Oxford, London, 1984.

Bromley, D.: *Krishna Consciousness in the West*, Bucknell University Press, Lewisburg, 1989.

Brooks, E.: The Original Analects: Sayings of Confucius and His Successors. Columbia University Press, New York, 1988.

Bruhn, Klaus: *The Jina-Images of Deogarh*, MacMillan, Leiden, 1969.

Burke, Mary Louise: Swami Vivekananda in America: New Discoveries, Advaita Ashrama, Calcutta, 1966.

Chaudhary, M.: *Partition and the Curse of Rehabilitation*, Calcutta, Bengal Rehabilitation Organization, 1964.

Chaudhuri, Nirad: *Thy Hand, Great Anarch! India: 1921-1952*, London, Chatto & Windus, 1987.

Coomeraswamy, Ananda K.: *Buddha and the Gospel of Buddhism*, MacMillan, London, 1928.

Crawford, Cromwell S.: *Ram Mohan Roy: His Era and Ethics*, Acharya Press, New Delhi, 1984.

Dalton, Dennis : *Gandhi's Power : Nonviolence in Action*, New Delhi, OUP, 2001.

Danielou, Alain: *The Complete Kama Sutra*, Park Street Press, Rochester, 2000.

Dasgupta, Shahana: *Rani Lakshmibai: The Indian Heroine*, Rupa & Company, Calcutta, 2002.

Datta, V.N.: *Sati: Widow Burning in India*, Manohar, New Delhi, 1990.

David, M. D.: *John Wilson and his Institutions*, Mumbai, 1957.

De Bary: *Self and Society in Ming Thought*, Columbia University Press, New York, 1970.

De, Sushil Kumar: *Ancient Indian Erotics and Erotic Literature*, Firma K. L. Mukhopadhyay, Calcutta, 1959.

Deak, Istvan: The Lawful Revolution: Louis Kossuth and the Hungarians 1848-1849, Columbia University Press, 1979.

Dhar, Niranjan: *Vedanta and Bengal Renaissance*, Minerva Associates, Calcutta, 1977.

Dikshit, D.P. *Political History of the Chalukyas of Badami*. New Delhi: Abhinav, 1980.

Donat, K.: *Meditate the Tantric Yoga Way*, George Allen and Unwin, London, 1973.

Doniger, W.: *The Rig Veda: An Anthology*, Penguin, New York, 1981.

Duboi, Abbe: *Hindu Manners, Customs and Ceremonies*, Fifth Indian Impression, CUP, 1985.

Dwivedi, M.: *The Principal Upanishads*, Adyar Library, Madras, 1931.

Eaton, Richard M.: Sufis of Bijapur, 1300-1700: Social Roles of Sufis in Medieval India, Princeton University Press, Princeton, 1978.

Edwardes, Michael: *Battles of the Indian Mutiny*, London; B. T. Batsford Ltd., 1963.

Erickson, Erik H.: Gandhi's Truth: On the Origins of Militant Nonviolence, Norton, New York, 1970.

Farquhar, J.N.: *Modern Religious Movements in India*, Munshiram, New Delhi, 1967.

Fay, Peter Ward: *The Opium War, 1840-42*, University of North Carolina Press, 1975.

Fisher, Michael H.: The Politics of British Annexation of India - 1757- 1857, Oxford, 1996.

Frauwallner, E..: *History of Indian Philosophy*, Motilal, Delhi, 1973.

Gambhirananda, S.: *Brahma Sutra Shamkar Bhasya*, Adavita Ashrama, Calcutta, 1977.

Gambhirananda, Swami: *Brahma Sutra Shamkar Bhasya*, Adavita Ashrama, Calcutta, 1977.

Gandhi, M. K.: *The Story of My Experiment With Trust*, Washington, Public Affairs Press, 1948.

Garbe, R.: *The Philosophy of Ancient India*, Chicago University Press, Chicago, 1899.

Goradia, Nayana: *Lord Curzon: The Last of the British Moghuls*, New Delhi, Oxford University Press, 1993.

Goudriaan, T.: *Ritual and Speculation in Early Tantrism*, State University of New York Press, New York, 1992.

Gough, A.E.: The Philosophy of the Upanisads and Ancient Indian Metaphysics, MacMillan, London, 1882.

Grant, G. P.: *Philosophy in the Mass Age*, Copp Clark, Toronto, 1959.

Grisenold, H.D.: *Insights into Modern Hinduism*, Oxford, New York, 1934.

Growse, F. S.: *The Ramayana of Tulasidasa*, Motilal Banarsidass, Delhi, 1995.

Gurumurthy, S. : *Hindu Heritage, Assimilative, Not Divisive*, Vigil, Madras 1993.

Haich, E.: *Sexual Energy and Yoga*, Aurora Press, New York, 1982.

Hasan, Murhirul: Legacy of a Divided Nation: India's Muslims Since Independence, New Delhi, Oxford, 1997.

Hasan, Mushirul: *India's Partition: Process, Strategy and Mobilization*, New Delhi, Oxford UP, 1993.

*Heifetz, Hank: The Origin of the Young God: Kalidasa's Kumara-*sambhava, University of California Press, Berkeley, 1985.

Heimann, Betty: *Facets of Indian Thought*, Geroge Allen & Unwin, London, 1964.

Heinsath, Charles: *Indian Nationalism and Hindu Social Reform*, Princeton University Press, Princeton, 1964.

Heschel, J.: *God in Search of Man: A Philosophy of Judaism*, Noonday Press, New York, 1997.

Hirschman, Edwin: White Mutiny: The Ilbert Bill Crisis in India and the Genesis of the Indian National Congress, New Delhi, Heritage, 1980.

Hixon, L.: Mother of the Universe: Visions of the Goddess, Tantric Hymns of Enlightenment, Quest Books, Wheaton, 1994.

Hopkins, J.: *Kalachakra Tantra Rite of Initiation*, Wisdom Publications, Boston, 1982.

Hopkirk, Peter: The Great Game: The Struggle for Empire in Central Asia, Kodansha, 1992.

Hume, R.E.: *The Thirteen Principle Upanishads,* Oxford University Press, London, 1971.

Hutchins, Francis: *Spontaneous Revolution: The Quit India Movement,* New Delhi, Manohar, 1971.

Irene, S.: *Vedic Heritage Teaching Program.* Arsha Vidya Gurukulam, Coimbatore, 1994.

Iyar, K.: *Vedanta: The Science of Reality,* Ganesh and Co., Mardas, 1930.

Iyengar, B.K.S.: *Light on the Yoga Sutras of Patanjali,* Aquarian Press, London 1993.

Jacob, K.: *Religion and Ethics in Advaita,* C.M.S. Press, Kottayam, 1982.

Jafar, Malik Muhammad: *Jinnah as a Parliamentarian,* Lahore, Afzar Publications, 1977.

Jain, Kailash Chand, *Lord Mahavira and His Times,* Saraswati Press, Delhi, 1974.

James, Lawrence: *The Rise and Fall of the British Empire,* St. Martin's, 1997.

James, Robert Rhodes: *The British Revolution, 1880-1939,* New York, Knopf, 1976.

Jean, M.: *Tantrik Yoga,* The Aquarian Press, Wellingborough, 1970.

John, B.: *Mantras: Sacred Words of Power,* George Allen and Unwin, London, 1977.

John, Elsner: Pilgrimage: Past and Present in the World Religions, Harvard University Press, Cambridge, 1995.

John, K.: *The Origin and Development of the State Cult of Confucius,* Paragon Book, New York, 1966.

Karmarkar, D.: *Sankara's Advaita,* Karnatak University, Dharwar, 1976.

Kaushik, Asha : Globalization, Democracy and Culture : Situating Gandhian Alternatives, Jaipur, Pointer, 2002.

Kaviraj, G.: *Aspects of Indian Thought,* University of Burdwan, Calcutta, 1966.

Kavlekar, K.K. : Non-Brahmin Movement in Southern India, 1873- 1949, Kolhapur, Shivaji University, 19790

Keith, A.B. : *Rigveda Brahmanas,* Harvard University Press, Cambridge, 1920.

Keith, Arthur Berriedale: *The Religion and Philosophy of the Veda and* Upanishads, MacMillan, Delhi, 1925.

Kishwar, Madhu : Religion at the Service of Nationalism, and Other Essays, OUP, Delhi, 1998.

Klaus, K.: *A Survey of Hinduism,* State University of New York Press, Albany, 1989.

Knipe, M.: *Hinduism: Experiments in the Sacred,* Harper, San Francisco, 1991.

Knott, K.: *Hinduism, A Very Short Introduction,* Oxford University Press, New York, 1998.

Kosambi, D. D. : The Culture and Civilisation of Ancient India in Historical Outline, London, Routledge and Kegan Paul, 1956.

Kottackal, Jacob: *Religion and Ethics in Advaita,* C.M.S. Press, Kottayam, 1982.

Kuiper, F.B.J. : *Aryans in the Rigveda,* Rodopi, Amsterdam, 1991.

Kuppuswamy, Sastri S.: Compromises in the History of Advaitic Thought, Kalyani Press, Madras, 1940.

Louis, Fischer: Essential Gandhi: An Anthology of His Writings, Vintage, New York, 1983.

Low, D. A. and Brasted, Howard: *Freedom, Trauma, Continuities: Northern India and Independence,* New Delhi, Sage Publications, 1998.

Maheshwari, Shriram: Rural Development in India: A Public Policy Approach, New Delhi, Sage, 1995.

Makhan, L.: *The Ramayana of Valmiki,* Munshiram Manoharlal, New Delhi, 1978.

Mathew, Arnold: *Culture and Anarchy,* The University Press, Cambridge, 1935.

Mayer, A. : Caste in an Indian Village: Change and Continuity 1954- 1992, Delhi, OUP, 1996.

Mazumder, Sukhendu : Politico-Economic Ideas of Mahatma Gandhi: Their Relevance in the Present Day, New Delhi, Concept Pub., 2004.

Mearns, David J.: Shiva's Other Children: Religion and Social Identity amongst Overseas Indians, Sage, Walnut Creek, 1995.

Mearns, J.: Shiva's Other Children: Religion and Social Identity amongst Overseas Indians, Sage, Walnut Creek, 1995.

Mehra, Parshotam: *A Dictionary of Modern Indian History, 1707-1947*, New Delhi, Oxford University Press, 1985.

Metcalf, Thomas R.: *The Aftermath of the Revolt: India, 1857-1870*, Princeton, Princeton University, 1964.

Mohan, K.: *The Mahabharata*, Munshiram Manoharlal, Delhi 1997.

Mookerjee, Ajit: *Kali The Feminine Force*, Thames and Hudson, London, 1988.

Mookerji, Satkari: *Modern Polity and Vedanta*, Sanskrit College, Calcutta, 1972.

Moon, Penderel: *The British Conquest and Dominion of India*, London, Duckworth, 1989.

Morris-Jones, W.H.: *The Government and Politics of India*, London, Hutchinson, 1971.

Nanda, B. R. : *Gandhi and His Critics*, Oxford University Press, Delhi, 1993.

Neale, Walter C.: Economic Change in Rural India: Land Tenure and Reform in the United Provinces, 1800-1955, New Haven, 1962.

Nevile, P.: *Lahore: A Sentimental Journey*, New Delhi, Penguin, 1993.

Oddie, G.A. : *Hindu and Christian in South-East India*, London, Curzon Press, 1991.

Pathak, Dr S.P.: *Jhansi during the British Rule*, Ramanand Vidya Bhawan, Delhi, 1987.

Preston, Diana: *The Boxer Rebellion*, Berkley Books, 2000.

Raimundo Panikkar: *The Vedic Experience: Mantramanjari*, Longman Todd, London, 1977.

Raja, C. Kunhan : *The Taittiriya Sarvanukramani of Yaska*, Madras, 1931.

Ramamurti, A.: *Advaitic Mysticism of Sankara*, Visvabharati, Santiniketan, 1974.

Ranajit Guha: *A Construction of Humanism in Colonial India*, CASA, Amsterdam, 1993.

Renou, Louis: *The Nature of Dharmashastra*, Walker and Co., New York, 1997.

Robson, Brian: *Sir Hugh Rose and the Central India Campaign*, Sutton Publishing Ltd for the Army Records Society, UK, 2000.

Satyapal Verma: *Role of Reason in Sankara Vedanta*, Parimal Publication, Delhi, 1992.

Savarkar, Vinayak Damodar : *The Indian War of Independence* 1857 Rajdhani Granthagar, Delhi, 1988.

Scheftelowitz, Isidor : Die Kasmirische Rezension von Katyayanas Sarvanukramani, Zeitschrift fur Indologie und Iranistik, 1922.

Shukla, D. N.: *Vastu-Shastra,* Motilal Banarsidass, Delhi, 1966.

Singh, Birendra Kumar: Early Chalukyas of Vatapi, circa A.D. 500 to 757, Delhi, Eastern Book Linkers, 1991.

Smith, Col. J. T. : *Silver and the India Exchanges,* Effingham Wilson, London, 1876.

Strauss, L.: *Political Philosophy,* The Bobbs Merrill Co., New York, 1975.

Swami Vishnu Tirtha: *Devatma Shakti,* Swami Shivom Tirth, Rishikesh, 1962.

Talageri, Shrikant : *Aryan Invasion Theory and Indian Nationalism,* Voice of India, Delhi, 1993.

Tejomayananda, Swami: *Hindu Culture: An Introduction,* Chinmaya Publications, Piercy, 1993.

Thapar, Romila : *Ashoka and the Decline of the Mauryas,* London, Oxford University Press, 1961.

Thompson, Edward: *The Making of the Indian Princes,* Oxford University Press, London, 1943.

Trautmann, Thomas R.: Kautilya and the Arthasastra: A Statistical Study, Leiden, Brill, 1971.

Trimingham, J.: *Sufi Orders in Islam,* Oxford University Press, New York, 1998.

Utpat, V.N.: *Riddles of Buddha and Ambedkar,* Itihas Patrika Prakashan, Thane 1988.

Vable, D.: *The Arya Samaj. Hindu without Hinduism.* Vikas Publ., Delhi, 1983.

Vedalankar, Pandit Nardev : *Basic Teachings of Hinduism,* Veda Niketan, Durban, 1978.

Visvantha, K.: *Essentials of Hinduism,* Narosa Pub. House, New Delhi, 1989.

Wendy Doniger: *Siva: The Erotic Ascetic,* Oxford University Press, Delhi, 1998.

Zaidi, A. Moin: *Evolution of Muslim political Thought in India,* New Delhi: S. Chand, 1975-79

Index

D

E

F

G

H

I

K

L

M

O

P

R

S

T

U

V

W

Y

□□□